D0933684

HOW MUCH TRUTH
DO WE TELL THE CHILDREN?
The Politics of Children's Literature

Marxist Dimensions, Vol. 1
Series Editor: James Lawler

Marxist Dimensions is a book series by MEP Publications containing contributions by various authors around a unified theme. Proposals for additional books in this series are welcome.

About the editor of this volume

Betty Bacon is a retired librarian, author of five children's books and a number of critical articles, and a former teacher in the Library School at the University of California, Berkeley.

Acknowledgments

First thanks go to Professor James Lawler of the Philosophy Department at State University of New York at Buffalo, general editor of the book series *Marxist Dimensions*. With admirable care and patience, he guided the book through its various stages of development and was a major influence on its final shape.

Thanks in particular to the following friends and colleagues who read the manuscript in whole or in part and offered useful suggestions and words of support: Russell Bartley, Julian Boyd, Dorothy Bryant, David Englestein, Betty Halpern, June Jordan, Jack Kurzweil, Ina Lawson, Claire Shallit, Ursula Sherman, Joel Taxel, Binnie Tate Wilkin, and Jack Zipes. And very special thanks to the late George Bacon who, suffering through innumerable rereadings and discussions of problems, was consistently cheerful and supportive.

Betty Bacon

HOW MUCH TRUTH
DO WE TELL THE CHILDREN?
The Politics of Children's Literature

Edited by

Betty Bacon

MEP Publications
Minneapolis

MEP Publications
c/o Anthropology Department
University of Minnesota
215 Ford Hall; 224 Church Street S.E.
Minneapolis, MN 55455

Library of Congress Cataloging-in-Publication Data
How much truth do we tell the children?
   (Marxist Dimensions ; vol. 1)
   Includes bibliographies.
   1. Children's literature — Political aspects.
2. Children's literature — Social aspects   I. Bacon,
Betty, 1914 —   . II. Series.
PN1009.5.P64H69   1988   809′.93358   87-22663
ISBN 0-930656-55-5
ISBN 0-930656-56-3 (pbk.)

Printed in the United States of America

CONTENTS

Introduction

Betty Bacon

To read *Charlotte's Web* is to experience the values of an American dream. The ultimate human issues of love and death, friendship and greed, change and growth are set against the background of an earlier rural time. The characters, human and otherwise, react with each other, deal decisively with their lives, and in good, democratic fashion organize the support of the folk around them. And the tale is told in a language exquisitely crafted in image and rhythm. The reader shares the joy and sadness and a conviction that it is possible to cope with problems and to shape one's own life.

All this happens because the reader is *involved,* has experienced Coleridge's "willing suspension of disbelief," and has lived in the story. Child or adult, the reader accepts a set of assumptions about what is "good," what is useful for a "successful" and "happy" life. In "real life," outside the book, the reading experience strengthens and reinforces these assumptions.

The English critic, Terry Eagleton, puts it this way: "From the infant school to the University faculty, literature is a vital instrument for the insertion of individuals into the perceptual and symbolic forms of the dominant ideological formation, able to accomplish this function with a 'naturalness,' spontaneity and experiential immediacy possible to no other ideological practice."[1]

Charlotte's Web is gentle and humane and is a reflection of positive values. Other children's classics, springing from a different aspect of capitalistic society, have agendas—hidden or not—that transmit a less benevolent message to young readers. As Eagleton says: "Literature is . . . a crucial mechanism by which the language and ideology of an imperialistic class establishes its hegemony, or by which a subordinated state, class or region preserves and perpetuates at the ideological level an historical identity shattered or eroded at the political."[2]

Take, for example, that innocent book of hilariously cavorting elephants, *The Story of Babar*. Both Edmund Leach,[3] the anthropologist, and Ariel Dorfman, the Chilean critic, have perceived in it openly expressed racism and European chauvinism. One has only to ask who is superior in Babar's society, who is dominant within the story, to see how obviously this works. Dorfman takes a sharp look at the world of those charming elephants:

> The admirer of Babar will not only find palpable evidence that there are "developed" countries and others which do not exhibit characteristics of progress or modernity, and are therefore perceived as "backward," but also there is a set of "solutions" to such an "abnormal" predicament. Even before he can read . . . the child has come into contact with an implicit history that justifies and rationalizes the motives behind an international situation in which some countries have everything and other countries almost nothing.[4]

And the reality is masked by a cloak of carefree innocence which blocks awkward questions. As Dorfman notes further:

> When it comes to children's books . . . everything should be "just entertainment." Politics, being part of a serious and solemn, not to say boring or even painful universe, can't conceivably be part of this. Taste, tradition, habit disallow it.[5]

Another Latin American scholar, the Brazilian educator Paulo Freire writes: "What the elites of today want, although they do not denounce popular education . . . cynically and openly, [is] for the people not to think."[6]

And also, we might add, to accept without question a particular set of ideas. The Council on Interracial Books for Children has put out a manual for the content analysis of books for young readers. The introduction states:

> In any given society, children's books generally reflect the needs of those who dominate the society. A major need is to maintain and fortify the structure of relations between dominators and dominated. The prevailing values are supportive of the existing structure.[7]

A case in point is the so-called "young adult problem novel." This is a popular commercial genre confined largely to the United States. In such a book, a young person is confronted with a serious "relevant" problem — drug abuse, or maladjustment at school, or family break-up, or unwanted pregnancy, or the presence of a senile grandparent, or in one case even a murder. The book is built around the process of the young protagonist's "accepting" the problem on its own terms and "adjusting" to it without doing anything much to change the situation. In many cases, the individual problem has social causes, but such basic problems are never dealt with in books of this type. As Binnie Tate Wilkin states in her book, *Survival Themes in Books for Children,* these stories are "full of pathos which moves young people to tears, but ingredients for recognizing the problem and/or possible solutions are absent."[8]

Conspicuous by their absence are books about the labor movement. It is as if today's labor struggles had no relationship whatever to millions of American families, as if they were of no concern to millions of children whose lives are touched and to millions of teenagers who can look forward to being participants in the near future. The one exception is Barbara Corcoran's *Strike!* The story of a high school boy confronted by a teachers' strike, it is certainly contemporary and a welcome breakthrough, although it is seriously marred by middle class attitudes. Even historical novels of the 1930s depression days deal only with the desperation of trying to make ends meet and make no use of the drama and excitement of the strikes and struggles of the time. Only Marilyn Sachs's *Call Me Ruth* and Athena V. Lord's *A Spirit to Ride the Whirlwind* deal with strikes—of the New York garment workers and the Lowell mill girls, respectively.

If there are few books for young readers about American labor, there is no fiction at all that gives an honest picture of life in a socialist society. Either stories set in socialist countries simply do not exist, or like Felice Holman's *The Wild Children,* they join the Cold War. (In this story of a homeless child after the Russian Revolution, every supporter of the Revolution is a monster and all opponents are kindly and heroic. Apparently, the author never heard of Makarenko—see note 1, page 92). U.S. foreign policy at its most conservative is reflected in the vast majority of books about other countries—from a substantial book for older children about the Philippines that is loud in its praises of Marcos to a slim volume with many pictures entitled *The Enchantment of . . . El Salvador.* In this area of children's literature the ideology of the dominant is hardly ever questioned.

Only in the last twenty-five years, through widespread popular struggle, has this ideology come to be widely questioned where racism and sexism are concerned. The Civil Rights movement of the 1960s and the women's movement of the 1970s have raised the popular consciousness so that even publishers are sensitive to ethnic and gender slurs. There is now a small brilliant Black children's literature, as I indicate in my own essay. But there is a tendency, among both writers and critics of children's books, to regard racism and sexism as morally "bad" in themselves, totally divorced from the imperialist drive for profits that uses them to keep wages down and the working class divided against itself.

Children's literature is essentially a product of and for the middle class created by the rise of the capitalist system. As Leeson points out in his essay (page 15), the literature in its modern sense began to flourish in England in the seventeenth and eighteenth centuries, created by and for the middle class. Raymond Williams, in *Marxism and Literature,* writes: "In modern class societies the selection of characters almost always indicates an assumed or conscious class position."⁹ In the United States this is evident in children's books, where white urban and suburban families are almost invariably middle class professionals, whereas urban working-class characters are Black. (Two notable exceptions are Virginia Hamilton's *The House of Dies Drear* about the son of a Black college professor, and Beverly Cleary's medal-winning *Dear Mr. Henshaw* about a white boy whose father is a truck driver. It should be pointed out that both of these writers are highly original in style and thought, with never a trite character or situation.)

It's a limited world. In the introduction to his book, *Reading and Righting,* Leeson writes, historically "in place of a story which adult and child believed together, was created a story which the adult did not believe but the youngster was expected to do so. More was lost than belief. . . . [There] developed a printed fiction in which the writers—and the main characters—were drawn from one social stratum [i.e., the middle class—Ed.]. The rest became culturally invisible."¹⁰ For example, most present-day stories with a rural background are laid in a world of small individually owned farms. The modern world of large-scale, mechanized agriculture is totally absent, and according to one concerned educator, today's farm children simply ignore the books that do not speak of the rural life they know only too well.¹¹

Strangely enough, there is more reality in fantasy. Both the symbols of capitalist society and the aspirations of working people—from the medieval peasant to the present-day oppressed—are embodied in stories. It all began, of course, with the folk tales, the stories which adult and child did indeed believe together. Zipes calls on us to break the spell of "conventional notions of literature so that we can discover our individual communal potential for infusing our everyday reality with the utopias we glean from the tales."¹² Chukovsky, the poet of nonsense for children, underlines the sense of nonsense when he writes:

The reading of topsy-turvies, tall tales, fairy tales, and fantasies to children is only one way of achieving the goal [of the correct understanding of reality]. . . . But it is necessary to use it with assurance, with energy, and with courage, remembering that this is not a children's diversion—not merely a diversion, that is—but a most useful mental effort. . . . With the help of fantasies, tall tales, fairy tales, and topsy-turvies of every type, children confirm their realistic orientation to reality.[13]

The child learns to understand reality by playing with it and thus confirming his own confidence that he knows what is real and what is not.

Fantasy cannot escape the society from which it springs, and its magical symbols can—and often do—signify negative values. Zanger demonstrates this in his analysis of middle class attitudes toward the industrial working class in nineteenth century England as exemplified in the classic fantasies of that era. Yet, from the days of Thomas More's *Utopia,* literary fantasies (as distinct from folk tales, where the process is less conscious) can point the way to something *else,* something *different.* That may well account for some of the present burgeoning popularity of science fiction, a distinct trend in books for young readers. Richard Adams's *Watership Down* (whatever faults it may have in depicting the relations between male and female rabbits) narrates very clearly in symbolic terms the successful struggle against a Hitlerian state. Even more openly, Robert O'Brien's *Mrs. Frisby and the Rats of NIMH* points a lesson to human beings by creating a rats' Utopia. (It is worth noting that, in the case of both books, the sociopolitical meaning was completely eliminated when they were made into movie cartoons.)

I once asked a distinguished writer of science fiction, "In your books, why is the future always the return to a kind of remote past instead of a journey forward into something new?" Nodding sadly, the writer replied: "Because I cannot imagine what that kind of future would be like." Yet the capacity to envision another way of life, another type of social organization, is one of the basic ingredients of fundamental social change. It is no coincidence that writers and educators in socialist countries place the highest value on qualities of imagination. Eliseo Diego, Cuban poet, critic, and theoretician on children's literature, says frankly, "Fantasy and imaginative thinking are . . . a major aspect of children's literature in Cuba, a way of awakening in children their latent dormant capacity for creative thinking, to influence their

sensibilities and awareness of the world around them."[14]
A new children's literature for a new society does not arise
suddenly from a void. Present-day Cubans are lucky in having a
unique tradition on which to build. Imagine Washington at Valley
Forge or Bolívar in Venezuela or Lenin in London spending several
months writing and publishing a magazine for children! In 1889,
the Cuban revolutionary leader, José Martí, a political exile in New
York, published four issues of *La Edad de Oro – The Golden Age.*[15]
Poet and playwright, Martí put his considerable talents to work and
wrote a number of stories, articles, and poems for the children of
Latin America, "the hope of the world," that are still highly
readable today and have set a standard for modern Cuban children's literature. In her essay Alga Marina Elizagaray, assistant
Minister of Culture, tells something of her struggles in helping to
create an indigenous Cuban children's literature and to bring the
world's literary riches to Cuban children.

After the Russian Revolution, Maxim Gorky, already a world-
famous writer, and Nadezhda Krupskaya, Lenin's wife and a leader
in her own right, were both passionately committed to the creation
of a *socialist* children's literature of the highest literary quality. In
the process of organizing the first children's libraries after the
Russian Revolution, Krupskaya defined the ideal:

> Children's book authors must have the ability to describe
> objects and phenomena in their total concreteness and within
> their relationships and developmental stages. Further they must
> possess the ability to transmit to the child's mind a correct
> appraisal of these phenomena. . . . The dialectic method is just
> as important within children's literature as it is for all mass
> education efforts. . . . One should not idealize reality – children
> easily discover untruthful descriptions – yet one must know how
> to help children understand our times and how to influence
> them.[16]

Although Maxim Gorky himself wrote only a few stories for
children, he was tireless in emphasizing the importance of children's literature in the new society. In a 1930 magazine article, he
wrote of "the rise of the new personality which is being shaped
in the fire of the 'concentrated energy' of the builders of the new
world."[17]
In those years, a number of books for young people were written
in the great tradition of nineteenth century Russian fiction. Striking
among them was the now classic novel by Valentin Kataev, *The
Lonely White Sail,* published in 1936 and often called the "Soviet

Tom Sawyer." Indeed, the two books resemble each other in a number of ways, but whereas Twain's Tom and Huck go their own way and never really enter wholeheartedly into the struggles of their time, Petya and his streetwise friend Gavrik find themselves in the center of the 1905 Revolution in Odessa. Yet Petya and Gavrik are like Tom and Huck in being constantly active, often funny, and always intensely real. This tradition of the junior novel continues in the Soviet Union today.

The advantages of a *heritage* of children's literature are demonstrated all too clearly in an article by Vidaluz Meneses Robleto about the present state of the art in Nicaragua. Without a Martí or a Gorky, and under the nation's constant need "to sacrifice its developing resources to defend its sovereignty," Nicaraguan writers have produced folk tales, riddles, carols, and above all poetry.[18] This seems like a short step forward, yet it is a remarkable achievement in a country that was more than half illiterate until recently and before that was flooded with Donald Duck and Superman.

To what degree is expression of the values of a society a conscious process? Gorky stated without reservation, "I know of no art which is not didactic, and I do not think that didacticism is capable of diminishing the influence of art upon the imagination, mind, and will of the reader."[19] Obviously, this process need not be deliberate. But the writer for children in particular, often views literature openly as a teaching mechanism and sees the adult writer as a responsible educator of the less experienced child. Eliseo Diego comments:

> There's no sense denying that reading material is a way of inducing moral values, of bringing children to appreciate what is good. You can use, for instance, a short story very subtly to awaken racial prejudice in the child, or you can use it to do exactly the opposite. But it is very clear that, when it comes to children, things must be done subtly, not obviously. Children like to draw their own conclusions.[20]

Some well-intentioned writers in the United States, wishing to combat negative values they see in children's literature, write books painstakingly structured around positive themes. The result is what a librarian friend of mine calls a "worthy" book as distinct from a "good" book. And what Dorothy Bryant, the novelist, in her advice to beginning writers, calls one of "the nastier forms of child abuse."[21] Leeson sees a trend today in which "moral and esthetic values are set against one another, and there is a renewed and powerful insistence on the didactic purpose of children's writing."[22]

The Council on Interracial Books for Children has been accused of fostering a mechanical approach that concentrates heavily on content to the detriment of the very literary qualities that delight and ensnare the reader and give the content personal meaning. In its own defense, the Council states in the introduction to its book-evaluation handbook:

> There is no automatic correlation between good values and good writing. . . . If we have emphasized content more than form, it is because good form has always been in demand but good content has not. Stylistic values are already recognized; human values are not—*at this time.* And these are the times that concern us.[23]

According to the Cuban critics Diego and Elizagaray, children's books must be beautiful to look at, they must be well written, they must have something to say and must say it with imagination and subtlety, and all this "without, of course, ignoring ideological content" (Elizagaray, p. 88, this volume). A tall order indeed! But by no means impossible. A prime example of a book that meets all of these standards is *Call Me Ruth* by Marilyn Sachs. Trade union organization, the special exploitation in the turn-of-the-century garment industry, the capacity of women for growth and leadership, anti-Semitism, the effect of the "melting pot" on the children of immigrants—all these can be clearly identified. But this book is not a dissertation on any of them; it is a human story of real people acting in real situations. Spare, sharp writing—witty, realistic dialogue—suspenseful plotting—unremitting pace—delicately balanced human relationships—all these keep the reader enmeshed in a story of a past that explains much about why we are the way we are today. If the book is a lesson in class consciousness for modern readers, it is because the principle is made real in terms of human living, and that living the reader shares through the writer's skill.

In widely varying ways the essays in this book all have a certain common view of children's literature. It is, the writers agree, a product of the social order within which it arises and as a rule expresses, consciously or unconsciously, its dominant social, political, ethical, and moral values. These values the essayists see as those of the bourgeoisie and of the middle class within the capitalist system of England and the United States. Racism, sexism, and national chauvinism are discussed within this class context. (The essays by Cuban and Soviet writers express a different set of major concerns, yet by this very fact serve to show the relationship of children's literature to the matrix society.) Other aspects of literature, education, psychology, and esthetics are discussed in terms of the historical process surrounding them.

The essays are arranged in nine sections:

The first one brings together three essays that point to the ways in which capitalist values are projected to children through various forms of literature. Leeson's essay, "The Middling Sort," connects the beginnings of modern children's literature with the rise of the middle class in England and shows, through analysis of three major classics, how well this new literary development suited the class needs of both creators and audience. With razor-sharp wit in "How to Read Donald Duck and Other Innocent Literature for Children," Dorfman and Mattelart, two Chilean exiles, expose the distorted bourgeois myths projected onto children in the comics and in the popular literature written for children's "entertainment." "Censorship or Selection?" by the editors of the no-longer-published British journal, *Children's Books Bulletin,* takes on a touchy subject and points to the censorial limitations placed upon writers for children by publishers and the demands of the capitalist marketplace.

The second section points to the development of nonfiction, that stepchild of children's literature, its uses and its abuses. Foremost Russian writer of his day, Maxim Gorky envisions a postrevolutionary literature for children that will open the whole world to them and lists the themes he considers most important.[24] As a sidelight on Gorky's own statement of purpose, Ron Walter pays tribute to Gorky's major role in establishing a rich socialist children's literature in the USSR. In almost ludicrous contrast, Goodman's essay, "From Lemonade Stands to Wall Street," examines the general run of U.S. books explaining economics to children, and with a fine sense of irony describes how the profit motive is dominant in all of them, exploitation is ignored, and other economic systems simply do not exist.

"Fantasy as Reality" is the theme of section three, in which four essays reveal the reality that lies beneath the surface imaginings of folk tales, fairy tales, and literary fantasies for children. Deeply concerned with both the historical background and the psychological meaning of folk tales, Zipes uses a critical examination of Bruno Bettelheim's theory to take a fresh look at psychoanalytic views on internalization and to present new insights on the production and use of folk tales. Zanger uses three classic examples of nineteenth century English fantasy and in each one examines the sharp and highly emotional divisions between the agreeable, refined protagonists and the threatening and hideous "others" lurking out there somewhere. He relates this situation to the historic reality of the Victorian upper middle class and the new industrial proletariat. Elizagaray, who has devoted her life to the creation of a Cuban children's literature, writes of her efforts to produce versions and adaptations of tales from many countries for storytelling and, in doing so, she enunciates the esthetic and ideological objectives of a socialist children's literature. Moynihan exposes the unstated ideologies in American children's fantasy (plus *Winnie-the-Pooh)* and, among other books examined, marks the populism in *The Wizard of Oz* and the theme of "individual initiative conquers all" in *The Little Engine that Could.*

Section four examines racist distortions in the presentation of American minorities in books for young readers. Two essays express diverse views in analyzing Mark Twain's humor in *Huckleberry Finn.* Woodward and MacCann bring a new factor into the "Huckleberry Finn" controversy by viewing the book in relation to a majcr cultural movement of the period—the Black minstrel show, whereas Schmidt deals with the sharply ironic quality of Huck's and Jim's speech and views. Palomino points to the predominantly middle class characters and attitudes in books about Japanese Americans and counters these by leading the reader to three important and almost shockingly vivid books for young adults about working class Japanese-American families. Dealing with a third ethnic group, Lewis's "Are Indians Nicer Now?" documents in detail the stereotypical message which picture books give to young children about the nature and culture of Native North Americans in both Canada and the United States.[25]

"Whose History?" asks the title of the fifth section. Taxel answers the question by showing that large sections of colonial society have been totally omitted from children's books about the American Revolution and pointing to the consequently distorted picture that remains in the minds of most Americans. Sherman brings her long and specialized experience to bear on books for young readers about the Holocaust, pointing to conflicting trends and changing attitudes and a general tendency on the part of writers to back away from the full story. Lumpkin looks at the open racism in books on ancient Egypt which, with a few notable exceptions, portray early Egyptian culture as somehow non-African and miraculously European. MacCann's second piece, "Militarism in Juvenile Fiction," exposes the hyped-up patriotism of early war books, the racist attitudes toward certain "enemies," and a more realistic point of view in some novels about World War II.

Two essays on biography comprise section six. Jurich answers her question, "What's left out of biography for children?" by pointing up the flat, one-sided, almost mock heroic characterizations that abound in biographies for young people and comparing a biography of Andrew Carnegie, in which he is portrayed as the ultimate and faultless American success story, with one of Karl Marx, which depicts him as the devil incarnate. Saul's "Living Proof" analyzes several biographies of Marie Curie in great detail, comparing them with the actual facts of her life and showing how by their omissions they present the young reader with a false picture of life possibilities.[26]

In section seven, my own piece, "I Play It Cool and Dig All Jive," considers various types of English in children's books, examines the nature of Black English and its literary use, and scrutinizes the class nature of the insistence on standard English.

Two class-conscious writers of children's books from highly different societies speak their piece about how they see themselves and their work in section eight. Walter, a Black writer in the United States, views her children's books not only as literary creations but as instruments for social change. Barto, one of the most widely read children's poets in the Soviet Union, describes the ways in which she feels the illustrations to her poems have influenced children's appreciation of them and goes on to some general comments on the content of a socialist children's literature.

In the final section, Soviet educator Sukhomlinsky underlines the ultimate purpose of books for children—not only the development of their own personal creativity but also a concept of beauty in which human beings find "respect of human dignity" and "affirmation of the most just relations between men."

This collection is a first attempt in the United States to bring together a group of essays that in general apply the principles of historical materialism to the field of children's literature. There is a great need in this country to develop a body of Marxist literary criticism in relation to books for young readers. In its entirety the subject touches on esthetics, sociology, history, psychology, education; it is literary, theoretical, and practical.

There are so many unanswered questions. What influence do books really have on young readers? How does this influence operate? Can books really combat racism? Educator Herbert Kohl says that "learning to read and learning to be articulate about one's own life can be considered one activity."[27] What does this say to the writer for children? What is the role of criticism in the development of a children's literature as commercially determined as it is in the United States? The questions multiply. It is to be hoped that this book will stimulate further discussion and argument in the struggle to find answers. The children have everything to gain from such effort on the part of their elders.

NOTES

1. Terry Eagleton, *Criticism and Ideology: A Study in Marxist Literary Theory* (London: New Left Books, 1976), 56.
2. Ibid., 55.
3. Edmund Leach, "Babar's Civilization Analysed," in *Only Connect: Readings in Children's Literature,* ed. by Sheila Egoff, G. T. Stubbs, and L. F. Ashley. 2nd ed. (Toronto: Oxford Univ. Press, 1980), 176–82.
4. Ariel Dorfman, *The Empire's Old Clothes: What the Lone Ranger, Babar, and Other Innocent Heroes Do to Our Minds* (New York: Pantheon Books, 1983), 22–23.
5. Ibid., 64.
6. Paulo Freire, *Pedagogy of the Oppressed,* trans. by Myra Bergman Ramos (New York: Seabury Press, 1970), 127.
7. *Human—and Anti-Human—Values in Children's Books: A Content Rating Instrument for Educators and Concerned Parents,* prepared by the Racism and Sexism Resource Center for Educators (New York: Council on Interracial Books for Children. 1976), 1.
8. Binnie Tate Wilkin, *Survival Themes in Books for Children and Young People* (Metuchen, NJ: Scarecrow Press, 1978), 138.
9. Raymond Williams, *Marxism and Literature* (Oxford: Oxford Univ. Press, 1977), 175.
10. Robert Leeson, *Reading and Righting: The Past, Present and Future of Fiction for the Young* (London: Wm. Collins & Sons, 1985), 11.
11. Mary Jane Roggenbuck, "Motivating Farm Children to Read," in *Motivating Children and Young Adults to Read,* ed. by James L. Thomas and Ruth H. Loving (Phoenix: Oryx Press, 1979.
12. Jack Zipes, *Breaking the Magic Spell: Radical Theories of Folk and Fairy Tales* (Austin: Univ. of Texas, 1979), xi.

13. Kornei Chukovsky, *From Two to Five,* trans. by Miriam Morton, rev. ed. (Berkeley: Univ. of California Press, 1968), 113.

14. Interview with Eliseo Diego, quoted in Karen Wald and Betty Bacon, "New Literacy and New People: Children and Books in Cuba," *Journal of Reading* 25 (Dec. 1981): 252.

15. José Martí, *La Edad de Oro* (Havana, Gente Nueva, 1978).

16. Nadezhda Konstantinovna Krupskaya, "About Children's Literature," trans. from the German by Sybille Jagusch, in *Phaedrus: An International Annual of Children's Literature Research* 8 (1981): 12.

17. Maxim Gorky, *Culture and the People* (New York: International Publishers, 1939), 107.

18. Vidaluz Meneses Robleto, "Nicaragua," in "Survey of Latin American Children's Literature," *Phaedrus* 10 (1985): 30–32.

19. Gorky, *Culture and the People*, 145–46.

20. Diego, in Wald and Bacon, 253.

21. Dorothy Bryant, *Writing a Novel* (Berkeley: Ata Books, 1978), 29.

22. Leeson, 10.

23. Racism and Sexism Resource Center for Educators, 22.

24. M. Ilin, whose books on science and technology published in the 1930s and 1940s set a new standard for nonfiction for young readers in many parts of the world (including the United States), followed Gorky's themes almost exactly, especially in his series on human development, *How Man Became a Giant, The Giant Widens his World,* and *Giant at the Crossroads.*

25. The vocal and unremitting struggle of native peoples and their allies through such organizations as the American Indian Movement has brought about some small improvement. The books Lewis analyzes so cogently are unfortunately found on many school and library shelves, but there are a few others— Paul Goble's well told and elegantly illustrated episodes in the history of the plains nations; Gerald McDermott's Caldecott Medal winner, *Arrow to the Sun; Ishi, Last of His Tribe,* by Theodora Kroeber; and even my own *People at the Edge of the World* about the often ignored people of central California.

26. Both these essays present a justifiably negative picture of biographies for young people. It should be pointed out, however, that there are a few exceptions. In the 1930s and '40s,

Nina Brown Baker set out to present the revolutionary heroes of other countries to American youngsters and produced sympathetic biographies of Juarez, Sun Yat-Sen, and then— boldly—Lenin. She was followed by Shirley Graham who wrote the first full-bodied biographies of Black leaders from Paul Robeson to Frederick Douglass and restored Phillis Wheatley to her rightful place in U.S. literature. Subsequently, Iris Noble started writing for young people with a biography of Clarence Darrow and shook up conventional attitudes with a book that treated Cleopatra as a political ruler instead of a sex object. On the west coast, Ruth Franchere wrote about two California rebels—Jack London and Cesar Chavez. Milton Meltzer put the life of his friend Langston Hughes on paper in a well-written, finely-crafted account. It must be borne in mind, however, that these are indeed exceptions, and the general run of biographies for young people are well characterized by Jurich and Saul.

27. Herbert Kohl, *Reading, How to* (New York: Bantam Books, 1974), 175.

Part 1. Class Value-Judgments

The "Middling Sort":
The People of the Book 1500–1850

Robert Leeson

They called themselves the "middling sort"—merchant, craft master, scrivener, lawyer. Cunning, courageous, never idle, they were as able to fire a cannon as to invent it. The Spaniards called them "Protestant Pirates," and they mastered the Grandee abroad in the sixteenth century, as they mastered the Cavaliers at home in the seventeenth. Restless and reckless, sober and cautious, their eyes on the future, in this world or the next, they were above all individualists, a cloud of atoms held together by the conviction that they were of a special kind ("Men of high degree are vanity, men of low degree are a lie," said the 63rd Psalm). Always a minority, balanced between the poor and the rich, they were ready to turn to one or another in time of crisis: ready to lead movements of protest, able to detach themselves to make deals with the powers that be. Endlessly seeking more freedoms, more rights, they were endlessly anxious that those rights should not be dispensed too widely. Their ranks thus contained the noblest of liberators and the worst of hypocrites, religious bigots and enlightened educators.

Their quest for influence and power went on over three centuries, along with their quest for understanding of themselves and their world. And in that quest their chief means was the book, from the Bible (their guarantee of knowing what God said without taking the word of the priest for it) to the novel (the "guarantee that the individual will always be more than one billionth part of

From *Reading and Righting* © Robert Leeson 1985. Published by Collins (London: 1985); reprinted by kind permission of the publisher and the author.

Robert Leeson is a journalist and the author of sixteen books for young people; he is active in the Writers in Schools program in England.

a billion," as William Golding told the Nobel Prize Jury in December 1983).

For them the book, print and trade were linked from the start. Caxton's stated reason for working out a uniform English text was the difficulties which dialect differences placed in the way of merchants as they bought and sold around the country. Freedom to trade (against the court monopolists of Charles I), freedom to print, sell, read and comment on the Bible and other books (against the edicts of his bishops): these were the aims which brought the middling sort with their servants and journeymen on to the battlefields of the Civil War in the 1640s. The notion of Cromwell's soldiers, marching with Bibles in their knapsacks, is a myth, but a powerful one.

Hard core of this army and clearest single voice among the middling sort were the Puritans. They were in fact as diverse themselves as the middling sort, and much misunderstood today, when "Puritan" often refers to the critic and the censor. Originally, in the sixteenth century, it stood for a purifying force in religious and social life. It was indeed a force for revolutionary social change. Only if one sees the Puritans' actions as part of a long struggle to change society, can one throw light on this strange mixture of the liberating and the repressive.

The Puritans opened their assault on the bishops' control of the printing presses in 1640 by complaining of "lascivious, idle and unprofitable ballads" selling in London. The bishops, they alleged, were not truly interested in morality but only wanted to suppress reforming, Puritan ideas. In 1641, the Star Chamber was abolished and with it went Crown-Church control over the presses. During the Civil War and the short-lived Commonwealth Government that followed, the number of presses trebled to sixty. From them came a flood of pamphlets and books on almost every topic. For some Puritans, the Presbyterians, there was too much freedom. But Milton, Cromwell's foreign secretary for a while, defended free publication in his *Areopagitica* —"Give me the liberty to know, to utter and to argue freely."

Strict control of the presses was clamped down again, when the Monarchy was restored in 1660. Charles II and his restored bishops, by insisting that they sign the 39 Articles of the Church of England, which they refused to do, drove many of their Puritan opponents out of the church, university and the grammar schools which the church controlled. These people, the Dissenters, or, as they were later known, the Nonconformists, formed the most active element in a social opposition which as before found its expression in literature, in writing and teaching. The Rule of the Saints for which they had fought was postponed, but they had faith, they could work and wait for the future—if not they, then their children would reach the Promised Land. Their contribution to a new, printed literature for the young was to be crucial in the next century and a half.

New ideas were in the air. A new class of well-to-do people wanted education—in book terms—for their children. They wanted books that would teach, not the "feigned fables" and "vain fantasies" of the oral tradition. But the teachings must appeal to the growing mind. There was a demand for new editions of books like *Aesop's Fables*—entertaining tales with the moral made clear. Even Charles I's unpopular censor, L'Estrange, in private a man with enlightened views on education, produced an edition of *Aesop*.

In this new era censorship in its old form could not last. The undertow of the movement toward free trade, beneath all the political and religious battles, was too strong. And in the 1690s the presses were going full blast again, not just in London and the university towns, but throughout the country. Some printers served the didactic trade, some the frivolous; some, opportunistically, served both. As Harvey Darton says in his *Children's Books in England* (1932), "Penny Merriments and Penny Godlinesses" poured from the presses. There were books for those who could afford them (a book cost a good deal more than a pair of breeches), chapbooks or installment "parts" of books, or ballad sheets, for those who could not. Those who could not read, the majority in farm, village or town, would turn to someone else who could, to read for them. The process by which the reader would replace the story-teller had begun.

The Puritan-Dissenters' part in the making of the new literature is a remarkable one. It is said, with some truth, that they aimed above all with their writing to teach truth, Godliness, and morality to the young. It is also said that they were against fiction, against fantasy and the imagination, that they frowned on enjoyment in the young, preferring to concentrate children's minds on approaching death and repentance to avoid damnation. They introduced the touching death-bed/conversion scene, the climax of many a children's (and adults') story for two centuries to come. But all these aspects of their work need closer examination, because they are not what they seem.

Preoccupation with death and death-beds is not surprising in writers like John Bunyan, Thomas White, James Janeway, Thomas Willis and other Puritans who had experienced war, fire, and plague; who lived at a time when, even in peacetime, life was short. But the Puritan interest in the gateway between this life and the next is at one with their interest in childhood, in nurture, conduct and morality, honesty and industry. It is an interest in the future; and in a future, different, better society. The wickedness of this world is not simply a complaint about the human condition, but also a critique of the way things are run. God, said Hugh Peters, Cromwell's chaplain, did not want the Saints to stand around with their hands in their pockets waiting for his Kingdom to come on earth.

Janeway, who published his *Token For Children* in 1671, is noted for his grim insistence on life's end. But his promise to his child readers that "in heaven they shall never be beat any more, they shall never be sick or in pain any more" breathes a quite contrary spirit of warmth—of better life in a different order. Like Bunyan, Janeway lived "in two worlds at once," says Harvey Darton *(Children's Books in England)*. In modern terms we recognize, through the religious language and talk of the next world, the revolutionary import of what they were saying.

It is interesting, too, that in making their sober, didactic points, these writers, from the lesser-known right up to the great Bunyan, were far from unimaginative. Willis uses vivid imagery in his *The Key to Knowledge* (1682); White indulges in comic exaggeration in *A Little Book For Little Children* (1660). In striving to produce a body of reading matter which would convey a message to the young different from the ancient store of folk tales with their giants, ghosts and goblins, the "Godly" book led on toward a new fiction, despite all the protestations of those who produced it.

The process is contradictory and fascinating. On the surface it is a battle between "fiction," or "vain fantasy," and "truth," between the didactic and the fantastic, between morality and entertainment. But underneath it runs the struggle between an old way of life and scale of values, and a new. The new, to gain an audience, turned constantly, perhaps often unconsciously, to the forms and conventions of the old, with its still powerful and enduring appeal.

John Foxe's *The Book of Martyrs* (1563) was a Puritan manifesto, a kind of counter-attack to the saints' lives published by the Catholic Church. Both were, in their way, religious versions of the old folk-heroes, half human, half spirit. But the saints' lives had compromised themselves in the battle with the pagan tale by including miracles, giving dubious authority to tales of magic. For its readers, Foxe's book was not like either saints' tale or folk tale. It was *true*. It was about real people, about events in current times. It was about the heroes of a social group under pressure. Their stories were more violent and horrific than any of the folk tales of the sixteenth century, which the Puritan Reginald Scot declared "servants have affrighted us with since we were children." Foxe's *Book of Martyrs* was to rob generations of children of sleep just as effectively. But because its purpose was acceptable, it was given as a Sunday School prize right until the twentieth century. As the real events which inspired it vanished into the past, it became like the tales of old, a part of the folklore of a new society, a new class, ready for fictional appeal, not instruction.

One can see this complex process working itself out in three books published between the 1670s and the 1720s. All best-sellers, all written at first for adults, all became immensely popular with children. They are John Bunyan's *Pilgrim's Progress* (1678), Jonathan Swift's *Gulliver's Travels* (1726) and *Robinson Crusoe* by Daniel Defoe (1719). Two are written by Dissenters, Bunyan and Defoe, the other by an unorthodox Minister of the Church, Swift.

Like all the folk tales before them, they are about a quest, a test for the hero and an eventual reward. They all convey lessons and messages through the use of vivid imagery. The authors were all propagandists. They had all written pamphlets for wide distribution using clear and simple English. But all three books are "fictions." The characters are invented people (although Defoe used a real-life castaway, Selkirk, as the model for his Crusoe). All three stories were accepted as true by those who read them, just as audiences had accepted folk tales as true. They were accepted by those who condemned the stories of the oral tradition as "abominable absurdities," "occult and inexplicable causes" or "fantastic visions." These new stories were in their way fantasies, but unlike the old, they were not "vain"—their purpose was clear, it was asserted, not assumed like that of the folk tale.

In his journey toward the celestial city Christian *(Pilgrim's Progress)* leaves his family behind. But they are not forgotten as are the families of the departing folk hero or heroine. Eventually they follow him. Like the folk hero, Christian meets dragons, giants, enchantments, visions, and he wins a kingdom. Bunyan and his readers knew such victories to be denied them here and now. So they must win them in the spirit.

Giant Despair of Doubting Castle is a real figure of folk tale and can be accepted as such by children even today. He is also a psychological experience—symbolizing the personal doubt and depression that can come to an individual, or the social despair that can overcome a frustrated and persecuted group. By inventing Christian, by making him as recognizable as any real life martyr, *Pilgrim's Progress* carries the reality of Foxe's book over into fiction. Blending the substance of a religious allegory with the structure and conventions of the folk tale, Bunyan points the way forward to the novel. Bunyan had served in the army, been tried in court, and kept in prison. But his book, unlike Foxe's, was not an imaginative reconstruction of actual happenings; it was a truthful imagining of the way the world goes, created in Bunyan's mind, aided by his own experience.

The folk tale had human beings and nonhuman spirits, which disturbed the Puritans. Bunyan resolves the problem by locating them all in the human mind. Human attitudes and moral outlooks are also implicit in the struggles of the old folk tale. But these have journeyed so far from their origins that by now the attitudes are buried almost invisibly within the story. Thus the fantasy appears to be vain (modern commentators sometimes assume the folk tale has no moral because they cannot discern it). Bunyan in his tale makes the Giants and Dragons openly display and represent moral (or immoral) qualities. His attitude, his outlook is asserted and proclaimed, whereas in the long re-told, developed and stylized folk tale, all attitudes are assumed.

Bunyan thus took one of the crucial steps in the creation of the fiction of the printed word. First the new content, the new message, the new meaning must be declared, asserted. For the middling sort, this book said where they stood. It also declared that they existed. If you do not appear in the stories of your society's culture, you do not exist. You are "invisible," culturally. Christian, the hero, typical Puritan craftsman like John Bunyan, was proof that his kind of people existed. And they had to go on asserting their values until these became so much a part of the whole society's way of life that they could be taken for granted, assumed. Thus the development of printed fiction is a journey from assertion to assumption. Until Bunyan's Pilgrim made his *real* journey, the new book story could not escape from the old oral tale. It had to be true, before it could become fiction again. Without the new morality the tale would not be worth telling. Without the authority of age-old forms of story-telling, the new story could not win the audience and thus survive.

Gulliver's journey is like the folk journey, in that it takes him into different kingdoms. These seem unlike the real world. They have their own rules, though, and Swift was well versed in lore about alternative fairy worlds. And they reflect that world in which we live. Among the tiny people, the giants, the graceful horses and the grotesque humanoids, we meet again all the faults and follies of humanity.

Again, as with Bunyan, the young can read what they like from *Gulliver's Travels,* taking it as a fantastic adventure among imaginary people. In maturity they can read it as a satire on the rich and great. At a distance, now, we can see, perhaps more faintly, these same two levels of understanding operating in the story-culture of the oral tradition. With the new literature, expressing the known experience of the modern world, we see these things more clearly.

Crusoe's journey is that of *explorer,* like Gulliver's. But Crusoe's journey is also that of *conqueror.* Crusoe is human, and superhuman. He makes engaging mistakes, but he triumphs over incredible difficulties. He stands in for the reader, doing what the reader would wish to be able to do, to survive in danger and a hostile environment. And, for the eighteenth century English of the middling sort, he does more. He takes over a native population, after rescuing them from more "savage" enemies. His phrase "my people perfectly subjected" is significant. For in the real England in which he lived, Defoe looked in vain among the competing merchants and craft masters and rebellious journeymen, for what he called the "Great Principle of Subordination," that social order in which all would willingly accept their place.

Then, as later, the finding and making of Empire were seen as the solution to never-ending social trouble at home. Crusoe was to provide the model for hundreds of similar and worse adventures abroad, written specifically for the young in the next two hundred years, as England set out to subject the world. As the King, in *Gulliver's Travels,* put it:

> A crew of pirates . . . see a harmless people, are entertained with kindness, they give the country a new name, they take formal possession of it for the King, they set up a rotten plank or a stone for memorial, they murder two dozen of the natives, bring away a couple more by force for a sample, return home and get their pardon. Here commences a new Dominion acquired with a title by Divine Right.

The new literature, the new era for society, were launched. The means to wealth and power for the middling sort were coming to hand. Where they had invested faith in the future, they were to invest in more material things. But their greatest investment, for the future, was in their own children.

How to Read Donald Duck and Other Innocent Literature for Children

Ariel Dorfman and Armand Mattelart

There can be no doubt that children's literature is a genre like any other, monopolized by specialized subsectors within the culture industry. Some dedicate themselves to the adventure story, some to mystery, others to the erotic novel, etc. But at least the latter are directed toward an amorphous public, which buys at random. In the case of the children's genre, however, there is a virtually biologically captive, predetermined audience.

Children's comics are devised by adults, whose work is determined and justified by their idea of what a child is or should be. Often, they even cite "scientific" sources or ancient traditions ("it is popular wisdom, dating from time immemorial") in order to explain the nature of the public's needs. In reality, however, these adults are not about to tell stories which would jeopardize the future they are planning for their children.

So the comics show the child as a miniature adult, enjoying an idealized, gilded infancy which is really nothing but the adult projection of some magic era beyond the reach of the harsh discord of daily life. It is a plan for salvation which presupposes a primal stage within every existence, sheltered from contradictions

Reprinted in shortened form from Ariel Dorfman and Armand Mattelart, *How to Read Donald Duck: Imperialist Ideology in the Disney Comic,* David Kunzle, translator, p. 30–76. New York: International General, 1984 (2nd Edition Enlarged). Copyright © International General 1975, 1984. Reprinted by permission.

Ariel Dorfman and Armand Mattelart are Chilean exiles. Dorfman writes for newspapers in Latin America, Europe, and the United States and is the author of a novel, *Widows,* and of *The Empire's Old Clothes.* Mattelart has written studies on communications and popular culture. *How to Read Donald Duck* has appeared in eleven languages. David Kunzle, who translated it into English, is professor of art at the University of California, Los Angeles.

and permitting imaginative escape. Juvenile literature, embodying purity, spontaneity, and natural virtue, while lacking in sex and violence, represents earthly paradise. It guarantees man's own redemption as an adult: as long as there are children, he will have the pretext and means for self-gratification with the spectacle of his own dreams. In his children's reading, man stages and performs over and over again the supposedly unproblematical scenes of his inner refuge. Regaling himself with his own legend, he falls into tautology; he admires himself in the mirror, thinking it to be a window. But the child playing down there in the garden is the purified adult looking back at himself.

So it is the adult who produces the comics, and the child who consumes them. The role of the apparent child actor, who reigns over this uncontaminated world, is at once that of audience and dummy for his father's ventriloquism. The father denies his progeny a voice of his own, and as in any authoritarian society, he establishes himself as the other's sole interpreter and spokesman. All the little fellow can do is to let his father represent him.

But wait a minute, ladies and gentlemen! Perhaps children really *are* like that?

Indeed, the adults set out to prove that this literature is essential to the child, satisfying his eager demands. But this is a closed circuit: children have been conditioned by the magazines and the culture which spawned them. They tend to reflect in their daily lives the characteristics they are supposed to possess in order to win affection, acceptance, and rewards; in order to grow up properly and integrate into society. The Disney world is sustained by rewards and punishments; it hides an iron hand with the velvet glove. Considered, by definition, unfit to choose from the alternatives available to adults, the youngsters intuit "natural" behavior, happily accepting that their imagination be channelled into incontestable ethical and esthetic ideals. Juvenile literature is justified by the children it has generated through a vicious circle.

Thus, adults create for themselves a childhood embodying their own angelical aspirations, which offer consolation, hope and a guarantee of a "better," but unchanging, future. This "new reality," this autonomous realm of magic, is artfully isolated from the reality of the everyday. Adult values are projected onto the child, as if childhood was a special domain where these values could be protected uncritically. In Disney, the two strata—adult and child—are not to be considered as antagonistic; they fuse in a single embrace, and history becomes biology. The identity of parent and child inhibits the emergence of true generational conflicts. The pure child will replace the corrupt father, preserving the latter's values. The future (the child) reaffirms the present (the adult), which, in turn, transmits the past. The apparent independence which the father benevolently bestows upon this little territory of his creation is the very means of assuring his supremacy.

But there is more: this lovely, simple, smooth, translucent, chaste and pacific region, which has been promoted as Salvation, is unconsciously infiltrated by a multiplicity of adult conflicts and contradictions. This transparent world is designed both to conceal and reveal latent traces of real and painful tensions. The parent suffers this split consciousness without being aware of his inner turmoil. Nostalgically, he appropriates the "natural disposition" of the child in order to conceal the guilt arising from his own fall from grace; it is the price of redemption for his own condition. By the standards of his angelic model, he must judge himself as guilty; as much as he needs this land of enchantment and salvation, he could never imagine it with the necessary purity. He could never turn into his own child. But this salvation only offers him an imperfect escape; it can never be so pure as to block off all his real life problems.

In juvenile literature, the adult, corroded by the trivia of every-day life, blindly defends his image of youth and innocence. Because of this, it is perhaps the best (and least expected) place to study the disguises and truths of contemporary man. For the adult, in protecting his dream-image of youth, hides the fear that to penetrate it would destroy his dreams and reveal the reality it conceals.

Thus, *the imagination of the child is conceived as the past and future utopia of the adult.* But set up as an inner realm of fantasy, this model of his Origin and his Ideal Future Society lends itself to the free assimilation of all his woes. It enables the adult to partake of his own demons, provided they have been coated in the syrup of paradise, and that they travel there with the passport of innocence.

The much vaunted and very inviting fantasy world of Disney systematically cuts the earthly roots of his characters. Their charm supposedly lies in their familiarity, their resemblance to ordinary, common or garden variety of people who cross our path every day. But, in Disney, characters only function by virtue of a suppression of *real* and concrete factors; that is, their personal history, their birth and death, and their whole development in between, as they grow and change. Since they are not engendered by any biological act, Disney characters may aspire to immortality: whatever apparent, momentary sufferings are inflicted on them in the course of their adventures, they have been liberated, at least, from the curse of the body.

By eliminating a character's effective past, and at the same time denying him the opportunity of self-examination in respect to his present predicament, Disney denies him the only perspective from which he can look at himself, other than from the world in which he has always been submerged. The future cannot serve him either: reality is unchanging.

The generation gap is not only obliterated between the child, who reads the comic, and the parent, who buys it, but also within the comic itself by a process of substitution in which the uncles can always be replaced by the nephews.[1] Since there is no father, constant replacement and displacement of the uncle is painless. Since he is not genetically responsible for the youngster, it is not treasonable to overrule him. It is as if the uncle were never really king, an appropriate term since we are dealing with fairy tales, but only regent, watching over the throne until its legitimate heir, the young Prince Charming, eventually comes to assume it.

But the physical absence of the father does not mean the absence of paternal power. Far from it, the relations between Disney characters are much more vertical and authoritarian than those of the most tyrannical real life home, where a harsh discipline can still be softened by sharing, love, mother, siblings, solidarity, and mutual aid. Moreover, in the real life home, the maturing child is always exposed to new alternatives and standards of behavior, as he responds to pressures from outside the family. But since power in Disney is wielded not by a father, but by an uncle, it becomes arbitrary.

Patriarchy in our society is defended, by the patriarchs, as a matter of biological predetermination (undoubtedly sustained by a social structure which institutionalizes the education of the child as primarily a family responsibility). Uncle-authority, on the other hand, not having been conferred by the father (the uncle's brothers and sisters, who must in theory have given birth to the nephews, simply do not exist), is of purely *de facto* origin, rather than a natural right. It is a contractual relationship masquerading as a natural relationship, a tyranny which does not even assume the responsibility of breeding. And one cannot rebel against it in the name of nature; one cannot say to an uncle "you are a bad father."

Within this family perimeter, no one loves anyone else, there is never an expression of affection or loyalty toward another human being. In any moment of suffering, a person is alone; there is no disinterested or friendly helping hand. One encounters, at best, a sense of pity, derived from a view of the other as some cripple or beggar, some old down-and-out deserving of our charity. Let us take the most extreme example: the famous love between Mickey and Pluto. Although Mickey certainly shows a charitable kind of affection for his dog, the latter is always under the obligation to demonstrate his usefulness and heroism. In one episode, having behaved very badly and having been locked up in the cellar as punishment, Pluto redeems himself by catching a thief (there is always one around). The police give Mickey a hundred-dollar reward, and offer another hundred to buy the dog itself, but Mickey refuses to sell: "O.K. Pluto, you cost me around fifty dollars in damages this afternoon, but this reward leaves me with a good profit." Commercial relations are common coin here, even in so "maternal" a bond as that between Mickey and his blood-hound.

With Scrooge McDuck, it is of course worse. In one episode, the nephews, exhausted after six months scouring the Gobi desert on Scrooge's behalf, are upbraided for having taken so long, and are paid one dollar for their pains. They flee thankfully, in fear of yet more forced labor. It never occurs to them to object, to stay put and to demand better treatment.

But McDuck obliges them to depart once more, sick as they are, in search of a coin weighing several tons, for which the avaricious millionaire is evidently prepared to pay a few cents. It turns out that the gigantic coin is a forgery and Scrooge has to buy the authentic one. Donald smiles in relief: "Now that you have the true Hunka Junka, Uncle Scrooge, we can all take a rest." The tyrant replies: "Not until you return that counterfeit hunk of junk and bring back my pennies!" The ducks are depicted in the last picture like slaves in ancient Egypt, pushing the rock to its destiny at the other end of the globe. Instead of coming to the realization that he ought to open his mouth to say *no,* Donald reaches the very opposite conclusion: "Me and my big mouth!" Not even a complaint is permitted against this unquestioned supremacy. What are the consequences of Daisy's Aunt Tizzy discovering a year later that Daisy had dared to attend a dance she disapproved of? "I'm going . . . and I am cutting *you* out of my will, Daisy! Goodbye!"

There is no room for love in this world. The youngsters admire a distant uncle (Unca Zak McWak) who invented a "spray to kill appleworms." "The whole world is thankful to him for that. . . . He's famous . . . and rich," the nephews exclaim. Donald sensibly replies, "Bah! *Brains, fame* and *fortune* aren't *everything.*" "Oh, no? What's left?" ask Huey, Dewey, and Louie in unison. And

Donald is at a loss for words: "er . . . um . . . let's see now . . . uh-h. . . ."

So the child's "natural disposition" evidently serves Disney only insofar as it lends innocence to the adult world, and serves the myth of childhood. Meanwhile, it has been stripped of the true qualities of children: their unbounded, open (and therefore manipulable) trustfulness, their creative spontaneity (as Piaget has shown), their incredible capacity for unreserved, unconditional love, and their imagination which overflows around and through and within the objects which surround them. Beneath all the charm of the sweet little creatures of Disney, on the other hand, lurks the law of the jungle: envy, ruthlessness, cruelty, terror, blackmail, exploitation of the weak. Lacking vehicles for their natural affection, children learn through Disney fear and hatred.

It is not Disney's critics, but Disney himself who is to be accused of disrupting the home; it is Disney who is the worst enemy of family harmony.

Every Disney character stands either on one side or the other of the power demarcation line. All those below are bound to obedience, submission, discipline, humility. Those above are free to employ constant coercion: threats, moral and physical repression, and economic domination (i.e., control over the means of subsistence). The relationship of powerful to powerless is also expressed in a less aggressive, more paternalistic way, through gifts, to the vassals. It is a world of permanent profit and bonus. It is only natural that the Duckburg Women's Clubs are always engaged in good works: the dispossessed eagerly accept whatever charity can be had for the begging.

The world of Disney is a nineteenth century orphanage. With this difference: there is no outside, and the orphans have nowhere to flee to. In spite of all their global traveling, and their crazy and feverish mobility, the characters remain trapped within, and doomed to return to, the same power structure. The elasticity of physical space conceals the true rigidity of the relationships within which the characters are imprisoned. The mere fact of being older or richer or more beautiful in this world confers authority. The less fortunate regard their subjection as natural. They spend all day complaining about the slavemaster, but they would rather obey his craziest order than challenge him.

The imaginative world of the child has become the political utopia of a social class. In the Disney comics, one never meets a member of the working or proletarian classes, and nothing is the product of an industrial process. But this does not mean that the worker is absent. On the contrary: he is present under two masks, that of the noble savage and that of the criminal-lumpen. Both groups serve to destroy the worker as a class reality, and preserve certain myths which the bourgeoisie have from the very beginning been fabricating and adding to in order to conceal and domesticate the enemy, impede his solidarity, and make him function smoothly within the system and cooperate in his own ideological enslavement.

In order to rationalize their dominance and justify their privileged position, the bourgeoisie divided the world of the dominated as follows: first, the peasant sector, which is harmless, natural, truthful, ingenuous, spontaneous, infantile, and static; second, the urban sector, which is threatening, teeming, dirty, suspicious, calculating, embittered, vicious, and essentially mobile. The peasant acquires in this process of mythification the exclusive property of being "popular," and becomes installed as a folk-guardian of everything produced and preserved by the people. Far from the influence of the steaming urban centers, he is purified through a cyclical return to the primitive virtues of the earth. The myth of the people as noble savage—the people as a child who must be protected for its own good—arose in order to justify the domination of a class. The peasants were the only ones capable of becoming incontrovertible vehicles for the permanent validity of bourgeois ideals. Juvenile literature fed on these "popular" myths and served as a constant allegorical testimony to what the people were supposed to be.

Each great urban civilization (Alexandria for Theocritus, Rome for Virgil, the modern era for Sannazaro, Montemayor, Shakespeare, Cervantes, d'Urfey) created its pastoral myth: an extra-social Eden chaste and pure. Together with this evangelical bucolism, there emerged a picturesque literature teeming with ruffians, vagabonds, gamblers, gluttons, etc., who reveal the true nature of urban man; mobile, degenerate, irredeemable. The world was divided between the lay heaven of the shepherds, and the terrestrial inferno of the unemployed. At the same time, a utopian literature flourished (Thomas More, Tommaso Campanella), projecting into the future, on the basis of an optimism fostered by technology and a pessimism resulting from the breakdown of medieval unity, the ecstatic realm of social perfection. The rising bourgeoisie, which gave the necessary momentum to the voyages of discovery, found innumerable peoples who theoretically corresponded to their pastoral-utopian schemata; their ideal of universal Christian reason proclaimed by Erasmian humanism. Thus the division between positive-popular-rustic and negative-popular-proletarian was overwhelmingly reinforced. The new continents were colonized in the name of this division; to prove that, removed from original sin and mercantilist taint, these continents might be the site for the ideal history which the bourgeoisie had once imagined for themselves at home. An ideal history which was ruined and threatened by the constant opposition of the idle, filthy, teeming, promiscuous, and extortionary proletarians.

In spite of the failure in Latin America, in spite of the failure in Africa, Oceania, and in Asia, the myth never lost its vitality. On the contrary, it served as a constant spur in the only country which was able to develop it still further. By opening the frontier further and further, the United States elaborated the myth and eventually gave birth to a "Way of Life," and to an ideology shared by the infernal Disney — a man who in trying to open and close the frontier of the child's imagination, based himself precisely on those now-antiquated myths which gave rise to his own country.

It is surely undeniable nowadays that all man's real and concrete achievements derive from his effort and his work. Although nature provides the raw materials, man must struggle to make a living from them. If this were not so, we would still be in Eden.

In the world of Disney, no one has to work in order to produce. There is a constant round of buying, selling, and consuming, but to all appearances, none of the products involved has required any effort whatsoever to make. Nature is the great labor force, producing objects of human and social utility as if they were natural.

The human origin of the product — be it table, house, car, clothing, gold, coffee, wheat, or maize (which comes from *granaries,* direct from warehouses, rather than from the fields) — has been suppressed. The process of production has been eliminated, as has all reference to its genesis; the actors, the objects, the circumstances of the process never existed. What, in fact, has been erased is the paternity of the object, and the possibility to link it to the process of production.

This brings us back to the curious Disney family structure with the absence of natural paternity. The simultaneous lack of direct biological production and direct economic production is not coincidental. They both coincide and reinforce a dominant ideological structure which also seeks to eliminate the working class, the true producer of objects. And with it, the class struggle.

Disney exorcises history, magically expelling the socially (and biologically) reproductive element, leaving amorphous, rootless, and inoffensive products—without sweat, without blood, without effort, and without the misery which they inevitably sow in the life of the working class. There is a term which would be like dynamite to Disney, like a scapular to a vampire, like electricity convulsing a frog: social class. That is why Disney must publicize his creations as universal, beyond frontiers; they reach all homes, they reach all countries. O immortal Disney, international patrimony, reaching all children everywhere, everywhere, everywhere.

Just as a Disney character leaves his normal surroundings to undertake fantasy adventures free of the usual time-space limitations of Duckburg, or undergo the most absurd extravaganzas in the most innocent of urban occupations, so it is similarly proposed that children transcend the concrete reality of their life, and surrender to the "magic" and "adventure" of the magazines. The segregation of the child's world between the everyday and the enchanted begins in the comics themselves, which take the first step in teaching children, from their tenderest years, to separate work from leisure, and humdrum reality from the play of their imagination. Apparently, their habitual world is that of unimaginative work, whereas the world of the comic is that of fantasy-filled leisure. Children are once again split between matter and spirit, and encouraged to eliminate the imaginary from the real surrounding world. To defend this type of comic on the grounds that it feeds the "overflowing imagination" of the child who tends, supposedly, by his very nature to reject his immediate surroundings, is really to inject into children the escapist needs of contemporary society. A society so imprisoned in its own oppressive, dead-end world that it is constrained to dream up perversely "innocent" utopias. The adult's self-protective escapist dreams impel the child to abandon its integrated childhood existence. Later, adults use this "natural" fantasy trait of childhood to lessen their own anxiety and alienation from their daily work.

Entertainment, as it is understood by the capitalist mass culture, tries to reconcile everything—work with leisure, the commonplace with the imaginary, the social with the extrasocial, body with soul, production with consumption, city with countryside—while veiling the contradictions arising from their interrelationships. All the conflicts of the real world, the nerve centers of bourgeois society, are purified in the imagination in order to be absorbed and co-opted into the world of entertainment. Simply to call Disney a liar is to miss the target. Lies are easily exposed. The laundering process in Disney, as in all the mass media, is much more complex. Disney's social class has molded the world in a certain clearly defined and functional way which corresponds to *its* needs. The bourgeois imagination does not ignore this reality, but seizes it and returns it, veneered with innocence, to the consumer. Once it is interpreted as a magical, marvelous paradigm of his own common experience, the reader then can consume his own contradiction in whitewashed form. This permits him to continue viewing and living these conflicts with the innocence and helplessness of a child. He enters the future without having resolved or even understood the problems of the present.

NOTES

1. Donald Duck as Uncle Donald to Huey, Dewey, and Louie; also, Uncle Scrooge.

Censorship or Selection? A British View

Editors of *Children's Books Bulletin*

Wherever and whenever the issues of sexism, racism and class bias in children's books are raised – at conferences, in discussions with groups or individuals – sooner or later someone will mention censorship and suggest that, whatever the merits of the case, the issue of the content of children's books is somehow out of bounds. Publishers and writers are especially quick to suspect censorial motives in those who wish to discuss a book's content or message.

The accusation that those who concern themselves with the content and availability of children's books are advocating censorship remains unsubstantiated. Scaremongering about "black lists" (sic) of undesirable titles at recent children's book conferences is hardly helpful. But let us consider the arguments.

Fear of censorship is most often expressed by people who have had no experience of censorship – i.e., the seizure or banning (and destruction) of printed works, usually through the deployment of the army or police. Examples of the suppression of literature in countries round the world can easily be cited from recent times, and they run parallel with the repression of the exponents or believers in the ideas expressed in that literature. Literature has always been seen to be important and powerful.

There is an all too prevalent assumption that the writing, production and distribution of children's books is free and open, spontaneous and natural and, if guided at all, then only by considerations of quality and taste, natural things those, and of profit, natural too in this society of ours. Certainly there is little public recognition of the decision-making that lies behind the production of every published book, and behind the appearance of that book in a bookshop or on the shelves of a public or school library.

The recent excited rejection by "quality" children's book publishers of the idea of guidelines to assist them in coping with

From *Children's Books Bulletin* (London), No. 3, (Spring 1980): 2–3.
Children's Books Bulletin was a journal devoted to children's literature reflecting the lives of working people and other areas not covered in the mainstream journals in the field.

newly developed awareness of sexism in children's books, on the grounds that their use would lead to unjustifiable interference in the literary process, is incomprehensible when one considers the editor's role. For editors interfere in the literary process and are expected to do so, thereby helping a book to fruition by supporting the writer or illustrator, sometimes even encouraging the rewriting of passages from a different point of view or suggesting changes of focus or plot. For the most part this editorial role is entirely positive and leads to a close cooperative relationship between editors and their writers and illustrators. It is unthinkable, within this framework of mutual cooperation, that concern about sexism (or other kinds of bias) could not be tackled, perhaps with the help of guidelines, on much the same level as discussions about, for example, punctuation or illogicalities in a plot.

In addition, it is rarely recognized that this editorial interference is, and always has been, concerned with questions of content. Recent examples of editorial "censorship" in children's books include the excision of the passage describing mutual sexual exploration from the 1978 Puffin edition of Jean MacGibbon's *Hal* (Heinemann 1974). Petronella Breinburg's picture book *Doctor Sean* (Bodley Head) was adapted for the alert U.S. market with the qualification of the sexist assumptions. In 1978 Penguin books published simultaneously in hardback and paperback (Kestrel and Puffin) *The Puffin Book of Flags* by J.C.G. George, a guide to the world's flags and their meaning. Shortly after publication the Puffin edition was called in – the annotation to one of the flags (Vietnam) had, by an oversight, not been changed before publication. The unacceptable annotation was:

> Vietnam is in south-east Asia. Its flag is blood red with a five-pointed yellow star in the centre. The colour represents the ruthlessness and the star the godlessness of its new masters, the communists.

This annotation was promptly amended. What is interesting about this incident is that it is a clear demonstration of the kind of editorial changes for social and political reasons which are made all the time as part of the editing process.

Publishers can thus be seen as significant forces of control of what literature is available to children, and also of the ways that children's literature is made available – the size of print runs, which books go into paperback, etc. But perhaps the most "censorial" role that editors play is in the selection of the manuscripts that they will publish (a selection made from thousands submitted) and in the commissioning of most nonfiction titles and some fiction.

The way a publicity department pushes (or does not push) books plays a significant role in deciding which titles end up in major book stores, libraries and schools. If anyone is "censoring" children's books, it is the editors and their publishing colleagues.

Teachers and librarians are the largest buyers of children's books and thus their tastes, preferences, and knowledge of the field crucially affect the range of books available to children. With few bookshops committed to children's books, the field is left open to dynamic mail order firms who also, of course, select. (Heffer's first children's book mail order catalogue lists 17 different editions of *Alice in Wonderland* but no Ashley, Dhondy or Leeson, to name but a few.) There must be many consumers of children's books from the parent to the school librarian or school bookshop organizer who feel that there is a "censorial" conspiracy at work, so difficult is it to get hold of the children's books of their choice.

All this to underline the obvious, that children's books are stalked by interference and by selection—a good deal of it censorial—from their inception to the moment they reach the young reader's hand. It may seem frivolous to classify these moments of selection as "censorship" when one recalls the systematic censorship of books, newspapers and journals and the physical intimidation of writers that is ongoing in such countries as Uruguay and Argentina,[1] but such a classification is no more extreme than the accusation of censorship leveled at those who are seeking to raise awareness about the manifestations of bias, distortions, and omissions in children's books. If both processes are to be termed "censorship," then the fundamental difference between the two must be recognized. The first seeks to control and *restrict* what is available. The second, by pointing out omissions and distortions and posing alternatives, seeks to *increase* the range of options available to children in their literature. Thus, as a direct result of the campaigning work of the Women's Movement in Britain in the last decade, many publishers are now aware that few children's books reflect women's history and women's present day contribution to society, and efforts are being made to rectify this omission.

So why is the fear of censorship so often raised when bias in children's literature is up for discussion? Perhaps a fear of social change has something to do with it, and in particular the fear of the emergent Black movement and the need to confront one's own racism; the fear of the Women's Movement and of a society in which women have equal opportunities and status; a fear of Socialism, of equal opportunities for everyone. But there is also an anguished concern for the creative imagination of the writer and illustrator, the delicate flower of art and literature which needs protecting from extraneous, insensitive influences.

Let us reaffirm once and for all that writers and illustrators of children's books have every right to write and illustrate as they please, to be involved or not involved in debates about children's books, as they please. Certainly, writers and illustrators should not be chivvied and harassed as they create, although for some, of course, social change is in itself a source of inspiration and creativity.

It is important, however, that the parameters of the critical debate *around* children's books should be extended to include consideration of content as well as esthetics. This is an approach now shared by many who work with children and their books — teachers, librarians, parents, etc. It is not insignificant that Britain, where the critical debate about children's books has for so long been dominated by children's book writers and their running dogs, there has been a strong reaction to the new criticism. It is strange that children's book writers accept as fair comment being told in the review columns of *The Times* that they cannot write, but cry censorship when a reviewer points out that a particular book is, for example, sexist.

Some of the ways that editors can extend their editorial practices to include a consideration of bias are touched on above. For some editors this is already normal practice. Let us be clear that this is not intended to *eliminate* bias but to give a writer or illustrator (often unaware of manifestations of bias) the *choice* as to whether bias remains or not. Publish and be damned certainly, but at least be clear about what it is that you are publishing and do not then try to control the critical appraisal of that book by crying wolf/censorship.

For the selectors of children's books — teachers, librarians, parents, booksellers, etc. — the lack of clear debate about censorship has not helped them in their search to understand and face the challenges of choosing books today. With limited funds and limited shelf space, what should they choose and why? For them open debate about bias in children's books has been more than welcome.

NOTES

1. This essay was written in 1980 before political changes in Argentina — Ed.

Part 2. Children's Questions/Adult Answers: Nonfiction

On Themes

Maxim Gorky

The problem of themes in books for children is, of course, a problem of the line of social education to be followed with respect to children.

In our country education is tantamount to revolutionizing, that is to say, liberating children's minds from modes of thinking laid down by their fathers' and ancestors' past, ridding them of delusions rooted in centuries of a conservative way of life – one built on the class struggle and the individual's striving to defend himself and to assert individualism and nationalism as "eternal" forms and laws of social behavior.

Children should be brought up in such a way as to preclude, even in their games, any conscious or unconscious attraction to the past; hence the need to reveal to children the processes that took place in the past. This cannot be achieved merely through acquaintance with facts, ideas and theories, but only through giving them stories about labor processes and the way in which these processes have produced facts, which in their turn have brought forward notions, ideas and theories. It should be shown that freedom of thought is possible only given complete freedom of labor life-activity, something that has never obtained under conditions of the capitalist system, but obtains under the socialist system.

The various ways in which facts and processes have affected thought should be kept in mind. This variety is to be seen not only in everyday life, but also in science, where so-called "firmly

From Maxim Gorky, *On Literature: Selected Articles,* translated by Julius Katzer and Ivy Litvinov (Moscow: Progress Publishers, n.d.), 185–97; reprinted by kind permission of the Progress Publishers.

Maxim Gorky (1868–1936) wrote books for children, as well as the fiction, essays and autobiography which established his reputation as one of the greatest Russian authors. This essay was written as a speech in 1933.

established facts" not infrequently play a conservative role, keeping thought captive to "the obvious" and thereby checking the speed and the freedom of the process of cognition. A "truth" – an instrument of cognition and its temporary point of departure – is very often an expression of a personal conscious or instinctive striving on the part of a "producer" of that truth toward quietude and power over other minds; that is why, in defiance of criticism, a truth is frequently presented as an immutable and "eternal" law, as "faith."

It is quite possible that the hypothesis of "entropy" – the tendency of energy to arrive at a state of rest – is merely an expression of a tired mind's urge to achieve a state of rest or calm. In the same way the theory of "compensation," which claims that physiological defects of the organism are balanced by an increase in brain power, is a teaching whose basic idea, if transposed into the field of sociology, would justify shameful abnormalities in social relations, in the manner attempted by Malthus and many other bourgeois thinkers. These men proceeded from facts, but it was only the genius of Marx that was able to lay bare the processes that created the facts; Marx alone showed that the basic cause of mankind's tragic life and sufferings has been the rift between clever hands and the clever mind.

In one of his early books the biologist Oliver Lodge, a materialist in his youth and a mystic in his old age, asserted that thinking arose from pain-sensations as the chemical reaction of the nerve cell to blows and buffets coming from the outer world. Lengthy and incessant collisions between some primitive organism and its surroundings led to the emergence of a neuro-cerebral organ of sense, which later developed into touch, sight, hearing, taste and smell. In man's prehistoric ancestor this organ ultimately produced the instinct of self-preservation, prompting that ancestor to arm himself for the struggle against phenomena that threatened his health and life. At a certain ancient stage of their development men were no more "social" than wolves are today. However, man, that relative of the ape, was able to develop his fore-limbs with ever greater effect, so that his hands, his clever hands, became the force that elevated him from his animal environment, encouraged the rapid growth of his brain, finally organizing him into what we have today – the skillful producer of metals, precision tools, apparatuses and machines, the gifted pianist, the surgeon who works almost miracles, and so on and so forth.

The above does not in the least minimize the influence of social relations on the growth and development of thought, but that came much later. We must show children how historical man emerged from the "darkness of the ages," and show him at the dawn of his semi-conscious labor processes; children should have some idea of the path traveled by man from the inventor of the flint axe down to Stephenson and Diesel, from the creator of tales and legends down to the great teachings of Marx, who has shown us the highway to the working people's radiant future. When they come into a new world, that of free labor facilitated with the aid of technology, the world of a classless society, children must realize the tremendous importance of manual labor and the way it affects not only the forms but the qualities of matter and, by subjugating its elemental forces, gives it a "second nature."

It is incontestable that thinking is nothing but the reflection in man's brain of the actually and objectively existent world of matter, whose most complex and marvelous product is man's neuro-cerebral tissue. Children, however, must absolutely know that had freedom of labor activity not been hampered and limited throughout the course of history by the self-interest and greed of the master classes, working mankind would have reached a level far higher than that of present-day "world culture," which has been built on the bones of the working people and cemented with their blood. All things are, of course, "conditioned," but with us history is no longer a fetish, and we are fashioning it according to plan. We must emphasize with special force the decisive significance of the freedom of labor. From the example of the bourgeois world we can see that capitalism is more and more resolutely denying its own "culture," since the latter is becoming hostile toward it. On the other hand, the example of the free play of labor energy in the Union of Soviet Socialist Republics gives us the indisputable right to show how rapidly, variedly and durably collective labor has enriched our huge country, and how in the space of fifteen years the firm foundations of a new culture have been laid down. Using numerous examples of the manner in which the phenomena of the objective world are distortedly and crookedly reflected in the bourgeois mind, we must show children how and why a correct and balanced perception of the world has been distorted. And again, we must elevate to the proper level a conception of historical working man as the vessel of an energy that organizes and transforms the world, and is moreover creating his "second nature"—the culture of socialism.

Man, the bearer of energy that organizes the world, is creating a "second nature"—culture; man is an organ of Nature created by that Nature so as to enable her, as it were, to know herself and become transformed—that is what should be brought home to children's understanding. From the age of six or seven they should begin to realize the wonderful work done by thought and the significance of social phenomena, and should be taught some idea of their own abilities. That is why children should begin their acquaintance with life with stories of the distant past, the inception of labor processes and the organizing work of thought.

It should be remembered that the history of the creation of culture was begun by people who were helpless, illiterate, and totally absorbed in the struggle for existence and against the hostile forces of Nature and wild beasts. Bourgeois historians of culture usually depict primitive man, that member of the clan collective, as a thinker who was perturbed by problems like: what are sleep and death? what created the earth? why was man created? However, man of those times was engaged in ceaseless physical exertion and self-defense; he was first and foremost a creator of real facts and had no time for abstract thought. As was realized by Marx's all-embracing mind, it was under the influence of labor processes that "reality turned into idea." Primitive man's methods of self-education were simple in the extreme: he understood the compelling need to become stronger than the wild beasts; before learning to overcome these animals he became aware of that possibility, this being expressed in legends about Samson and Hercules, the lion-killers. He felt no other need to create gods than the assumption that his strength and abilities might reach fantastic proportions. He was not wrong in assuming this: the finest of primitive craftsmen came to be depicted by his fellow-men as having overcome the tremendous opposition offered by Nature and matter. The most ancient myths knew no other gods but such that were endowed with some skill: they were expert smiths, hunters, herdsmen, sailors, musicians or carpenters; the goddesses also knew crafts, such as spinning, cooking, and healing. What has been termed the "religious creativity of primitive man" was in essence artistic creativity, without the least admixture of mysticism. The latter appeared on the scene when, divorced from the collective for some reason or other, the individual began to realize the absence of any meaning in his existence and his helplessness against Nature and especially against the power of the collective, which very properly demanded that the individual perform labor on a level with all others. It is hardly feasible that the primitive family and clan could tolerate in their midst members that were idlers, loafers or shirkers from the collective labor of finding food and protecting life; such people were probably done away with.

Man also began to think in abstract and mystical terms when he grew old, feeble, and fear-ridden at the imminence of death. Fear may cause panic in a collective, but panic cannot be lengthy or suppress the collective's biological energy. Catastrophes like volcanic activity, earthquakes or periodical floods never led to migrations of peoples. Vedaism and Buddhism are the most pessimistic of faiths, but this has not prevented the Hindus from living and multiplying. The Indo-German philosophy of Schopenhauer and Hartmann has not perceptibly increased the number of suicides even in bourgeois society, with all its rifts and fissions.

As has already been mentioned, man's fear of life, of all that is "incognizable"—a feature peculiar to the individualist—derives from a sense of his own insignificance. The individualists learned to utilize their own fear by trying to induce working people to accept it as sublime wisdom, as penetration into mysteries beyond the reach of reason. It is quite probable that fear-ridden idlers and infirm old men were founders of mystical faiths, organizers of cults, and their first priests.

The entire course of bourgeois history presents numerous instances of a premature weariness of thought and the fear experienced by the bourgeoisie at the conclusions they themselves have drawn. The closer we approach our times, the more frequent these instances become. The nineteenth and the twentieth centuries particularly abound in cases of materialistic and scientific-revolutionary thinkers reverting to reaction and mysticism. Bourgeois society's senility is confirmed by the weariness of thought displayed in practice by such people as Oliver Lodge, Virchow, Mendeleyev, Crookes, Richet and other "men of science."

To successfully create fiction and educative literature for children we need the following: first, writers of talent capable of writing simply, interestingly and meaningfully; then, editors of culture, with sufficient political and literary training, and, finally, the technical facilities to guarantee the timely publication and due quality of books for children. Such goals cannot be achieved overnight.

Of special importance is the goal of *providing children with books that will tell them of the origin of private property and how that property is the main obstacle to man's development today.* This goal can be achieved through a series of books on history, through keen political pamphlets and through satires directed against proprietary survivals in conditions of the Soviet land, among adults and children.

Prior to the Revolution quite a number of books were published dealing with Western countries; for instance, books by Vodovozova. Most of these books dealt with the subject in a superficial manner, life in various countries being depicted from the exterior, and certain immutable characteristics being attributed to their peoples. For instance, humor was presented as a feature of the French, calmness of the British, while all Dutch women were supposed to wear their national head-dress on all occasions. Of course none of these books ever made mention of the class struggle.

Nevertheless these books aroused children's interest in the life and culture of Western countries and induced them to study foreign languages.

We must get our leading writers and artists to produce books and albums about the peoples of the world, while the peoples of the U.S.S.R. can best be described by specialists on local lore and studies and by members of the numerous expeditions scattered throughout the length and breadth of the Union. These will be able to describe the life and customs of the various nationalities in the process of change and development, thereby inculcating sentiments of internationalism in children.

It is of the utmost importance that representatives of the national minorities be drawn into the creation of such books, particularly students at higher schools and at special institutes catering to the peoples of the North and the East of our country.

In brief, we must develop all of children's literature on an entirely new principle, one that will, in a big way, encourage scientific and artistic thought in terms of images. This principle may be formulated as follows: a struggle is raging in human society for the liberation of the labor energy of the working masses from the yoke of property and the rule of the capitalists, a struggle for the transformation of Man's physical energy into intellectual energy, a struggle for control over the forces of Nature, for long life and good health for working mankind, for its world-wide unity and a free, all-round and unlimited development of men's abilities and talents. It is this principle that should form the foundation of all literature for children, of each and every book, beginning with those written for tiny tots. We must remember that there are no longer any fantastic tales and stories that are not grounded in labor and science, so that what children should be given are tales and stories based on the searchings and hypotheses of present-day scientific thought. Children must learn not only to count and measure, but also to imagine and foresee.

It should be remembered that primitive man's unequipped imagination foresaw that he would be able to fly in the air, live in water, travel on land at breath-taking speed and bring about changes in matter, etc. Today fancy and imagination can use the facts of scientific experience and thereby infinitely expand the creativity of reason. Among our inventors we can see people who have brought forth correct ideas of new machine-tools, machines and apparatuses, though their knowledge of mechanics may be imperfect. We must bring science to the assistance of the child's imagination and teach children to think of the future.

The power of Vladimir Lenin and his followers lies in their extraordinary faculty to foresee the future. In our literature there should be no sharp line between works of pure and science fiction. How can that be brought about? How can educative books be made effective and emotional?

In the first place—and I must emphasize this point—our books on the achievements of science and technology must reveal not only the ultimate results of human thought and experience, but acquaint the reader with the process of research work, displaying how the search for the correct method is carried on and difficulties are overcome.

Science and technology should not be depicted as a storehouse of ready-made discoveries and inventions, but as an arena of struggle, where concrete and living man overcomes the resistance offered by material and tradition.

Such books can and should be written by leading scientists, not by impersonal and intermediary compilers, who are prepared at any moment to concoct a feature-story, an article or an entire treatise on any subject and to the order of any publishing house. The conditions of Soviet life, which have driven the middlemen out of industry, must expel them from literature too.

Only with the immediate participation of genuine scientists and men of letters shall we be able to undertake publication of books devoted to making scientific knowledge widespread in forms of artistic value.

The bold and successful experience of several authors who have written books on the future of our construction work and destined for young readers, *i.e.,* Ilin *(New Russia's Primer)* and Paustovsky *(Kara-Bugaz),* shows that children can be addressed in simple and attractive language, without the least didacticism and on the most serious themes.

Simple and clear style is achieved not by lowering the level of literary standards but through consummate craftsmanship. The author who would cater to young readers must take account of the demands presented by their age, for otherwise he will produce a book with no "address," suited neither to child nor adult.

Apart from professional writers, literature for children should draw on the rich experience of life accumulated by "old-timers" and "seasoned" people, such as hunters, sailors, engineers, airmen, agronomists, workers at machine and tractor stations, and so on.

It stands to reason that I have sketched out merely the broad outlines of the work to be done, all this calling for careful and detailed study. With this aim in view a group of young scientists and writers should be organized without any delay.

Gorky and Soviet Children's Literature

Ron Walter

High-flying birds and burning hearts are typical images in the works of Maxim Gorky (1868–1936). His *Song of the Falcon* and *Song of the Stormy Petrel* were paeans to the forthcoming Revolution, and the image of Danko saving his people from the dark forest by holding his own ripped-out heart, burning like the sun, above his head is well-known to Gorky readers.

Gorky himself was all fire and flight. His brilliant humanitarian spirit soared above the world of narrow-minded politicking and for this reason he is regarded with a combination of respect, reverence, and awe in the Soviet Union by liberal and dissident thinkers as well as by orthodox communists—a rare accomplishment in a country where heroism is often determined by the ideological camp one belongs to. Though he is the acknowledged father of Socialist Realism, it is not so much Gorky's greatness as a writer, which is questionable, that Russians admire so deeply in him. Rather, it is his unique role in preserving life and culture in Bolshevik Russia. In the years directly following the Revolution, Gorky edited the only oppositionist newspaper in the country; singlehandedly preserved art works and architectural monuments from wanton destruction; saved countless lives (Lenin never refused a Gorky request for help or intervention); founded a large-scale literary translating house to save starving writers; and was a moral center around which gathered the best minds of Russia. Even in exile during NEP (1921–28), Gorky's influence was immense: a *Who's Who* of the writers of the twenties would show that virtually every writer of note regarded Gorky as something of a literary spiritual father. He maintained voluminous correspondence, reading all important literature of the day and giving valued advice to the authors. From the time of his permanent return to the Soviet Union till his death in 1936, Gorky worked indefatigably

From *Children's Literature* 6 (1977): 182–87 by permission of the publisher.

Former lecturer in Russian language and literature at the University of California, Irvine, Ron Walter has translated the work of a number of Russian poets.

on establishing a firm basis for his brainchild—the literature of Socialist Realism.

Gorky's writing and his humanitarian pursuits are well-known in the West. Almost unknown, however, is the great role he played in fostering children's literature in the Soviet Union. In fact, if any one figure can be said to be the "father" of Soviet children's literature, it certainly has to be Gorky (an appellation which may, to some degree, exculpate him from being the undeniable father of a rather hapless brainchild—Socialist Realism). Such parentage is not to be scoffed at, for Soviet children's literature is certainly one of the richest in the world, partially because Gorky incessantly encouraged the best Soviet writers to write children's literature, partially because the best writers have naturally moved toward children's literature to avoid writing obligatory tendentious literature, and partially because it appears that a collective society shows more concern for its children (albeit sometimes for the wrong reasons) than a free-enterprise society.

Gorky's concern for the well-being of children dates back, as it naturally should, to his own childhood. In one of his acknowledged best pieces of fiction, Part One of his well-known autobiographical trilogy, appropriately entitled *Childhood,* we see Gorky as a sensitive child exposed to arbitrary brutality (his grandfather, for example, was given to counting the daily sins of the children and ritualistically whipping them every Saturday for the accumulated transgressions of the week) and resolved to right the wrongs of the older generation when he himself grows up. (Among his later methods, incidentally, was often to recommend to children that they read his own *Childhood.*)

From early in his literary career Gorky showed concern for children by organizing holiday programs for poor children in his hometown of Nizhny Novgorod (since renamed Gorky), directing children's plays, helping to select books for children's libraries, not to mention writing children's stories himself. By 1910 his role in children's lives was sufficiently respected that he was invited to speak at the Third International Conference on Family Education in Brussels. He couldn't attend, but the letter he wrote the Conference represents the first in a long series of theoretical formulations of his views on children's literature. Gorky was a tireless propagandizer and in this letter, as in many others, he wrote with great feeling about the urgent need to have children read about the accomplishments of mankind, about the great role of reading in the raising of children and the formation of their world view. When he was the head of a publishing house during World War I he decided to put into effect the thoughts expressed in his letter by publishing a series of books for children on outstanding people written by recognized authorities. He wrote letters asking people to write biographies—H.G. Wells on Edison, Romain Rolland on Beethoven, Nansen on Columbus, Temiryazov on Darwin, and he himself would write on Garibaldi. These were to be books written for children, not adult literature usable by children. Though in the Soviet Union they are by now used to having children's literature written by top-rank writers, at the time the idea was revolutionary and indicative of Gorky's fervor and breadth of vision in promoting children's literature. When all his correspondents showed their willingness, Gorky went on to compose a long list of the world's best children's books, which he proposed to have translated and published in Russia. But all this was during a time of war and revolution—and severe paper shortages—so that Gorky's ambitious plan had to wait for more stable times. It eventually formed the basis of a similar project taken on by the world's first Government Children's Publishing House (Detgiz, then called Detizdat), which Gorky helped found in 1933. At the time he had to content himself with a more modest project, the founding of the new country's first children's journal, *Northern Lights,* published between 1919 and 1920, through which Gorky hoped to realize his dream of founding a solid new children's literature based on "respect for the power of reason, for the searches of science, for the great task of art—to make a person strong and beautiful," as he wrote in the editorial of the first issue. Once again, however, his vision far exceeded its realization as governmental pressures (Gorky readily employed ideological enemies of the revolution as children's writers) eventually caused the journal to fold.

With *Northern Lights* began Gorky's history of resistance to narrow political pressures in the area of children's literature. As the free development of Soviet literature was halted in the late twenties when Stalin and his minions came into firm control of the country, children's literature came under siege. The Russian Association of Proletarian Writers, an organ of the Party that had gained virtual hegemony over literary output, came out against, among other things, fantasy in children's literature. It was argued that the "new man" of the socialist world should develop from childhood a purely "realistic" view of the world. Having animals talk, for example, only encouraged retreat into an individualistic fantasy life characteristic of the old bourgeois world. The literary slogans of the day were "removal of the veils" and "for the living man"—both calls for a highly realistic literature accurately reflecting the evolving socialist world as it was. In children's literature the attitude was to regard a child as a small man and to appeal purely to his rational faculty, to write informational literature for him, to propagandize him from the dawn of his consciousness to become a sturdy builder of communism. The polemic excited by these views was intense and Gorky, ever the defender of culture, was in the thick of the battle, publishing a series of seminal articles in *Pravda* on his theory of children's literature. In these articles, from 1928–1930, we see Gorky as no less a propagandizer than his adversaries, no less interested in cultivating a socialist mentality in children and extirpating capitalistic values, but his views are incomparably better informed, based on long experience with children's mentalities. Gorky convincingly argues that a child naturally absorbs the external world through the medium of play, and it is through words as play that a child learns the subtleties and spirit of his native language. Furthermore, the fantasy and play elements in children's literature develop the sense of intuition, so that later in life the adult raised on a strong fantasy literature will be more likely to pass beyond the merely practical in his solutions to scientific, artistic, and life problems.

Gorky's theory of children's literature, as evolved during this polemic on the "right" way to cultivate young socialist minds as well as in later speeches and articles, could form a substantial study in itself. Here it is enough to observe that Gorky always maintained an extremely broad-based stance and was never narrowly didactic in his approach. True, in the spirit of the theory of Socialist Realism which he developed, his attitude toward children's literature was always tinged with romanticism, with the distinct tendency to see people as larger than life. So deep was his faith in the power of a book and so urgent his desire to extract from children their noblest instincts, their highest flights of imagination, their deepest respect for the accomplishments of their forebears, not to mention their most antiacquisitive impulses, that he felt perfectly justified in fostering the creation of a literature molded on the Dostoevskian formula of "realism in a higher sense." But within this general romantic bias Gorky consistently remained both the practical and theoretical enemy of the politicos, hacks, and Party hard-liners who were out to use children's literature to turn young people into pragmatic, obedient, orthodox communist thinkers.

Gorky's theoretical formulations were not based simply on his own literary ideas adapted for children. He constantly checked his ideas with children themselves. During the 1920s, for example, he maintained a lively correspondence with members of the so-called "Gorky Colony"—a group of three hundred or so boys being raised at a former reform school near Kiev, and with Anton Makarenko, their headmaster and disciplinarian. It was at Gorky's insistence, incidentally, that Makarenko, a household name in the Soviet Union in the area of children's education, wrote his magnum opus on his experience at the Gorky Colony, the *Pedagogical Poem* (translated recently into English under the title *The Road to Life*). And when Gorky embarked on another of his many grandiose projects, the founding of the government publishing house for children in 1933, he had letters sent all over the Soviet Union to children and children's organizations, asking them what kind of reading they wanted. The over two thousand replies he received were carefully analyzed and formed the basis for the many book contracts offered by the newly established enterprise.

It was Gorky's dream to establish children's literature in the Soviet Union as a pursuit equal in value to adult literature and to draw upon the best talent in the country to write it. When in 1934 Gorky presided over the first congress of Soviet writers he had the introductory general lecture on Soviet literature followed immediately by a report on the state of and possibilities for children's literature. It was certainly in large measure due to Gorky's influence that many of the Soviet Union's best writers, who normally wrote for adult audiences—Olesha, Zoshchenko, Kaverin, Kataev, Paustovsky, Prishvin, Aseev, Tikhonov, A. Tolstoy—also wrote for children. And Gorky himself set an example by writing a variety of tales for children filled with fanciful situations and imaginative language.

There can be no doubt that had it not been for Gorky, Soviet children's literature, which comparativists will someday discover to be one of the world's richest and most sophisticated bodies of contemporary children's literature, would not have developed so broadly or so freely. Gorky was the patron saint of Soviet children, constantly looking out for their interests, constantly inspiring writers to give their best to them, constantly withstanding political pressures to use children's literature as an instrument of narrow indoctrination. To this day his influence is strongly felt. Almost every Soviet book devoted to children's literature, a subject of considerable scholarship in the USSR, contains reminiscences of Gorky or articles about him or numerous references to his role in establishing Soviet children's literature on a firm foundation. In a country where pressures toward doctrinaire literature are constant, Soviet children are fortunate that Gorky's spirit is an enduring part of their heritage.

WORKS CITED

The sources of the material contained in this article are from numerous texts. The principal ones are given below:

Chernyavskaya, Ya. A. *Sovetskaya detskaya literatura*. Minsk: 1971.

Detskaya literatura 1967. Moscow: 1968.

Detskaya literatura 1970. Moscow: 1970.

Ivich, Alexandr. *Vospitanie detey*. Moscow: 1969.

Kon, L. *Sovetskaya detskaya literatura 1917–1929*. Moscow: 1960.

Levin, Dan. *Stormy Petrel: The Life and Work of Maxim Gorky*. New York: 1965.

Makarenko, Anton. *The Road to Life*. New York: 1973.

Medvedeva, N. B. *M. Gorkiy o detskoy literature*. Moscow: 1968.

Morton, Miriam. *A Harvest of Russian Children's Literature*. Berkeley: 1968.

Smirnova, Vera. *O detyakh i dlya detey*. Moscow: 1967.

Weil, Irwin. *Gorky, His Literary Development and Influence on Soviet Intellectual Life*. New York: 1966.

From Lemonade Stands to Wall Street: Children's Books' Messages About the Economy

Jan M. Goodman

Hey, Kids! Want to see how easy it is to make money in America? Invest in a lemonade stand today. Tomorrow, you'll be on Wall Street!

Of course, you'll need some *capital* to *invest*, but everyone has that. And you'll have to be careful of the changes in *supply and demand*, but if you're a shrewd business*man*, you'll use our *free market system* to your advantage.

You may have some *labor trouble*, but *negotiations* should cure that. Just be sure to agree to a *compromise* that will assure you a good *profit*. If you just invest wisely, you'll have quite a *nest egg* when you retire!

The text above summarizes the hype about the U.S. economy that pervades the vast majority of children's books about money. These economic primers present a grossly incomplete picture and an almost unquestioning acceptance of U.S. capitalism. Of little relevance to a child from a poor working-class family, the books mislead all children.

Fifteen nonfiction books were closely examined to identify the messages they convey to elementary school children. We focused on nonfiction books because they claim to present the "truth" about their subjects, and therefore, their messages are considered factual. The sample group was selected from *Children's Books in*

From *Interracial Books for Children Bulletin,* 16, nos. 2/3 (1985): 4–9, by permission of the publisher and the author.
Jan M. Goodman is an educator in Berkeley, California. After reading these books, she decided to leave the teaching professions.

Print 1984–85 listings under: Money, Economics, Business, Banking, Labor, Capitalism, Socialism and Industry. Public and school libraries in the San Francisco Bay Area were searched to find the books most commonly available for children in Grades K-6. (See bibliography at the end of this article).

The books examined fall into two basic categories: *guides for children about the principles of economics in our country* and *lessons for children in money management.* The *guides* present overviews of how the U.S. economy operates and, basically, articulate the concepts of capitalism in our country. The following sophisticated principles were introduced to even the youngest children: supply and demand; capital; investment; market value; inflation; recession; depression; unemployment; management and labor; wages and salaries.

The *lessons* offer children money-making ideas and advice on investment. These books include explanations of the U.S. banking system; specific instructions for record-keeping and budgeting; and suggestions about advertising, employee relations and customer service.

Most books use as examples child-owned and operated business ventures (lemonade stands, in particular) to simplify economic concepts for elementary schoolers. Unfortunately, an over-simplification results! In discussing the economy, the books provided the following inaccuracies, assumptions, and omissions:

Q. Who has money in America?

According to our sampling, almost all people in the U.S. have the money they need. "It's Here, There, Everywhere!" proclaims the title of Chapter Five in *Money: How to Get It and Keep It.* (Note the underlying assumption in the title: If everyone in this country followed the instructions in this handy book, there would be no poverty!)

Apparently, the only difference among us is how we spend the money we have. "It comes down to this," says *Barter, Bills and Banks.* "Money is meant to be a servant of man. If it is not managed wisely, it can easily become his master." Sexism aside, this suggests that people are poor because they are unwise managers of their money! The inadequacies and inequities of our economic system are not even hinted at.

Portrayals of the "average" U.S. family clearly reflect a middle- and upper middle-class bias. In *Nickels, Dimes, and Dollars* (published in 1980), the "typical American family" of "a man, a wife and two children" had an income of $2,000 a

month. This income level was far beyond the reach of many people
in our country.

Money: How To exhorts us: "Let's look at three people who
have money. They are similar to people you know, like relatives
and friends." Here the "typical Americans" are Mr. Johnson,
Mrs. Emery and Amy Brown, who each save $2,000 a year for 30
years! How odd it is that my relatives and friends do not save so
efficiently!

The book concludes, "Remember, money alone will probably
not make you happy. But you can gain much satisfaction by
making good and profitable use of whatever money you happen to
possess." Once again, we hear that all of us can become
wealthy—or wealthier—if only we invest well. Not one of these
fifteen books deals directly with the fact that many if not most
people in this country do not "happen to possess" money!

Although the majority of the books do acknowledge that wealth
is distributed unequally in the U.S., most seem to simply accept
this fact. Statistics about wealth and poverty in our country are
glaringly absent from all works examined. No book details the
small percentage of people who control the bulk of the money in
our society. Nor is there evidence of the large number of poor and
unemployed people in the U.S. (One book mentions the Depression
but minimizes its impact and desperation by presenting character
sketches of unhappy people who are simply sad and depressed
because they're out of work temporarily.) Certainly there is no
correlation made between wealth—or a lack of it—and a person's
race and/or gender.

The extent to which certain books accept the economic inequality
in this country is shocking. *Barter, Bills and Banks* states,
"Perhaps you've asked yourself why the U.S. doesn't go ahead
and print enough money so that everyone could be rich." It then
explains, "Unfortunately, it's not a very practical suggestion. For
the problem is not providing everybody with enough money. The
fact is, we do have the machinery to print enough money to give
each person a million dollars. The problem is supplying the goods
and services to meet the demands of the people." The book
elaborates on the disaster that would ensue: "If the United States
printed a lot of money, people would begin to buy things much
quicker than they could be made."

The following rationalization is provided by *Prices Go Up, Prices
Go Down:* "You might even dream of a store that has no prices.
. . . But a store without prices would be crowded with people.
And everyone would want everything. What would the store owner

do? How would he or she decide who gets what?" The author presents the solution to this horrible dilemma: "Prices are a good way of deciding who gets what. Whoever is willing and able to pay the price of a bicycle should be able to buy one."

These two books warn us of the terrible problems that would result if people had equal access to wealth. There simply would not be enough goods and services for everybody. According to these books, a very acceptable solution to this problem is to assure that a proportion of our families cannot afford what they need! Furthermore, youngsters are told not to dream of economic reform; it is simply too inconvenient and would turn our free market into utter chaos!

Q. What is the difference between rich and poor in America?

Rarely do these books present a realistic portrayal of poverty in the U.S. Rather, they imply that everyone has enough to live on, but that rich and poor people spend their money differently! Note this simplistic excerpt from *Nickels, Dimes, and Dollars:* "Studies by government groups . . . have shown that money is spent in nearly the same way in many households. The major difference from one family to another is food costs. Although the actual amount of money spent on food is much the same, high-income households use a smaller proportion of their money while low-income families use a larger proportion."

Money: How To elaborates on this theme: "Many wealthy people pay all their living expenses with money their investments earn." However, the book offers no explanation as to how poor people manage to live on extremely limited incomes!

Other books de-emphasize the difference between rich and poor by making generalizations. *From Barter to Banking* says, "These days, nearly everyone uses credit—for convenience and even safety, since a credit card can mean less cash to carry around. The plastic credit card, with its raised name and number is, of course, a modern, almost revolutionary form of money." Unfortunately, this is the *only* instance where anything revolutionary is mentioned in these books.

Barter, Bills and Banks also tempts its readers with buying power that only a small percentage of U.S. families have: "The advantage of a credit card is convenience. You can buy gas, eat in a big restaurant, buy clothing, fly back and forth to Europe, and at the end of the month, receive only one bill!" Do you wonder *who* can pay that bill?

Q. Who has jobs in America?

Several of the books feature groups of children happily co-existing, each with his or her business. Given that unemployment is rarely mentioned, these young entrepreneurs leave the reader with the impression that everyone in this country has a job. *How To Turn Up into Down* is quite explicit on this point, presenting a children's community where "You're all making enough in profit and wages to get what you need and what you want."

A few books do refer to the fact that some people are unemployed in this country, but usually this message is distorted. *Nickels, Dimes and Dollars* states, "Not everyone works, however, or is a member of a family with an income. Many people are too old or too sick to work." In addition to being ageist and handicappist, this presents the misinformation that everyone who is able to work in our country has a job.

A Kid's Guide to the Economy, one of the better books, adds to this inaccurate message. Tony and Hamilton are discussing the value of people as resources. But Tony regrets, "You can't even bet on people. Look at how many nitwits kill themselves off in auto accidents. Others drop out or are too old or sick to work." Here, readers get the impression that the worker should be blamed if s/he doesn't have a job, and that old and sick people have no value, since they can't work.

Unemployed people are further faulted for their lack of work in *How To Turn Up into Down.* In this book, the main character, who (needless to say) has a lemonade business, is faced with an increase in the price of sugar. Because she wants to make a good profit, she must lay off her employee, Johnny. The text states, "What Johnny becomes is part of the unemployment problem." Johnny is presented as a problem not for the business owner, but, rather, for society. There is no suggestion that the young entrepreneur reduce her profit and keep Johnny employed.

In this book's sequel, *How To Turn Lemons into Money,* we encounter Johnny once again. He is still employed at the lemonade stand but he is tired of squeezing lemons. Johnny threatens to go on strike, which the author describes as "labor trouble." Finally, Johnny and his boss reach a compromise, and she agrees to purchase a lemon squeezing machine. Johnny returns to work, but not for long. His boss realizes that she doesn't need him anymore because she's got a machine to do his job!

Poor Johnny has learned a hard lesson: Do not fight for better working conditions or you will negotiate yourself out of a job. His boss, meanwhile, is never challenged on her business ethics!

Q. In America, what work is valued and who does that work?

These books remain true to form in their distortion of economic life in the U.S. Time and time again, the business owner's point of view is presented, with little or no mention of the workers. In addition, workers are only valued as accessories to a good profit. In only one instance does a child voice his frustration as a worker. (This occurs in *A Kid's Guide* when an angry young employee confronts his boss about her high profit margin. "I've been exploited!" he shouts.) In fact, the only in-depth view of a worker's perspective is found in *Labor Unions,* which chronicles the history of labor struggles. The other reference to the oppression of workers is found, ironically, in the very conservative 1964 work, *Communism: An American View!*

These books scarcely validate the importance of women in the U.S. economy. A large majority of the illustrations feature men in positions of power—as bankers, business owners, executives. Women are either "out of the picture" or in service roles—as secretaries and other helpers.

To supplement the sexism in illustrations, the books offer the following commentaries:

> Usually, it is the father who works to earn the money that the family needs (*Spending Money*).

The labor force in the U.S. totals about eighty million people. . . . This number includes only those who sell their labor for money. Therefore, a housewife who performs many essential services for her family is not part of the labor force. Since she is not paid for the work she does at home, the government, which collects information on the labor force, has no way of placing a value on her services or determining how many hours she works, and therefore, does not count her in the labor force (*Learning about People Working For You*).

The two titles cited above were published in the late 1960s, so we might excuse their stereotypical portrayals of women and their devaluing of women's work. It is, however, harder to excuse the librarian who has kept these biased books readily available for children of the 1980s!

The Banking Book, which consistently uses male pronouns in describing how banks operate, concedes, "By the way, even though we have been calling the bank President 'he,' 'he' could just as easily be 'she.' Many women in the United States are presidents and officers of banks." Ironically, the book's one attempt to counter sexism unrealistically presents a field which is still dominated by (white) men.

Two books contain hypothetical situations that suggest that women have little knowledge or good judgment about money management. Says *Money: How To*: "A month later, Mr. Porcorelli dies in Florida, and Mrs. Porcorelli inherits his stock. Knowing nothing of business, she wants to sell the shares to her brother. . . ."

Nickels, Dimes, and Dollars presents the following "real-life" example:

> Suppose the wife in a family finds a job for which she needs a car. To celebrate the new job, she and her husband obtain a bank loan and purchase a $10,000 car. Shortly after she starts working, the wife becomes terribly ill and has to give up her job. As a result, she and her husband have no way of paying back the loan.

The car is repossessed and the reader is left with the sense that a woman's job choice may jeopardize her family's finances—and that she can't hold a job without becoming terribly ill!

Although male and female children are equally featured as business owners in these books, white children far outnumber Black children (who are only identifiable by shaded-in faces). In addition, there is no mention of other people of color. Readers may accurately conclude that the primary beneficiaries of U.S. capitalism are white males—but they will certainly learn nothing of the involvement of other people in our economy.

Q. Are there viable alternatives to the American economic system?

With two exceptions, these books present a lop-sided view of U.S. capitalism. The young reader gets the sense that all is well, because our free enterprise system, balanced by laws of supply and demand, is successful.

One book—*A Kid's Guide to the Economy*—poses some thought-provoking questions: "Is it fair that some people or countries are wealthy and others are poor? Should everyone have *total* freedom to get rich? Are we overworking the earth?" This same book, the best of those examined, discusses the pros and cons of capitalism: "Critics say that capitalism builds a rich, but not a just, society. Along with liberty came risk and inequality." And of socialism: "Critics say that socialist governments achieve equality and security by making all decisions and clamping down on personal freedom and comfort."

Communism: An American View confronts the American system directly: "All of us have wondered why things happen as they do — why one man works hard and gets richer and his neighbor works just as hard and gets poorer. But most of us stop with wondering. We decide that the problem is too hard, and give it up. Karl Marx never gave it up."

However, after such a powerful start, the book quickly becomes disappointing. The author repeatedly points out the drawbacks of the Communist system, stating that it "denies people freedom of the mind." Later, he concludes, "In the least capitalistic countries . . . Communism has been established at the cost of terrible civil wars and the loss of lives running into the millions!" Such is the inevitable high price paid for radical change.

Even *A Kid's Guide,* which claims to be objective in presenting several alternative economic systems to its readers, ends up on a procapitalistic note. "In the past, free citizens . . . have prospered most. Capitalists . . . stand a good chance of improving their economic quality of life."

Other books take an even stronger anti-Communist stand. *Prices Go Up* asserts, "There are often long lines outside stores without a free economy. There is just not enough of certain items. The demand for these items is much greater than the supply." This is a bleak picture of life in Russia and China. In the U.S., we have far better solutions to these long lines. Only the rich will get these certain items!

Q. What does all this mean?

Hey kids! Got the message? Now you have all the information you need to become young entrepreneurs and make big profits! Weren't these books helpful? Remember, the more you understand about our economy, the more you can make your money work for you.

What? You don't have any money to invest? You don't know where to get any capital? There must be something you can do. Keep reading! I'm sure you'll find an answer somewhere.

At a very early age, our country begins to indoctrinate our children with a strongly procapitalist view. The books analyzed for this article are powerful tools that influence elementary schoolers to accept and perpetuate the inequalities of the system if they can afford to do so! It is no wonder that middle-class aspirations pervade our culture, though they are only in reach of a fraction of our people.

We were unable to locate any books that present an accurate and balanced view of economic life in our country, but we hope they exist. We ask readers to inform us of any material with a progressive perspective.

WORKS CITED

Adler, David A. *All Kinds of Money.* Illustrated by Tom Huffman. Franklin Watts, 1984.

— — —. *Prices Go Up, Prices Go Down.* Illustrated by Tom Huffman. Franklin Watts, 1984.

Armstrong, Louise. *How To Turn Lemons into Money.* Illustrated by Bill Basso. Harcourt Brace Jovanovich, 1976.

— — —. *How To Turn Up into Down.* Illustrated by Bill Basso. Harcourt Brace Jovanovich, 1978.

Fodor, R. V. *Nickels, Dimes, and Dollars.* Morrow, 1980.

James, Elizabeth, and Carol Birkin. *How To Grow a Hundred Dollars.* Illustrated by Joel Schick. Lothrop, Lee & Shepard, 1979.

Johnson, Gerald W. *Communism: An American's View.* Illustrated by Leonard Everett Fisher. Morrow, 1964.

Maher, John E., and S. Stowell Symmes. *Learning about People Working for You.* Illustrated by Arthur Wallower. Franklin Watts, 1969.

Morgan, Tom. *Money, Money, Money: How To Get It and Keep It.* Putnam, 1978.

Riedel, Manfred G. *A Kid's Guide to the Economy.* Prentice-Hall, 1976.

Rossomando, Frederick, Florence Leventhal and Marilyn Szymaszek. *Spending Money.* Illustrated by Gioia Fiammenghi. Franklin Watts, 1967.

Scott, Elaine. *The Banking Book.* Illustrated by Kathie Abrams. Frederick Warne, 1981.

Sims, Carolyn. *Labor Unions in the United States.* Franklin Watts, 1971.

Tarshis, Barry. *Barter, Bills and Banks.* Illustrated by Ric Estrada. Messner, 1970.

Wade, William. *From Barter to Banking.* Crowell-Collier, 1967.

Part 3. Fantasy as Reality

On the Use and Abuse of Folk and Fairy Tales with Children: Bruno Bettelheim's Moralistic Magic Wand

Jack Zipes

Bruno Bettelheim was impelled to write his book *The Uses of Enchantment*[1] out of dissatisfaction "with much of the literature intended to develop the child's mind and personality, because it fails to stimulate and nurture those resources he needs most in order to cope with his difficult inner problems."[2] Therefore, he explored the great potential of folk tales as literary models for children since "more can be learned from them about the inner problems of human beings, and of the right solutions to their predicaments in any society, than from any other type of story within a child's comprehension" (p. 5). This is, indeed, a grand statement on behalf of the folk tale's powers. However, despite his good intentions and moral concern in the welfare of children, Bettelheim's book disseminates false notions about the original intent of Freudian psychoanalytic theory and about the literary quality of folk tales and leaves the reader in a state of mystification. Not only is the manner in which Bettelheim would *impose* meaning onto child development through the therapeutic use of the folk tale authoritarian and unscientific,[3] but his stance is symptomatic of numerous humanitarian educators who perpetuate the diseases they desire to cure.

This is not to dismiss Bettelheim's book in its totality. Since folk and fairy tales have played and continue to play a significant

Reprinted from *Breaking the Magic Spell: Radical Theories of Folk and Fairy Tales*, Univ. of Texas Press, 1979, 160–77, by permission of the author.

Jack Zipes is professor of comparative literature at the University of Florida in Gainesville, coeditor of *New German Critique*, and author of a number of books including a history of *Little Red Riding Hood*.

role in the socialization process, a thorough study of Bettelheim's position is crucial for grasping whether the tales can be used more effectively in helping children (and adults) come into their own. A critical examination of his theory may ultimately lead to a fresh look at contemporary psychoanalytic views on internalization and new insights about the production and usage of folk and fairy tales.

Bettelheim's major thesis is a simple one: "the form and structure of fairy tales suggest images to the child by which he can structure his daydreams and with them give better direction to his life" (p. 7). In other words, the folk tale liberates the child's subconscious so that he or she can work through conflicts and experiences which would otherwise be repressed and perhaps cause psychological disturbances. According to Bettelheim, folk tales present existential dilemmas in a clear-cut manner so that the child can easily grasp the underlying meanings of the conflicts. Most folk tales are an imaginative depiction of healthy human development and help children understand the motives behind their rebellion against parents and the fear of growing up. The conclusions of most folk tales portray the achievement of psychological independence, moral maturity, and sexual confidence. Obviously, as Bettelheim admits, there are other approaches to folk tales. But, he maintains that it is primarily the psychological approach which uncovers the hidden meanings of the tales and their overwhelming importance for child development.

Characteristic of Bettelheim's orthodox Freudian approach is the arbitrary way in which he makes excessive claims for the therapeutic power of the folk tale and then diagnoses the power to fit his strait-jacket theory about neurosis and the family. For instance, he unabashedly asserts that "unlike any other form of literature, they [folk tales] direct the child to discover his identity and calling" (p. 24). Then he narrows the psychological meaning in a reductionistic manner: "the content of the chosen tale has nothing to do with the patient's external life but much to do with his inner problems, which seem incomprehensible and hence unsolvable" (p. 25). Such flat assertions, common throughout the book, rest on shaky grounds. Bettelheim provides no documentation to prove that the folk tale is better than any other imaginative or nonfiction literature for helping children develop their character. Moreover, Bettelheim has a one-dimensional way of examining the relation of literature to the psyche. To suggest that the external life is isolated from the inner life and that there is a literature which primarily addresses itself to the inner problems of a reader completely eliminates the dialectical relationship between essence and appearance. Existence is divorced from the imagination, and a static realm is erected which resembles the laboratory of an orthodox Freudian mind that is bent on conducting experiments with what *ought* to be happening in the child's inner realm.

The categorical imperative used by Bettelheim constantly prevents him from achieving his purpose of uncovering the significance of folk tales for child development. Folk tales are said to personify and illustrate inner conflicts, and Bettelheim wants to demonstrate to his adult readers how a child views folk tales and reality so that they can be more enlightened in their dealings with children. This stance is in actual contradiction to his previous argument that children must be allowed freedom to interpret the tales and that adults must not impose interpretation. It is the authority, Bettelheim, who *claims to know* how children subconsciously view the tales and who imposes this psychoanalytic mode of interpreting tales on adults. In turn they ought to use his approach if they care for children. This moral argumentation has nothing to do with a more scientific explanation of the tales and how they can be used to aid children in their development. Everything remains in Bettelheim's own realm of reified Freudian formulas which restrain the possibilities for a vital interaction between the tale and the child and between the adult and the child.

This can immediately be seen when he presents his theoretical explanation of how folk tales clarify the meaning of conflicts for children and how they provide for resolution. Like many cultural censors of morality, Bettelheim believes that only literature which is harmonious and orderly should be fed to the delicate souls of children who should be sheltered from harsh reality. Thus, the folk tale is perfect. In contrast to myths, fables, and legends, folk tales are allegedly optimistic because they allow for hope and the solution of problems. In addition, they involve a conflict between the reality and pleasure principles and show how a certain amount of pleasure can be retained while the demands of reality are respected (as in the example of the oldest pig in *The Three Little Pigs*). Indiscriminately using the discoveries of Piaget, who has demonstrated (among other things) that the child's thinking up till the ages of nine or ten is animistic, Bettelheim explains how the magic and fantastic images in the folk tale enable the child subjectively to come to terms with reality. The adventures in the folk tale allow for vicarious satisfaction of unfulfilled desires and subconscious drives (pp. 56–57) and permit the child to sublimate those desires and drives at a time when conscious recognition would shatter or shake the child's character structure which is not yet secure. The folk tale provides freedom for the child's imagination in that it deals at first with a problematic real situation which is then imaginatively transformed. The narrative breaks down spatial and temporal limits and leads the child into the self, but it also leads him or her back into reality. Bettelheim argues against true-to-life stories for child development because they impinge upon the imagination of the child and act repressively as would the rational interference of an adult. In contrast, the folk tale transforms reality in such a way that the child can cope with it. Like the symbols of the id, ego, and superego, which Freud created as operative constructs, the folk-tale symbols represent separate entities of the child's inner sanctum, and their representation in a folk tale (for a child) shows how order can be made out of chaos (p. 75). In particular, the folk tale demonstrates how each element (ego, id, superego) must be given its due and integrated if character structure is to develop without disturbance.

Many folk tales like *Brother and Sister* show how the animalistic (male/id) must be integrated with the spiritual component (female/ego, superego) to permit human qualities to blossom: "Integration of the disparate aspects of our personality can be gained only after the asocial, destructive, and unjust have been done away with; and this cannot be achieved until we have reached full maturity, as symbolized by sister's giving birth to a child and developing mothering attitudes" (p. 83). At the bottom of all the chaos and conflict which children experience are parents, leading Bettelheim to make the following claim: "Maybe if more of our adolescents had been brought up on fairy tales, they would (unconsciously) remain aware of the fact that their conflict is not with the adult world, or society, but really only with their parents" (pp. 98–99). In other words, the ambivalent attachments to one's parents are the roots of all evil and must be worked out by the child (particularly the Oedipal conflicts) if a well-integrated personality is to be achieved. Symbolically folk tales are the most clear and distinct representations of children's anxieties and unconscious drives, and therefore they can stimulate children to explore their imaginations for resolutions to the conflicts with their parents. They are like guidebooks for achieving true identity and a true state of independence. Thus now we know what becoming a ruler over a kingdom means, and Bettelheim can conclude his first part by advising adults again to take an active part in the telling of the tale but not to interpret it for the child. The participation will (like the psychiatrist) bring the child and parent closer together by magically restoring order to the child's mind.

This theory is fallacious on two levels, the psychoanalytic and the literary. Not only does Bettelheim misinterpret some of Freud's key notions about psychoanalysis, but he also twists the meanings of the literature to suit his peculiar theory of child development. The intended "humanitarian" goals of his study are undermined by his rigid Freudian abstractions which prop up irrational and arbitrary forms of social behavior whose norms and values children are supposed to adapt. The patterns of the folk tales allegedly foster ideal normative behavior which children are to internalize; yet, some of these literary patterns like the forms of social behavior are repressive constructs which violate the imagination of both children and adults alike. Let me clarify both charges against Bettelheim, his betrayal of the radical essence of Freudianism and his corruption of the literary meaning of the folk tale.

The critical task of Freud's psychoanalytic theory was to demonstrate the manifold ways in which society made it impossible for the individual to achieve autonomy. His purpose was to expose the inner forces which hinder full development of the individual and cause psychic disturbances because of external pressures and conditions. His work in theory was to destroy illusions which society creates about the possibility of achieving autonomy and a happy life so that the individual could elaborate meaning out of the antagonistic relationship between self and society.

Yet, in *Civilisation and Its Discontents,* Freud made clear just how repressive society was and how limited and varied the possibilities were to attain freedom and happiness.

> The liberty of the individual is not a benefit of culture. It was the greatest before any culture, though indeed it had little value at that time, because the individual was hardly in a position to defend it. Liberty has undergone restrictions through the evolution of civilization, and justice demands that these restrictions shall apply to all. . . . [4]

What is significant in Freud's work is that he located the cause for psychosis and all mental sicknesses in the historical and materialistic development of social conditions. He may have misconstrued some theories which were based on inconclusive and partial data, but the basis of his research for studying the relationship of the human psyche to civilization was dialectical and provided the fundamentals for a social science that could be altered as the social conditions changed. Bettelheim not only fails to develop Freud's far-reaching findings for application to the massive changes in society and the human psyche, but he actually eliminates the dialectic from Freud's method. He holds the family primarily responsible for the conflicts a child experiences, thus not locating it as *one of the mediating agencies* through which civilization causes repression. Even worse, he employs Freudian terminology like a puritanical parson encouraging parents to have faith in the almighty power of the folk tale which will lead children through the valley of fear into the kingdom of grace. Gone is the dialectical antagonistic relationship between society and the individual. If anything, it is misplaced between child and family which shifts the real cause for repression and thus dilutes the dialectics. Bettelheim would have us believe that the child can voluntaristically work through internalized problems with the aid of a folk tale and become a well-adjusted, autonomous individual. Once familial conflicts are grasped and solved, happiness is just down the road. By assuming such a position, Bettelheim unwittingly becomes an apologist for a "civilized" society noted for its abuse of children and its proclivity toward dehumanization. These negative tendencies of our contemporary society have been recorded not only by its critics but by its very own established news media which document the violation of human rights and violence of subjectivity every minute of every day.

In Bettelheim's discussion of folk tales and their use with children, there is no regard for the differences between children and their particular relationships to language which influences their receptivity to the linguistic and esthetic codes and patterns of literature. In fact, differences are virtually leveled out as if the education process were a democratizing experience and as if there were no codes, either in public or private language or in the folk tales themselves. This brings us to Bettelheim's misuse of the folk tale as an art form.

Though aware of the historical origins of the folk tale, Bettelheim fails to take into account that the symbols and patterns of the tales reflect specific forms of social behavior and activity which often can be traced back as far as the Ice and Megalithic Ages. As August Nitschke has documented in his book *Soziale Ordnungen im Spiegel der Märchen*,[5] the contemporary psychological labels attached to the symbols and patterns of the tales are contradicted by the actual historical and archaeological findings. According to the data, the normative behavior and labor processes of primitive peoples as depicted in the tales which they themselves cultivated cannot be explained by modern psychoanalytic theory. Properly speaking, any psychological approach to the folk tales would first have to investigate the socialization processes of primitive societies in a given historical era in order to provide an appropriate interpretation. Leaving aside the questionable methodology of the orthodox Freudians, who see penis envy and castration complexes everywhere in folk tales, and assuming that there is some validity to using folk tales therapeutically in educating children, one must still question the manner in which Bettelheim imposes meaning on the tales as well as his indiscriminate application of their meaning to children of all ages, sexes, and class backgrounds. As Nitschke demonstrates, the creative purpose and major themes of the folk tales did not concern harmony, but the depiction of changing social structures and alternative forms of behavior so that new developments and connections between humans and things could be better grasped by the people. Central to most tales is the concept of power. Where does it reside? Who wields it? Why? How can it be better wielded? Many of the tales bespeak a primitive or feudal ideology of "might makes right." Depending on the historical epoch, the tales portray either the possibilities for social participation or the reasons for social conflict. The immanent meaning of the tales has little to do with providing suitable direction for a contemporary child's life. From a contemporary perspective, the tales are filled with incidents of inexplicable abuse, maltreatment of women, negative images of minority groups, questionable sacrifices, and the exaltation of power.[6] Here I am only mentioning some of the more negative aspects of the tales which also contain positive features which will be discussed later. The point which I should like to make right now is that the psychological components and meanings can best be understood when first related to the contradictory developments of the historical period in which they originated.

To use the tales with children today as a means for therapeutic education demands first a historical understanding and secondly a careful delineation of the progressive and regressive ideological and psychological meanings of the tales. Here we are dealing with the entire question of reception. How does a child receive and perceive a given tale? It is necessary to ask whether a child actually knows what a king is. What does a king mean to a five-year-old, to an eight-year-old, to a girl or boy, to girls and boys of different races and class backgrounds? A prince who uses magical gifts which sometimes involve killing to become a king of a particular realm does not necessarily imply, as Bettelheim would have us believe, that the child (which child?) will psychologically comprehend this as a story about self-mastery. Could it not also serve to reinforce the aggressive instincts of a middle-class child to become more ego-centered, competitive, and achievement-oriented? Could not the code be understood by a lower-class child so as to reinforce the arbitrary power of authoritarian figures and to accept a strict hierarchical world? What is obviously necessary in working with the impact of the tales on children is a method which takes into consideration the aesthetics of reception. Such a method would have to investigate the possibilities for comprehension by children in the light of the dialectical relationship of a specific audience to the tale at a given moment in history.

The ultimate weakness of Bettelheim's methodology can be seen in the second part of his book which contains his case studies of popular folk tales. Let us look at his exhaustive treatment of *Cinderella* as an example of his approach. Bettelheim first discusses the various versions and cycles of the *Cinderella* story, in particular those of Basile and Perrault, and he diagnoses their major themes as those of sibling rivalry and the Oedipal complex. He then uses the basic plot of the Grimm version as the paradigmatic model for comprehending all the *Cinderella* stories. Actually no matter what tale is touched by Bettelheim's orthodox Freudian wand, it is always transformed into a symbolic parable of self-realization and healthy sexuality. Here, as usual, Bettelheim is concerned with the hidden meanings which work wonders on children. *Cinderella* teaches children about sibling rivalry and a young girl's endeavors to prove her worth. It is significant that Cinderella is given "dirty" work to do since that reflects her own low self-esteem as well as the guilt she feels for desiring her father. Her thwarted Oedipal desires must be overcome if she is to prove her real worth and achieve complete sexuality. The hardships which Cinderella must endure are tests that involve the development of personality.

Using Erik Erikson's model of the human life cycle, Bettelheim talks about the "phase-specific psychosocial crises" which an individual must go through in order to become the "ideal human being." In the case of Cinderella, she goes through five phases of the human life cycle to develop basic trust (the relationship with her original good mother), autonomy (acceptance of her role in the family), initiative (the planting of the twig), industry (her hard labors), and identity (her insistence that the prince see both her dirty and her beautiful side). Bettelheim is particularly penetrating on this last point.

In the slipper ceremony, which signifies the betrothal of Cinderella and the prince, he selects her because in symbolic fashion she is the uncastrated woman who relieves him of his castration anxiety which would interfere with a happy marital relationship. She selects him because he appreciates her in her "dirty" sexual aspects, lovingly accepts her vagina in the form of the slipper, and approves of her desire for a penis, symbolized by her tiny foot fitting into the slipper – vagina. . . . But as she slips her foot into the slipper, she asserts that she, too, will be active in their sexual relationship: she will do things, too. And she also gives the assurance that she is not and never was lacking in anything. (p. 271)

It is quite clear that the virginal Cinderella is the most suitable for Prince Charming because her step-sisters in their act of self-mutilation reveal through the blood (menstrual bleeding) that they are sexually too aggressive and cause the prince anxiety. In sum, *Cinderella* as a story "guides the child from his greatest disappointments – Oedipal disillusionment, castration anxiety, low opinion of others – toward developing his autonomy, becoming industrious, and gaining a positive identity of his own" (p. 276). After reading Bettelheim's concluding remarks, one wonders why such books as Dale Carnegie's *How to Win Friends and Influence People* and *How to Succeed in Business* are necessary when we have folk tales.

In contrast to Bettelheim's moral primer about folk tales, Nitschke has demonstrated that *Cinderella* originated toward the end of the Ice Age. The norms of behavior and social activity depicted in *Cinderella* reveal that the tale revolves around a female who receives help and gifts from her dead mother who continues living in the form of a tree, and from animals. Nitschke explains in some detail that the society which produced tales similar to *Cinderella* was one of hunting and grazing in which the woman was accorded the place of honor. Death was not feared, and women were sacrificed so that they could return to life in the form of a plant or animal to help their children develop. Life was seen in sequences and as eternal. Thus, a human being participated in his or her own time and, through transformation after death, there was a renewal of time. Most important is the function of the female. She was at the center of this society and maintained it as a nurturing element. *Cinderella* does not reflect society undergoing great changes in production but a maintenance of the hunting and grazing society. However, when compared to tales of the early Ice Age, it does show how human beings have taken over center stage from animals, and the growing importance attached to the woman. Love and mutual self-respect are accomplished through the intercession of the mother.

Nitschke's explanation of the historical origins and meaning of *Cinderella* obviously cannot be grasped by children. But it does set the framework for a psychoanalytical approach which must first consider the people and their social behavior if it wants to establish the psychological essence of a tale. The same thing holds true for the retelling of the tale today, but in a slightly different manner. And here the implications of the tale are remarkably different from what they were in the Ice Age. Instead of having a tale which does homage to women, we have a tale which is an insult to women. Here I want to concentrate on just one aspect of *Cinderella* to question the relevance Bettelheim bestows upon it. In the American society today where women have been in the vanguard of the equal rights movement, where female sexuality has undergone great changes, where the central agency of socialization of boys and girls has shifted from the family to the mass media, schools, and the bureaucratic state,[7] a tale like *Cinderella* cannot (neither explicitly nor implicitly) guide children to order their inner worlds and to lead fuller, happier sexual lives. Though it is difficult to speculate how an individual child might react to *Cinderella,* certainly the adult reader and interpreter must ask the following questions: Why is the stepmother shown to be wicked and not the father? Why is Cinderella essentially passive? (How Bettelheim twists the meaning to see Cinderella as active is actually another one of his Freudian magic tricks.) Why do girls have to quarrel over a man? How do children react to a Cinderella who is industrious, dutiful, virginal, and passive? Are all men handsome? Is marriage the end goal of life? Is it important to marry rich men? This small list of questions suggests that the ideological and psychological pattern and message of *Cinderella* do nothing more than reinforce sexist values and a Puritan ethos that serves a society which fosters competition and achievement for survival. Admittedly this is a harsh indictment of *Cinderella* as a tale. Certainly I do not want to make it responsible for the upkeep of the entire capitalist system. However, the critique of *Cinderella* is meant to show how suspect Bettelheim's theory and methodology are. There is something ultimately pathetic and insidious about Bettelheim's approach to folk tales. It is pathetic because he apparently wants to make a sincere contribution in fighting the dehumanization of life. It is insidious because his banal theory covers up the processes and social mediations which contribute most to the dehumanization. Fundamentally, his instructions on how to use the folk tales can only lead to their abuse. Our task is to explore the possibilities for their positive utilization with children.

There is no doubt but that folk tales are alluring, not only to children but to adults. Their imaginative conception of other worlds in which repressed dreams, needs, and wishes might be fulfilled has long since motivated the common people to transmit and cultivate the tales in an oral tradition. As Johannes Merkel and Dieter Richter have demonstrated in their important study *Märchen, Phantasie und soziales Lernen*,[8] the folk tales were often censored and outlawed during the early phase of the bourgeoisie's rise to power because their fantastic components which encouraged imaginative play and free exploration were hostile to capitalist rationalization and the Protestant ethos. Once the bourgeoisie's power was firmly established, the tales were no longer considered immoral and dangerous, but their publication and distribution for children were actually encouraged toward the end of the nineteenth century. The tales took on a compensatory function for children and adults alike who experienced nothing but the frustration of their imaginations in society. Within the framework of a capitalist socioeconomic system the tales became a safety valve for adults and children and acted to pacify the discontents. Like other forms of fantastic literature—and it is significant that science fiction rises also at the end of the nineteenth century—the tales no longer served their original purpose of clarifying social and natural phenomena but became forms of refuge and escape in that they made up for what people could not realize in society. This does not mean that the radical content of the imaginative symbols in folk tales and other forms of fantastic literature have been completely distilled. As Herbert Marcuse has suggested, "the truth value of imagination relates not only to the past but also to the future: the forms of freedom and happiness which it invokes claim to deliver the historical *reality*. In its refusal to accept as final the limitations imposed upon freedom and happiness by the reality principle, in its refusal to forget what *can be*, lies the critical function of phantasy."[9] Still, the question remains as to how to make the artistic forms conceived by the imagination operative *in society*. In other words, how can the imagination and imaginative literature transcend compensation?

In essence, Bettelheim's book discusses the use of the folk tale to compensate for social repression. But folk tales and other fantastic literature can be used to suggest ways to *realize* greater pleasure and freedom in society. Let us take Oscar Wilde's literary fairy tale, *The Selfish Giant*, as an example. The plot is simple. It involves a giant who chases children out of his garden, erects a wall, and puts up a sign "Trespassers will be Prosecuted!" Because he does this, spring and summer refuse to come to his garden, and he suffers from cold and loneliness. One day he notices through his window that the children had crept through a hole in the wall and had climbed up a tree. In that part of the garden inhabited by the children it suddenly turns spring, and the giant realizes how selfish he has been. After that he opens up his garden to all the children and learns to share in their happiness. Because of this he attains heaven upon his death.

I do not want to explore the different meanings of this tale in depth, for this would involve a consideration of Wilde's behavior, socialist perspective and personal philosophy in light of the repression of Victorian society. My main concern is to touch upon the general meaning which, on both a literary and a psychological level, might have an impact on children today. The language and symbols of the tale are such that it is probably comprehensible to all children regardless of sex, race, and background. The major theme involves collectivity versus individualism and the struggle over private property. The children band together and represent a principle of social interaction, sharing and joy while the giant obviously represents arbitrary power and greed. It is interesting that the tale depicts the alienation of the persecutor and how joy can only come through collectivity. Naturally it is possible to talk about the story in psychoanalytic terms: the fear of sexuality and parents, the id learning that there is a deeper pleasure to be attained by curbing its drive and participating in reality according to strictures of the superego. However, the message amounts to the same on an ideological and psychological level: the necessity for collective action and autonomous participation to attain pleasure, love, and recognition. What is even more important is that we are dealing with a literary fairy tale which illustrates through the imagination an alternative manner of behavior which *can be realized* in society. Wilde's tale is a valid critique of a society based on private property, a society which shuns children, and it provides hope that, if children stick together and use their initiative *(Hansel and Gretel* says this, too), they can convince their oppressors to change their ways. The children find a way into the giant's garden and show him the light, so to speak, and the process of overcoming his greed is depicted not as annihilation but a movement toward collective action. The focus is on intersubjective action which can nurture individual development.

There are numerous folk tales *(The Bremen Town Musicians, How Six Travelled Through the World)* and literary fairy tales which suggest means by which children can implement their imagination to promote collective action. I am not suggesting that it is only fantastic literature of this sort which should be used with children. In contrast to Bettelheim, I would argue that it is culturally repressive to dictate what forms of literature and types of tales are best suited for aiding a child's development. Folk tales, after all, were never conceived as tales for children, and there was never a special children's literature or culture until the late Middle Ages. Even now this distinction is somewhat arbitrary since children are exposed to all forms of art through the mass media, commercial outlets, and institutions of socialization. Bettelheim's argument for the folk tale is apparently an argument for fantastic literature over realistic literature as the best mode for solving a child's inner problems. But, once we realize that literature in and by itself does not work automatically to solve psychological problems, that realistic literature is not inherently repressive, and that the evaluation of literature cannot be discussed without considering its production and reception, we draw nearer to a more sober approach to the use of folk and fairy tales for children.

One could perhaps talk about certain interesting experiments which have been undertaken in West Germany:[10] the rewriting of folk tales from a socialist perspective, the conceiving of contemporary fairy tales written by adults and children which expose social contradictions and oppression, the active telling of folk and fairy tales which allow for a critical dialectical relationship between adults and children as the tale is told and interpreted.[11] Such radical use of folk and fairy tales is significant in that it demonstrates ways in which the imagination can be used to operate in society so that children and adults gain a greater sense of forces acting upon them and begin relating to one another in nonrepressive ways in their cultural work.[12]

The specific use of folk and fairy tales ultimately depends on the production and reception of the literature which is closely bound to the needs of the commodity market. Obviously, in American society it is near to impossible to control the Walt Disney industry and other conglomerates which mainly aim at making profit from the fantasy of children and adults. Educators sincerely interested in using fantastic or realistic literature to aid children in developing critical and imaginative capacities must first seek to alter the social organization of culture and work that is presently preventing self-realization and causing the disintegration of the individual. One cannot talk about the wounded child's psyche without talking about a social praxis which is geared toward ending the unfair speculation with lives that our socioeconomic system endorses. Cultural work with children must begin from a critical perspective of the production and market conditions of literature, and this involves using fantastic and realistic literature to make children aware of their potentialities and also aware of the social contradictions which will frustrate their full development. Any other approach will lead to illusions and lies. Thus, a concrete humanitarian engagement on behalf of children means utilizing the existing literature of all kinds while also creating new, more emancipatory forms so that the fallacies and merits of the literature become apparent as well as the fallacies and merits of society. There is no need to resort to methods of censorship or enchantment as Bettelheim does. But there is a need to develop effective means of enlightenment so that the repressed dreams, wishes, and needs of children and adults alike can be realized in a mutually beneficial way in the fight against what Freud called "cultural privation."

Folk and fairy tales remain an essential force in our cultural heritage, but they are not static literary models to be internalized for therapeutic consumption. Their value depends on how we actively produce and receive them in forms of social interaction which lead toward the creation of greater individual autonomy. Only by grasping and changing the forms of social interaction and work shall we be able to make full use of the utopian and fantastic projections of folk and fairy tales.

NOTES

1. New York, 1974. Throughout his book, Bettelheim uses the term fairy tale to indicate folk tale or *Volksmärchen*. Occasionally he will make a distinction between a folk fairy tale and a literary fairy tale *(Kunstmärchen)*, but more often than not he uses the term fairy tale indiscriminately. I shall employ the term folk tale when referring to the literature he discusses because it is largely of this variety.

2. Ibid., p. 4. Hereafter the page references to this book will be cited in the text.

3. Cf. the excellent critique of Bettelheim's book in this regard, James W. Heisig, "Bruno Bettelheim and the Fairy Tales," *Children's Literature,* 6 (1977), 93–115.

4. *Civilisation and Its Discontents,* trans. Joan Riviere, 5th ed. (London, 1951), 60, 63.

5. *Das frühe Europa,* vol. 1 (Stuttgart, 1976).

6. Cf. Robert Moore, "From Rags to Witches: Stereotypes and Anti-Humanism in Fairy Tales," *Interracial Books for Children Bulletin,* 7 (1975), 1–3. Moore's major thesis is that fairy tales are dangerous material for children since they present stereotypes which are based on racist and sexist ideologies. The only positive way to relate fairy tales to children is to expose the destructive nature of the tales. Moore goes to the opposite extreme of Bettelheim, and thus, like Bettelheim, he distorts the meaning of the tales and their possibilities for positive use with children.

7. Cf. Lee, Patrick C., and Robert Sussman Stewart. *Sex Differences: Cultural and Developmental Dimensions.* (1976), 15–22.

8. Berlin, 1974.

9. *Eros and Civilization* (New York, 1962), 135.

10. Cf. my article "Down with Heidi, Down with Struwwelpeter, Three Cheers for the Revolution: Towards a New Socialist Children's Literature in West Germany," *Children's Literature,* 5 (1976), 162–79.

11. Aside from the radical reutilization of fairy tales, there have been other interesting experiments in West Germany along the lines of Bettelheim's work. However, the educators do not make the extraordinary claims Bettelheim makes. See Felicitas Betz, *Märchen als Schlüssel zur Welt* (Munich, 1977) and Gisela Erberlein, *Autogenes Training mit Märchen—Ein Ratgeber für Eltern und Kinder* (Düsseldorf, 1976).

12. See Lena Foellbach, *Es war einmal kein König: Spiele für Kinder nach Märchen aus aller Welt* (Berlin, 1977). While Foellbach's experiments are far from being radical, they indicate a way in which one can rewrite fairy tales as plays with children and activate their consciousness of social interaction. Such work has been conducted in East Germany and in the West as well and provides the basis for the reinvigoration of the folk and fairy-tale tradition.

Goblins, Morlocks, and Weasels:
Classic Fantasy and the Industrial Revolution

Jules Zanger

Since most early English literature for young people had some didactic intention, the emergence of a wide range of fantasy in the late nineteenth and early twentieth centuries appeared to offer to the imaginative reader alternatives to the solid Victorian pieties. Earlier fantasies, like John Ruskin's Grimm-like *King of the Golden River* (1851) and Charles Kingsley's *The Water Babies* (1863) had been burdened by a great deal of fairly transparent allegorizing and overt moralizing. The newer fantasies tended to avoid this and appeared to focus much more singlemindedly upon appealing to the imaginations of their readers. Free from the instructional tone of the Peter Parley series and from the imperial exhortations of Marryat and Henty, fantasy seemed to open "magic casements" on worlds in which the young reader might wander, purely for pleasure, released for a time from the weighty burdens of duty, morality, and patriotism.

T. S. Eliot, in his essay "Religion and Christianity," warned us, however: " . . . It is just the literature we read for 'amusement' or 'purely for pleasure' that may have the greatest, and least suspected influence upon us." If we are to determine what was significant in British young people's literature at the close of the century, we must not turn only to the public idealizations of virtue set out so plainly for us in overtly didactic and "realistic" fictions for youth. We must turn also to the fantasies to discover the private nightmares of an England beset from

Reprinted from *Children's Literature in Education* 27 (Winter 1977), 154–62, by permission of the publisher, Agathon Press.

Jules Zanger is Professor of English at Southern Illinois University at Edwardsville, where he teaches American Literature. He is former president of the Midcontinent American Studies Association and has published widely in American Literature.

without and within by the forces of social breakdown. These night-mares were expressed in fictions whose surfaces seemed innocent and distant from the social and political upheavals threatening what many Englishmen considered England's Golden Age. Beneath the surface, however, the fearful images of disorder and revolution stirred uneasily, and in turn stirred the imaginations of generations of readers.

These fantasies stemmed from a variety of sources and took a variety of shapes. From traditional nursery fairy tales rooted in the works of Perrault, Grimm, and d'Aulnoy came the original adventure fantasies of George Macdonald and those who followed him. From the beast fables emerged such enchanting variations as Kenneth Grahame's *Wind in the Willows*. From the long tradition of travel literature, much of which had already bordered on the fantastic, came that most generative variation of all, H. G. Wells' *The Time Machine*.

In common, however, they shared what is a characteristic of much fantasy—a predilection for the past, or as a variant, a distrust of the future. This preference can be expressed explicitly as in Wells' dystopian vision of the future or, less directly, in the creation of worlds in which old magic still works, in which old gods still rule. It is expressed in the creation of an England which was rural, which was aristocratic, and which remained essentially Tory. It is a world of kings and princesses, of noble blood, and of houses of ancient lineage, and of equally ancient curses. The fantasies of late Victorian and of Edwardian England present us with a "green and pleasant land" which by its distance from the immediate and proximate reality of English life reveals its essential conservatism. Seen in this light, the dominant tone of English fantasy of this period can be said to be essentially elegiac, looking back at a world of country houses and yeoman cottages, of folk crafts and folk beliefs, of tradition and culture founded not on cities but on green fields. The elegiac tone of this literature, then, is not so much for the passing of the fairies as it is for the passing of a world in which it might still be possible to believe in fairies.

To the degree that the writers chose to embody their fictions in the mode of fantasy, they revealed their own predisposition toward tradition, toward the past, toward a preurban, preindustrial, pastoral England. They revealed equally their predispositions against the new and against change. In one sense, the fantasist was fighting nothing less than the Industrial Revolution and the transformations it had wrought upon the face of England. The "green and pleasant land" the writer depicts is under the attack of forces whose appearances change from fiction to fiction, but whose essential nature remains remarkably consistent.

To illustrate this, I would like to examine three fantasy classics of this period: George Macdonald's *The Princess and the Goblin* (1871), H. G. Wells' *The Time Machine* (1898), and Kenneth Grahame's *The Wind in the Willows* (1908). They represent something of the variety of late Victorian and of Edwardian fantasy, but also, that remarkable consistency of images and attitudes which haunted the English imagination at this time of transition.

In Macdonald's novel, the land over which the father of Princess Irene rules is undermined by great caverns inhabited by goblins who threaten to break out of their darkness and conquer the castle. These goblins, as Macdonald describes them, are quite unlike the traditional gnomes and kobolds and goblins of Germanic folklore. Instead of presenting them simply as another supernatural race, he evolves them out of a social, political, and economic context that is highly realistic. Of the goblins, he says:

> There was a legend current in the country, that at one time they lived above ground, and were very like other people. But for some reason or other, concerning which there were different legendary theories, the king had laid what they thought too severe taxes upon them, or had required observances of them they did not like, or had begun to treat them with more severity, in some way or other, and impose stricter laws; and the consequence was that they had all disappeared from the face of the country. According to the legend, however, instead of going to some other country, they had all taken refuge in the subterranean caverns. . . .[1]

Further, he tells us that in their subterranean lives they had been transformed.

> Those who had caught sight of them said that they had greatly altered in the course of generations; and no wonder, seeing they had lived away from the sun, in cold, and wet and dark places. They were now, not ordinarily ugly, but either absolutely hideous, or ludicrously grotesque both in face and form.[2]

These misshapen underground dwellers are prevented from kidnapping the Princess and conquering the kingdom only by the intervention of benevolent magical forces in the shape of a mysterious grandmother figure (a powerful Victorian icon), and the heroic activities of Curdie, a miner's boy of "noble blood" who succeeds in flooding the goblins' caverns and drowning them.

In H. G. Wells' *The Time Machine,* the implications of Macdonald's goblins become explicit. Here, the time traveler voyaging to the distant future discovers that the human race has evolved, in fact, into two races: the Eloi and the Morlocks. The Eloi are beautiful, delicate, surface dwellers whose lives consist of "playing gently, in bathing in the river, in making love in a half-playful fashion, in eating fruit, and sleeping."[3] The Morlocks are pale, deformed, underground creatures whom the traveler regards with physical loathing; he describes them variously as white spiders, worms, and rats. In attempting to explain the emergence of such two different races, he concludes:

> . . . the gradual widening of the merely temporary and social difference between the Capitalist and the labourer was the key to the whole position. . . . Even now, does not an East-end worker live in such artificial conditions as practically to be cut off from the natural surface of the earth? Again, the exclusive tendency of rich people — due, no doubt, to the increasing refinement of their education, and the widening gulf between them and the rude violence of the poor — is already leading to the closing, in their interest, of considerable portions of the surface of the land. . . . So, in the end, above ground you must have the Haves, pursuing pleasure and comfort and beauty, and below ground the Have-nots, the Workers getting continually adapted to the conditions of their labour.[4]

However, the ultimate horror the traveler discovers is that the Morlocks emerge nightly from their caverns to feed on the Eloi whom they raise as their cattle: the goblins have conquered the castle.

The third work I wish to discuss in this context seems at casual reading to be altogether different in subject, mood, and style from the books I have described. Yet even in Grahame's *Wind in the Willows,* the threatening presence of "the other" is felt. The ordered world of nineteenth-century England is represented by thinly disguised types: Water Rat as private gentleman with a touch of Oxbridge still lingering about him, Badger as bluff country squire, Toad of Toad Hall as landed aristocrat, Mole as emerging Mr. Polly. But even on this idealized bucolic setting, the shadow of the Wild Wood falls. The Wild Wood is inhabited by stoats and weasels and ferrets who overwhelm by their numbers the unwary who venture in. The climax of the novel occurs when the stoats, weasels, and ferrets pour out of the Wild Wood to capture Toad Hall, the great house of the district, and are finally driven back by the combined forces of Water Rat, Badger, Toad, and Mole. Like the Goblins and the Morlocks, the dwellers in the Wild Wood are described as physically repellent, with "little evil wedge-shaped" faces; like them, they are represented in the aggregate—living in great numbers under the ground:

> . . . every hole, far and near, and there were hundreds of them, seemed to possess its face, coming and going rapidly, all fixing on him glances of malice and hatred: all hard-eyed and evil and sharp.[5]

Like the Goblins and the Morlocks, they issue forth from their holes underground to threaten the world of sunlight and to overthrow established order.

The concern with the usurpation of established and legitimate authority is, of course, much older than the literature we have been examining. However, it emerges in this period with a frequency that at first appears remarkable for an age which was dominated by the longest reign of a legitimate monarch in English history and one for whom no problems of succession existed. This concern is explained, however, when we recall that in the period under discussion no fewer than nine heads of state were deposed, executed, or assassinated: the Emperor Maximillian of Mexico was deposed and executed in 1861; Queen Isabella of Spain was deposed and exiled in 1868; in 1881, Tsar Alexander II of Russia was assassinated; the Empress Elizabeth of Austria was murdered in 1898; King Umberto of Italy was shot to death in 1900; President William McKinley was murdered in 1901; King Alexander II and Queen Draga of Serbia were cut to pieces by assassins in 1903; King Carlos of Portugal was assassinated in 1907. During this same period, there were at least six attempts on the life of Queen Victoria herself. This pattern of events surely contributed to the sense of the precariousness of established authority that appears in the works we have discussed. It appears, as well, in fantasies as various as Dinah M. M. Craik's *The Little Lame Prince* (1874) where the rightful heir to the throne is replaced by his scheming uncle, in E. Nesbit's "The Princess and the Cat" (1905) where the Princess is removed and exiled by a revolutionary mob, and even in Lewis Carroll's *Sylvie and Bruno* (1889), which boasts both a scheming uncle and a revolutionary mob that at the opening of the novel is gathered under the palace windows alternately chanting for "more bread and less taxes," and "more taxes and less bread."

There emerges from the three very different fantasies of Macdonald, Wells, and Grahame what appears to be a single cluster of shared images and ideas. In all of these we are shown societies in conflict in which an established, traditional order is under attack. The authors enlist our sympathies in support of the traditional order, and we are made to regard the opponents of this establishment with fear and disgust. These opponents are presented as underdwellers who are deformed and twisted and who issue out from their subterranean holes in great hordes to usurp traditional authority.

In *The Golden Key,* a study of George Macdonald's fiction, R.L. Wolff conjectures that the goblins represent the "greedy cunning side of human nature tunneling away in the secret subterranean chambers of the subconscious and threatening to take possession of the castles of our mind."[6] Richard H. Reis, author of a more recent critical biography of Macdonald, criticizes Wolff for what he calls his "doctrinaire Freudianism" but in his own discussion of *The Princess and the Goblin,* he writes: "The Freudian hierarchy of ego (the Princess), superego (the fairy grandmother in the attic), and id (the goblins in the basement), is obvious enough, and their presence reflects Macdonald's independent discovery of these phenomena" (p. 81).[7] I would suggest that Macdonald's goblins, like Wells' Morlocks and Grahame's weasels, were at least as much representative of certain social and political phenomena of Victorian England as they were of the psychic impulses Wolff and Reis describe.

To understand the impact of these phenomena on the shape of fantasy, it will be necessary to review some of the events of the previous century. One of the by-products of Great Britain's success in the Napoleonic wars was the profound reduction in numbers of the army and navy. This, coupled with a sharp drop in demand for British manufactures after 1816, created great numbers of unemployed and hungry men. To these were added those agricultural laborers who had lost their communal grazing rights and those who had subsisted on the traditional cottage industries which the new machines had destroyed. The first major confrontation between the poor and the established order was the famous Peterloo massacre of 1819, in which armed yeomen cavalry charged a peaceful meeting of 60,000 working people carrying banners with revolutionary inscriptions. This first encounter established a pattern of conflict that was to be repeated frequently during the following years, with the significant difference that the crowds of unemployed which had been well-ordered at Peterloo were to grow increasingly violent, destructive, and revolutionary as the century wore on. When the Reform Bill of 1831 was rejected by the House of Lords, rioting broke out in Bristol during which the Manor House and the

Bishop's Palace were burned. The rioters were again broken by a cavalry charge. Increasingly, the industrial towns of the North and the mining districts especially became centers of revolutionary activity. In 1839, rioting began in Birmingham, and the town of Monmouth was attacked by miners with pitchforks and muskets, in the hopes that Wales, Lancashire, and Yorkshire would rise in revolt.

The climax of revolutionary activity came in 1842 when, after prolonged depression and closing of many factories and mines, starving mobs of unemployed and underpaid coal miners and operatives rose all through the north. During the month of August rioting spread from Staffordshire to Manchester, where furnaces and factories were shut down and police stations, courts, and great houses were gutted. Work throughout the industrial North was brought to a complete standstill. In response, the government called out the rural yeomanry in every Northern and Midland county, pitting farmers on horseback against the urban mobs. This confrontation was the perfect embodiment of the conflict between old and new, between rural and industrial England, and between past and future. In this case, Old England won, but the victory was at best a holding action. The insurrection failed, but the fearful memory of those pale-faced miners and operatives pouring out of their pits and hovels was to haunt the English imagination for a century. Even Thomas Carlyle, who was sympathetic to the working men, described the rioters of the Manchester insurrection as a "million-headed hydra" which had been trodden down "into its subterranean settlements again."[8]

Contributing to the numbers of native unemployed were the hordes of Irish peasants who throughout the century had migrated to England and exchanged rural starvation for urban starvation. In most of the great new industrial centers they constituted a hard core of ignorant and brutal paupers living in conditions of unbelievable filth, deprivation, and savagery. By 1844, two years, that is, *before* the great famine, there were over a million Irish in England. Their presence in the festering slums of the cities maintained a constant threat and reproach to Britain's security. Carlyle wrote of the Irish:

> He is the sorest evil this country had to strive with. In his rags and laughing savagery, he is there to undertake all work that can be done by mere strength of hand and back—for wages that will purchase him potatoes. . . . The uncivilized Irishman, not by his strength but by the opposite of strength,

drives the Saxon out, takes possession in his room. There abides he, in his squalor and unreason, in his falsity and drunken violence, as the ready made nucleus of degradation and disorder.[9]

The image of the Irish slum dwellers was to converge with that of the revolutionary miners and operatives to create an impression of the poor that emphasized their savagery, and above all, their otherness: to deny, that is, their common shared humanity. This sense of the alienness of the poor was heightened by the fact that as the industrial age wore on, the poor were growing physically different from the adequately fed. By the turn of the century, it was revealed that over sixty percent of Englishmen were unfit for the Army. Disturbed by this threat to its military strength, the government formed a Committee on Physical Deterioration which reported that "even allowing for dietary deficiencies imposed by ignorance, the differences between the physical condition of rich and poor children were gross, as a few statistics show. The average height of working class school boys was five inches below that of public school boys. . . ." The pale and stunted condition of the poor made it easier to regard them as belonging to another race and to further deny their humanity.

One important and influential work which recorded and reenforced this vision of the poor was Gustave Doré's popular *London, a Pilgrimage* (1872), an illustrated tour of London which had as its dramatic climax a visit to Whitechapel and the East End. This section of the work, which is illustrated by a series of engravings as horrifying as any he did for his edition of Dante's *Inferno,* recounts a visit Doré and Blanchard Jerrold, his collaborator, made to the East End under heavy police guard. The whole experience is described as an exploring expedition, or a sort of safari, to some hostile foreign land peopled by savages totally alien to the visitors:

> We dismiss our cab: it would be useless in the strange dark byeways to which we are bound: byeways the natives of which will look upon us as the Japanese looked upon the first European travellers in the streets of Jeddo. This missionary, the parish doctor, the rent collector (who must be a bold man indeed), the policeman, the detective, and the humble undertaker are the human beings from without our Alsatia who enter appearances in this weird and horrible Bluegate Fields; where in the open doorways lowbrowed ruffians and women who emphasize even their endearments with an oath, scowl at us in threatening groups as we pass, keeping carefully in the middle of the road. "Stick close together, gentlemen; this is a

very rough part," our careful guides tell us—some walking before, others behind—the local superintendent or Scotland Yard sergeant accosting each policeman on his beat, and now and then collecting two or three, and planting them at strategical points or openings, that cover our advance, and keep the country open behind us.[10]

The visit of Mole and Water Rat to the Wild Wood in Grahame's *Wind in the Willows* seems to me to show remarkable parallels to Doré's slumming expedition into Whitechapel. More generally, however, Doré's account reveals the astonishing distance that had come to exist between the poor and the middle and upper classes in late Victorian England, and helps explain the recurring fantasy patterns in its literature for young people.

The conditions that had contributed to these attitudes before 1870 were to continue well into the twentieth century. Throughout this time, the hostility toward and fear of the immigrant Irish were to be intensified by the activities of the Sinn Fein, the Invincibles, and the other Irish nationalist extremist groups. Labor unrest, especially among the miners and ironworkers, provided a constant ground base to the swan song of the Empire. The serious rioting that had been confined to the North in the 1840s erupted in London itself in the 1880s and broke windows in Pall Mall.

The fantasy literature that emerged from this time of unrest, of apprehension, and of guilt, was a literature that consistently created the Forces of Evil in shapes that reflected the fears and prejudices of the essentially middle-class audience—literate and leisured—for which it was written. It reflected their dread of revolution, their distrust of the alien, and their horror of the poor, and transformed these feelings into images that in the guise of fantasy reenforced and crystallized them. But beyond this, in these fantasies' depiction of social conflict, we see reflected the shift away from any transcendant moral or spiritual authority as the regulating institution in the human community. Instead, we see a greater emphasis upon what Leonard Krieger called "authoritative power" which can only secure obedience or conformity through the exercise of force or coercion, no matter how legitimate or lawful that power may be. It is symptomatic of this shift that the conflicts in the fantasies we have examined are all uniformly expressed and resolved by naked violence.

The impact of these fantasies upon subsequent fantasy writers is clear. There seems little doubt that the conservative concern with the worlds of Faerie, with the Elder Gods, with princes and ancient houses and ancient curses that dominated the great classics of the turn of the century still dominates our more recent classics. The Earthmen of Underland in C. S. Lewis' Narnia series, and the Orcs of Tolkien's *Lord of the Rings* are direct lineal descendants of Macdonald's goblins, Wells' Morlocks, and Grahame's denizens of the Wild Wood. In Tolkien's work, especially, the conflict between pre- and post-Industrial Revolution England is most clearly worked out, with the evils of Mordor as an embellished recapitulation of the evils of Birmingham and Manchester. In both Lewis' and Tolkien's works we find the same fear of the usurpation of power and the loss of the rightful king. In both works, the sympathies of the reader are enlisted absolutely on the side of a traditional, pastoral world whose establishment is aristocratic, benign, and supernaturally supported. In both works we see the forces of evil as, in every sense, beyond redemption.

The impact of these fantasies upon the social and political attitudes of the young people who read them is, of course, impossible to determine. In his essay "Words and Behavior," Aldous Huxley observed, "We know that the killing of men and women is wrong, and we are reluctant consciously to do what we know to be wrong. But when particular men and women are thought of merely as representative of a class that has previously been defined as evil and personified in the shape of a devil, then the reluctance to hurt or murder disappears. . . . When they have been called such names and assimilated to the accursed class to which such names apply, Brown, Jones, and Robinson cease to be conceived as what they really are—human persons—and become for the uses of this fatally inappropriate language mere vermin or, worse, demons whom it is right to destroy as thoroughly and as painfully as possible." Certainly, any such blanket assertion about the influence of these fantasies upon the sensibilities of their readers must remain unproved. Nevertheless, we can surely conjecture that the identification of the laboring poor, the unemployed, and the immigrant with the goblins, the Morlocks, and the stoats and weasels of the Wild Wood must have poorly served the young middle-class readers of these classics in the great labor of reconciliation that the twentieth century has demanded of them.

What does this all mean today? Certainly not that any fantasy should be included in or excluded from a curriculum on the basis of its roots in one or another political bias. Instead, I am advocating that as readers and teachers of fantasy we are obligated to clarify both for ourselves and for our students even the most problematical implications of this most-disarming literary mode.

NOTES

1. Macdonald. *The Princess and the Goblin*, 14–15.
2. Ibid.
3. Wells. *The Time Machine*, 34.
4. Ibid., 40.
5. Grahame. *The Wind in the Willows*, 35.
6. Wolff. *The Golden Key*, 166.
7. Reis. *George Macdonald*, 19, 81.
8. Carlyle. *Works*, vol. 13, 16.
9. Ibid., vol. 3, 55.
10. Doré and Blanchard. *London, a Pilgrimage*, 144-45.

WORKS CITED

Carlyle, Thomas. *Works*. Boston: Estes and Lauriat, 1884.

Doré, Gustave, and Blanchard Jerrold. *London, A Pilgrimage*. London: Grant; New York: Blom, 1972.

Eliot, T. S. "Religion and Literature" In *Essays, Ancient and Modern*. London: Faber and Faber; New York: Haskell, 1936.

Grahame, Kenneth. *The Wind in the Willows*. New York: Heritage Press, 1940.

Huxley, Aldous. *The Olive Tree*. New York and London: Harper, 1937.

Krieger, Leonard. "The Idea of Authority in the West." *American Historical Review* 82, no. 2 (1977).

Macdonald, George. *The Princess and the Goblin*. New York: Grosset and Dunlap, 1907.

Ries, R. H. *George Macdonald*. New York: Twayne, 1972.

Wells, H. G. *The Time Machine*. London: Heinemann; New York: Bantam, 1963.

Wolff, R. L. *The Golden Key*. New Haven: Yale University Press, 1961.

The Ability to Dream
Adaptations, Translations, Folklore

Alga Marina Elizagaray

Adaptations of books for children have always been a very controversial subject, arousing vehement arguments pro and con. Advocates of adaptations maintain that if children have not read certain books by the age of fifteen, they will never read them. Most young people end their studies in the humanities (literature, the arts, etc.) at around that age, when they finish high school and begin working, or go on to college to enroll in technical and scientific courses. In favor of adaptations, supporters point out that there are many titles for adults which could be made suitable for young people if certain passages and episodes which do not inspire a child's imagination were omitted, *provided* the author's work and style are respected. Having been exposed to the adaptation in their youth, adult readers may well want to go back to the original, complete work. Passionate defenders of adaptations assert that every work of literature is in some sense an adaptation. The themes, situations, and characters in books are limited and differentiated primarily through the style of the author. To tell a story is to relive it, to bring it to life in such a way that it draws the hypothetical reader into the story as a participant. And in its own way this is a kind of adaptation.

Reprinted by permission of the author from *En Torno a la Literatura Infantile* (Havana: Unión de Escritores y Artistas de Cuba, 1975), 161–75. Translated by Charlotte Bagby and Rosainés Aguirre.

Alga Marina Elizagaray is assistant minister of culture of Cuba, in charge of children's activities. She is also the author of several books of stories for children, has compiled a number of collections of children's writing, and has written a number of critical studies.

Conversely, adaptations of literature for younger readers evoke ideological, esthetic, psychological, and pedagogical criticisms, which give rise to impassioned discussions. Some opponents of adaptations maintain that a work of art is a creation with its own rhythm and balance, and to adapt it is to destroy its texture and its essential shape. There are also those who think that the suppression of certain themes gives a false idea of these very subjects. Such is the case with sex, since children find out about it through radio, movies, and television—especially within capitalist society. To avoid such themes appears naive and hypocritical. This position affirms that children need to be educated about important ideological questions and moral aspects of personality. The problem is to orient them correctly in relation to life's realities and to explain to them the "possibilities of resistance," as Makarenko[1] put it. Other opponents of adaptations maintain that when a work is simplified, readers grow passive and follow the line of least resistance. As a result, they lose the capacity to read more complex books and are left with a false idea of the original book. Why go to the trouble of reading the full work when you believe— unjustifiably, to be sure—that you know it already? Perhaps, the opponents of adaptations argue, it would be better to wait a few months or even years and then give young readers the original text. I must point out here that most of these criticisms are leveled at *digest*-type adaptations. We can easily remember the slanted publications issued by *Reader's Digest,* which were sold to our people up until the triumph of the Revolution.

My own point of view differs from both of these extreme, exclusive positions. For the past few years, I have dedicated myself in part to adapting juvenile stories for telling by our storytellers to the children who come to *Story Hours,* and I seldom agree with the way some adapters work.

The need for these adaptations—often based on previous translations—arose when the storytellers of the Red Nacional de Bibliotecas (the Cuban national library network) began to look for high-quality, well-written materials to use in the practice of their art. For this purpose, according to Eliseo Diego, it was essential to have on hand "written material of the highest quality, something not always within our reach because of the scarcity of good books and because most of the editions for children in our own language suffer from a deplorable linguistic poverty." In an effort to solve this problem, the Biblioteca Nacional José Martí (the national library of Cuba) began publishing the *Textos para narradores* (Texts for Storytellers).[2]

The purpose of our adaptations is primarily recreational and esthetic, without, of course, ignoring ideological content. Through
these stories and storytelling, we hope to develop and strengthen
children's imagination and language, which are so often neglected.
By respecting the original poetic element of the stories, our adaptations try to create that "willing suspension of disbelief" which
Coleridge held to be the secret of all art. Though these aspirations
might seem unduly ambitious, we believe this is a proper attitude
toward work ultimately intended for children.

To adapt a story is to modify it, a task not as easy as one
might think. Unfortunately, it is not like pruning a tree, because in
some cases a branch must be turned into a new trunk, and many
leaves have to be chopped off so that varicolored ones can grow.
This process requires knowledge, care, and some dexterity developed only with practice. Above all, we must respect the original
poetic values of the story, whether they were created by a
particular writer or by some unknown author rooted in the folklore
of a people.

Children take great pleasure in traditional folk tales. Moreover,
they provide an ample source of themes and situations which
contain all the wisdom and popular poetry of their origins. Therefore, we use this rich vein in our choice of material. Yet we must
always remember that these stories, since they did not arise as
sophisticated artistic creations, are sometimes full of primitive
violence, irrationality, and barbarian ancestral customs, which
should be eliminated—or at least softened—in adaptation for the
Cuban children of our own day.

In this task it is very important to search for the most authentic
version of a tale and the best Spanish translation. In this way, we
can compare the various versions—it they exist—and detect possible
omissions. With adaptations destined for storytelling, we want the
final version to give the storyteller enough room to develop her
own individual style of presenting the tale.

We have discussed a number of valid problems related to adaptations drawn from world and national folklore. We shall now
discuss similar questions about children's literature by individual
authors. In this case, adaptation is much harder since the stories
are more involved and lack the simple definite structure of popular
tales. Because these stories are generally more descriptive and complex, respect for the author's style and purpose must always be
present. Unfortunately, one does not have to be a magician to
succeed in transforming a giant of literature into a dwarf—it's all
too easy!

Here are the procedures we follow in making our adaptations: First, *analysis* of the story, breaking it down into primary and secondary elements and understanding the relationship between them—for example, in choosing characters vital to the structure of the narrative. Second, *selection* of a single sequence of scenes, eliminating anything that could distract attention, destroy the unity of the story, or prevent its visualization. In picking out the scenes, there are three methods: *omission, expansion,* and *alteration.* (The third method is used when the story is neither too long, nor too short, but needs only a change in the order of its elements for the child to enjoy and understand it.) But we must keep in mind, when using these devices, that it is better for the child to miss the meaning of a word or phrase than to lose the chance to listen to the beauty of the language.

Whatever the methods we use and the changes we make in the course of adaptation, we must be very sure that these alterations add real liveliness and interest to the story without detracting from its essence or the beauty of its style. We can put our own words into the mouth of any important character provided we know how to do it well and always provided the dialogue is in harmony with the character's integrity. If we lack this ability, or if we do not have time to develop it seriously, it is better to give up this work or at least put it off.

Adaptations for children should emphasize action and dialogue by omitting excessively long descriptions that are tiring and distracting; good adaptations should suggest instead of explaining; they should eliminate vulgar words and incidents that could provide harmful models; and finally, they should not force the plot into a *happy ending.* We must not overprotect children nor shut them up in a glass case. We must not deny that in this world death and sadness exist along with happiness, that good and evil are the two poles of the human condition—complex, varied, and often ambiguous. And so, we must teach children to confront the difficulties of daily human existence, but without unnecessary traumas. Good adaptations can help in this practical and straightforward task and, of course, move us toward our primary goal: *To encourage the ability to dream, indispensable to children.*

Alexander Nicolaievich Nesmeiánov, former president of the Academy of Sciences of the U.S.S.R. and one of the founders of modern organic chemistry, a man of science, not a poet, has said that the truly essential ability of the scientist—without which he would be blind—is this capacity to dream.

For many years, national, Latin American, and world folk tales have been the "work horse" in our daily struggle to provide adaptations for storytelling to children. But for us folklore is not an indiscriminate source of tales; on the contrary, we believe that, apart from its irrefutable value as a rich vein of spontaneous poetry, elements of sadomasochism quite often appear. While we do not share the attitude of excessive protection, neither can we condone frightening children by introducing them to extreme cruelty and horror before they are ready.

In general, children's appreciation of tales and fantasy has changed very little, if at all, since the days of Perrault or Martí. Nothing replaces the delight in the poetic and the marvelous which these stories bring to a child's eager sensitivity. When these stories are told or read to children, they are engrossed and willingly abandon a movie or a television program to listen. Of course, this happens only if the storyteller is a true artist, an authentic narrator capable of bewitching the audience with eloquent voice and gestures.

As Saint Exupéry remarks in *The Little Prince,* "What is essential is invisible to the eye," so we have to be extremely careful about the folklore we intend to give children. When we make adaptations, we must not only be sure that they conserve the freshness, lyricism, and wit of the original. We must also make certain that the language remains spontaneous and never descends into shoddiness. And most important, we must not tolerate anything objectionable from an ideological point of view.

In our collections of stories adapted for storytelling, we have materials taken from our rural, Afro-Cuban oral traditions, such as those gathered by Ramon Guirao in *Cuentos Negros de Cuba (Black Tales from Cuba),* and others directly recorded from Black elders. These stories have been re-created with a respect for the essence of the original, but enriched as much as possible in structure, dialogue, and language, so that they will appeal to children. From our national folklore, we have stories based on anecdotes and incidents in our epic liberation struggle of the last century and more recent episodes of the Cuban Revolution. Nor should we forget Cuban traditions as collected by Alvaro de la Iglesia in *Tradiciones Cubanas.*

From Latin American folklore we have adapted the tales of various South American countries — legends of the Incas of Peru, the Araucanians of Chile, the Mexicans, and others. Some were compiled by the Argentinian folklorist Rafael Jujena in his book, *Cuentos de la Mamá Vieja (Old Mama's Stories).* From world folklore, our repertory includes Norse, Spanish, North American,

English, and Hindu stories, as well as popular Russian, Chinese, Vietnamese, and other tales.

All normal children can distinguish perfectly well between reality and fantasy, and they may be harmed if they are deprived of something as important to their nature as fiction. We women remember playing in the make-believe kitchens that we improvised on our patios. The leaves of the plants were steaks, the tiny pebbles were rice, and so forth. Everything was cooked in imagination in little pots and served in pretty play dishes. But it never occurred to any little girl, either then or now, actually to eat those supposedly succulent meals. We used to say that it was just "pretend" and then give them to our dolls.

Childhood is the stage of human existence most apt to enjoy the esthetic experience. That it coincides with the greatest love for folk tales, is due to the following:

1. Folk tales are a product of popular imagination, capable of filling a basic human need for fantasy.

2. Characters in the folk tale are nearly always presented as archetypal figures and, in many cases, as symbols of human virtues and failings. The folkloric conception, with its primitive structure in which human acts and values operate within carefully marked limits, is an understandable result of the Manichean concept of good and evil, which is the mentality of childhood. Within these limits, bad is completely bad, and good is unmistakably good. In short, the longing for justice, strong in a child, is amply fulfilled by appropriate reward or punishment.

3. The child's mind is like a blank page, still untouched by the burden of cares, which life imposes, and which, on occasion, hinders human sensibility.

4. Children, like primitive people, the creators of these fantasies, need to empower themselves from this accumulation of vital experiences.

Finally, all young people's literature of true artistic quality, whether or not based on the folklore of a given people, develops children's sensitivity and enriches their inner life. Even if children do not yet have great imagination—just because it is still undeveloped—they look for it in stories. In this light, I recall the words of the poet Eliseo Diego, to whom I owe much of my concern and love for themes relating to childhood. He once said,

"Maybe it's not so important that children should *know* prematurely, but that they should *be*." In truth, without this initial conditioning, there would be no human being of the future, new in action and in thought, the integral human being needed by the society we are building. Nor would we have that beautiful motto of our Pioneers and Young Communists: "Seremos como el Ché." (We will be like Ché.) To quote Saint-Exupéry once again, let us never forget that "all grown-ups were once children."

NOTES

1. Anton Makarenko (1888–1939), pioneer Soviet educator who set up schools for homeless children after the Revolution; author of *The Road to Life, A Book for Parents,* and *Lectures on Education.* — Ed.
2. *Adaptaciones de Cuentos Para Niños de 1o y 2o Grados. 3o y 4o Grados. 5o y 6o Grados.* Booklets in this series constitute the *Colección Textos Para Narradores,* Departamento de Literatura y Narraciones Infantiles, Biblioteca Nacional "José Martí," Consejo Nacional de Cultura, Havana, various dates. The quotation is taken from the foreword to the series by Eliseo Diego, eminent Cuban poet, critic, translator of Grimm and Andersen, and tireless pioneer in the development of a truly fine Cuban children's literature. — Ed.

Ideologies in Children's Literature:
Some Preliminary Notes

Ruth B. Moynihan

Stories told or written for children are often indicators of the dominant values within a society. Various times and cultures reveal various attitudes, not only toward children but also toward life and society. As a Swedish specialist in children's literature recently said,

> Every age has felt the need to provide new instructions in its children's books on how life is to be lived. Thus children's books do not merely reflect the contemporary social scene and the problems of adult life; the simplified manner in which they treat their subjects also makes them something of magnifying glasses.[1]

The number of such magnifying glasses in our modern world is greater than ever before in history. An adequate discussion even of a particular era in one society could well be a major study. The purpose of this brief essay is merely to point out a few examples and to indicate some possibilities for further investigation.

The Wonderful Wizard of Oz, published in 1900 by Lyman Frank Baum, is one of the best known of American children's stories, but few have given much thought to the way in which its characters and plot reflect the political and social situation of the time. However, an article by Henry M. Littlefield recently described in detail the way the book serves as a populist parable. The Scarecrow, for example, represents Midwestern farmers, while the Tin Man represents the honest laborers bewitched by Eastern

Reprinted from *Children's Literature* 2 (1973), 166–72 by permission of the publisher.

Ruth B. Moynihan has lectured on history and women's studies at Yale and is the author of "Children on the Overland Trail."

industrialists (personified in the Wicked Witch of the East). The Cowardly Lion is a parody of William Jennings Bryan. The Wizard, says Littlefield, "might be any President from Grant to McKinley. He comes straight from the fair grounds in Omaha, Nebraska, and he symbolizes the American criterion for leadership — he is able to be everything to everybody."[2] But Dorothy's innocence and her loving kindness, along with the brains, heart, and courage of her friends (which were within them all along though they didn't know it), are sufficient to unmask even the formidable Wizard and to achieve Dorothy's goals — the freedom of her friends and her own return to reality among her hard-working relatives in Kansas.

If we compare *The Wizard of Oz* to the English classic for children, *Winnie the Pooh,* the contrast is startling. A. A. Milne's story takes place in a sheltered circumscribed world, the easy-going world of the English upper classes, where one lone child might live on a huge green estate with a dozen stuffed animals for playmates, and in a fantasy world where he himself was in complete control. Baum's book, on the other hand, reveals a world full of conflict and danger where the heroine lives in a harsh gray world with only a little dog for a playmate (but a live dog, not a stuffed one) and can only escape into fantasy by being hit on the head in a tornado. Furthermore, even the fantasy world is full of dangers and harrowing experiences. Dorothy and her friends must deal with events as they occur, while Milne's characters generally frame or manipulate events according to their own expectations.

Winnie the Pooh, published in England in 1926, has been tremendously popular in America as well, though perhaps not as influential as *The Wizard of Oz.* It is better known to the intelligentsia, probably, while *Oz* is better known to the "common man." *Pooh* reflects a disillusionment with the pre–World War I world and its leadership. It is a sustained low-key spoof on official bureaucracies, the adult world in general, and the adventure and travel tales of nineteenth century imperial Britain. Where many earlier fairy tales were full of seriousness and took pretentiousness for granted as necessary and good, A. A. Milne's tales are all humor — especially in regard to pretensions. The ideology is that of a bumbling imperfect world, though a generally kind-hearted and not at all dangerous one.

Let us look at one chapter as an illustration. Chapter VIII, called "In Which Christopher Robin Leads an Expotition to the North Pole," reveals even through its title its deliberate parody of such earlier literature as *Robinson Crusoe* or the works of Robert Louis Stevenson.

This particular story concerns an expedition to the North Pole which Christopher Robin is planning. When asked by Pooh Bear what it is, Christopher says, "It's just a thing you discover," since he isn't quite sure himself, and then goes on to explain that all his friends can come because "that's what an Expedition means. A long line of everybody." Pooh goes off to gather the friends and they set off. After passing a "dangerous" part of the river where Christopher claims there might be an "ambush," they settle down in the first grassy area to eat their provisions—the best part of the "expotition" to most of the participants. After Christopher takes Rabbit aside to check with him about just what the North Pole might look like, the crisis event occurs. Baby Roo falls in the water while washing his face. He thinks he's swimming, while everyone else tries desperately to rescue him. Finally Pooh rescues Roo with a long pole and is informed by Christopher Robin that he has also discovered the North Pole. They put a sign on the Pole to that effect and go home. Pooh, "feeling very proud of what he had done, had a little something to revive himself."

Within the story, each character carries a message, too. Eeyore, the donkey, is the complaining old, self-centered, hypocritical relative with whom society must be patient and forgiving. He doesn't ask things, he just tells people. He comes along only "to oblige" and everything is "all the same" to him, though when things start moving he says, "Don't Blame Me." He's a perennial wet blanket, full of self-pity, an eater of thistles who assumes that Pooh sits on them on purpose to keep them away from him. He preaches consideration, which he does not practice, and he "don't hold with all this washing" of Roo—"This modern Behind-the-ears nonsense." Finally, he's totally useless despite his painful efforts when it comes to rescuing Roo. The message is that the older generation is generally irrelevant, but well-meaning, and one must be nice to its members.

Owl is the intellectual who always knows about things, like the meaning of "ambush," and who tells "Interesting Anecdotes full of long words like Encyclopedia and Rhododendron" while his listeners fall asleep with boredom. In the emergency he explained that "in a case of Sudden and Temporary Immersion the Important Thing was to keep the Head Above Water," while the others hurried to the rescue. His knowledge is always either obvious or useless or both, but he is respected just for thinking and for his slightly mysterious potential usefulness.

Kanga is a spoof on motherhood. While she "explained to everybody proudly that this was the first time [Roo] had ever washed his face himself," he fell in the water and had a glorious time while she worried. The only female in the story, she represents a complacently sexist viewpoint — all women are mother figures and mothers are rather a nuisance most of the time. Piglet is a lovable coward in a world where there is nothing to be afraid of, while Rabbit has an unseemly number of relatives — message: fecundity is not really proper. Pooh is, of course, a "Bear of little brain" — the good and average person, and happily so. Presumably, the reader identifies with Christopher Robin, the paternalistic natural leader and protector simply by virtue of his superior birth, even though he is not much smarter or more capable.

It seems clear that this North Pole Expotition is intended to parody the great exploratory polar expeditions of the previous fifty years, especially those of Admiral Robert E. Peary. Peary had planned and provisioned several expeditions during the 1890s and even took his wife and new-born baby along. The Peary Arctic Club consisted of a few of his friends helping him towards his goal. Finally, on his sixth attempt in 1909, with much publicity, Peary succeeded in planting the American flag at the desolate site of the Pole. Milne's plot is debunking the imperial myth while preaching an easy-going, live-and-let-live myth. The leader doesn't know where he's going or what he's looking for, his friends and followers are mainly concerned with eating and enjoying themselves, the minor crisis as well as the major quest is resolved purely by accident by a bumbling good-natured hero, and everything is happy and okay because they all really love one another. The message is that goals don't matter so long as everyone enjoys himself and is kind to one another along the way. And in a way, the whole book suggests that reality itself, whatever that may be, doesn't matter much either if everyone is happy.

American books on the other hand, are usually firmly rooted in some aspect of reality and in the pursuit of specific goals. For example, *The Little Engine That Could* by Watty Piper, published in 1930 (and regularly reprinted ever since), clearly reflects the official optimism with which most of the nation entered the depression. Even though the "happy little engine," carrying all sorts of toys and good food to the children on the other side of the mountain, had broken down, apparently irreparably, and even though the shiny new Passenger Engine and the big strong Freight Engine and the Rusty Old Engine refused to help, the Little Blue

Engine which had never been over the mountain at all was willing to try. And, of course, it succeeded. As Hoover told the nation at that time, it was the willingness of all the little people to make temporary sacrifices and work a little harder which would soon solve the problems of the depression. And Roosevelt too, after 1933, as most historians agree, set all the little engines to work without really changing the system for wealth and industry.

The American myth of innocence, goodness, and determination which was so much a part of *The Wizard of Oz* is revealed again in this simple book. Furthermore, it implies that there is no need to be more than temporarily sad at the refusals of big business or wealth or the older generation (whose interest in toys and good food for children could not really be expected anyway), since there is bound to be a "little Blue Engine" who is equally capable and glad to help. The world of great passenger and freight engines is not really our concern. If we just keep hoping and trying, everything will be all right. There is nothing wrong with the system, only with small parts within it. "I think I can, I think I can" became the motto of a whole generation of depression parents and their children, while society's general structure remained unchanged.

A similar message shines out of *The Little House* by Virginia Lee Burton, winner of the Caldecott Award in 1942. An extremely simple, but endearing, story of the life history of a little house overwhelmed by urbanization and industrialization, the story is clearly a parable about the development of American society. This little house which had weathered the seasons for an untold number of years sees the beginning of the destruction of its country idyll with the coming of the first horseless carriage "down the winding country road." Inexorably, the car is followed by steam shovels, highways, houses, tenements, trolleys, subways, skyscrapers, and abandonment. "No one wanted to live in her and take care of her any more," but she remained because she was so well-built. Furthermore, her wise original builder had said, "This Little House shall never be sold for gold or silver and she will live to see our great-great-grandchildren's great-great-grandchildren living in her."

It is this stipulation which suggests that the house represents something more than just rural life. The house stands for a whole civilization and perhaps also for the American Constitution – the system of government which many conservatives felt was threatened by the New Deal as well as by increasing industrialization. The story preaches a nostalgia for the past and the rural innocence of snow and stars and apple trees and daisies. And when "the great-great-granddaughter of the man who built the Little House so well" recognized "the shabby Little House" in the midst of the hurly-burly city, there was an obvious solution—move it to the country. "Never again would she be curious about the city . . . A new moon was coming up . . . It was Spring . . . and all was quiet and peaceful in the country."

The flight to suburbia as a return to innocence and beauty is the message of *The Little House*. The world of the past was better, while the city and all of modern industrialization is evil and dirty. Nor is there any possible compromise or evolution, only escape. Even the class element is quite blatant, for it is only the well-to-do who can stop all the traffic to move a house out of the city. In this case it is also an "old" family, a fifth-generation family in 1942, which is thus representative of only a very small proportion of the population. (Interestingly enough, at approximately thirty years per generation, this also makes the house the same age as the Constitution.)

Horton Hears a Who! by Dr. Seuss, published in 1956, is a fantasy in form, but its ideology is very goal-oriented and socially concerned. While *Winnie the Pooh* centered on the on-going happiness of a group of mutually respectful but self-contained individuals, and *The Little House* on a nostalgic recreation of a lost rural past, *Horton* is, above all, concerned with the individual's crucial role as a member of society. And it is a society full of conflicts and antagonism, with constant crises and dangers, and social pressures of every sort.

The plot of *Horton* is very simple. A benevolent elephant hears a voice from a small speck of dust and immediately feels obligated to help and protect it "Because, after all,/ A person's a person, no matter how small." This refrain is repeated again and again as the elephant faces one crisis after another. First some kangaroos mock him, then some monkeys steal the clover with the speck of dust on it. They give it to Vlad Vlad-i-koff the "black-bottomed eagle" who obligingly flies off with it and drops it in a one hundred-mile wide field of clover. Horton toils after it "with groans, over stones/ That tattered his toenails and battered his bones" and then picks three million clovers before he discovers his speck of dust. The people on the speck are in real trouble (like the dolls and toys on the little train) because they had "landed so hard that our clocks have all stopped./Our tea-pots are broken. Our rocking-chairs smashed./ And our bicycle tires all blew up when we crashed." Horton promises once again to "stick by you small folks through thin and through thick!" But the kangaroos have decided to rope and cage the elephant for "chatting with persons who've never existed" and for "Such carryings-on in our peaceable jungle!" Furthermore, they are going to boil the dust speck in Beezle-Nut oil. (How mild was the disdain of the big Engines for the toys in comparison!)

The action now shifts to the people of *Who*-ville on the speck, since Horton can no longer protect them. Their only hope, and his, lies in shouting enough to make even the kangaroos hear. As Horton puts it, "you very small persons will not have to die/ If you make yourselves heard! *So come on, now, and TRY!*" They do try — desperately — but without success, until the Mayor "discovered one shirker," a very small one who "Was standing, just standing, and bouncing a Yo-Yo!" He lectured the lad that this was the "town's darkest hour! The time for all *Whos* who have blood that is red / To come to the aid of their country!" Finally, "that one small, extra Yopp put it over" and the Whos "proved they ARE persons, no matter how small./ And their whole world was saved by the Smallest of ALL!"

The ideological message of this story is so blatant that one is tempted to interpret it almost too specifically. For example, it seems to reflect the Cold War mentality of the Fifties — especially in the name of its arch-villain, the Eagle. It also teaches the general virtue of responsible paternalism — the big should take care of the little, the comfortable should protect the oppressed, no matter how great the cost. And then it further preaches that an individual's value is determined not by his own pleasure (playing with Yo-Yos), but only by his contribution to the whole, his active participation in achieving the goals of his society.

Horton is not a "middle-of-the-road" story. The preservers of the status quo are the kangaroos, and they are clearly evil. They also represent the pressures for social conformity and against "hearing voices." The ideal which Horton represents is that of the sensitive, spiritual, artistic, dedicated lone defender of humanity with all the world against him. There is a similarity to the Little Engine of 1930, but Horton is far less humble and the stakes are much higher. This is a life-and-death struggle, not just a matter of toys and good food. Horton's nonconformism is shown as right because it is in a good cause benefiting others — just playing and minding one's own business like the *Who* with the Yo-Yo is clearly immoral. (*Winnie the Pooh* characters would certainly be frowned upon in the *Horton* value system.)

One may suggest that Horton represents the messianic idealism which has been for so long a part of American tradition—with periodic eruptions on both the right and the left in internal affairs, and, in the twentieth century especially, on the international scene as well. Nixon, Johnson, and Kennedy could claim to be identified with Dr. Seuss's dedicated elephant just as well as Ellsberg, Dr. Spock, and Daniel Berrigan. Radical fighters for social justice come right out of the mainstream of American ideology, and violent confrontations are an accepted part of our world view.

In another way, *Horton* reveals the two main themes of a mass democratic society—the paradoxical importance of individual resistance to mass pressure for evil but cooperation with mass pressure for good. In such a society neither the large "elephant" nor the small "Who" is safe without the help of the other—and both are always in danger.

From the debunking of the Wizard in *Oz* and of the Empire in *Pooh,* America moved to an idealization of hopeful struggle in the face of difficulties in *The Little Engine* and of older rural values in the face of modernization in *The Little House.* And then in the Fifties we became newly aware of the irreconcilable conflicts of our mass modern society and also of the impossiblity of escape. A study of our children's literature in its historical context might have forecast both a Viet Nam type encounter and the youthful upheaval of the Sixties. Both adults and students were acting out the values they had absorbed at an early age. And those values were taught by their own parents and in their own books. An analysis of the most popular children's literature indeed provides a magnifying glass for its society.

NOTES

1. Mary Orvig, "One World in Children's Books?" The May Hill Arbuthnot Honor Lecture, *Top of the News,* June 1972, p. 40.
2. Henry M. Littlefield, "The Wizard of Oz: Parable on Populism," *American Quarterly* 16 (1964), 54.

Part 4. Views of Racist Stereotypes

Huckleberry Finn and the Traditions of Blackface Minstrelsy

Fredrick Woodard and Donnarae MacCann

Scholars and other commentators have generally maintained that Mark Twain's *The Adventures of Huckleberry Finn* is a broadly humanistic document. Twain's ability as a humorist and stylist, his effective satires and his advocacy — at times — of improved conditions for Black Americans have contributed to this judgment.[1]

However, in spite of the countless analyses of *Huck Finn,* the influence of "blackface minstrelsy" on this story is either barely mentioned or overlooked entirely, even though the tradition of white men blackening up to entertain other whites at the expense of Black people's humanity is at the center of *Huck Finn's* portrayal of Jim and other Blacks. This dimension is important to a full interpretation of the novel and should be considered essential to any classroom analysis of the book.

Minstrel performers were an important cultural influence in the last century. They were featured in circuses and other traveling shows, as well as in the afterpieces and entr'actes of the formal, "high art" theaters. In 1843, four white actors, the Virginia Minstrels, created an entire evening's entertainment of minstrel routines. By the middle of the nineteenth century more than one hundred professional troupes in "blackface" were touring the

From *Interracial Books for Children Bulletin* 15, nos. 1/2 (1984), 4–13 by permission of the publisher.

Fredrick Woodard is Associate Dean of Faculties and Professor of English and Afro-American Studies, University of Iowa. Donnarae MacCann is a columnist for *The Wilson Library Bulletin* and has coauthored *The Black American in Books for Children* (Scarecrow Press) and other books on children's literature.

U.S., with some performing in the White House.[2] According to sociologist Alan Green, the minstrel caricatures were so compelling to white audiences that "anyone after the early 1840s who wished to portray a humorous Negro on the stage had to conform to the minstrelsy pattern, and that included Negroes themselves."[3] By the latter part of the century, guidebooks for amateur performers were available to the general public.[4]

Minstrel actors blackened their faces with burnt cork and wore outlandish costumes. They swaggered about the stage boasting nonsensically about minor accomplishments or fabricating tales of grandiose deeds; they had riotous celebrations; they mutilated the English language; and they quarreled vehemently over trivial issues.

Nineteenth century American minstrelsy drew upon European traditions of using the mask of blackness to mock individuals or social forces. The conventions of clowning also played a part, since clowns in many cultures have blackened or whitened their faces, exaggerated the appearance of the mouth, eyes, and feet, used rustic dialects, and devised incongruous costumes. Clowns have filled a variety of social and esthetic functions, but U.S. blackface performers have been unique in their single-minded derogation of an oppressed group. In the U.S., aspects of African American culture were incorporated into the minstrel routines in a highly distorted form. The resulting ridiculous or paternalistic portrayals of Black Americans were particularly appealing to the white theater-going audience.

Educators who teach *Huck Finn* as a literary and historical bench mark need to recognize how Twain used minstrelsy and how he himself was, to some extent, socialized by it.

Twain called these blackface minstrel routines a "joy." "To my mind," he said, "minstrelsy was a thoroughly delightful thing, and a most competent laughter compeller. . . ." He described the broad dialect as "delightfully and satisfyingly funny."[5] As to the typical violent quarrels between two minstrel protagonists, Twain wrote:

> . . . a delightful jangle of assertion and contradiction would break out between the two; the quarrel would gather emphasis, the voices would grow louder and louder and more and more energetic and vindictive, and the two would rise and approach each other, shaking fists and instruments and threatening bloodshed. . . . Sometimes the quarrel would last five minutes, the two contestants shouting deadly threats in each other's faces with their noses not six inches apart, the house shrieking

with laughter all the while at this *happy and accurate imitation of the usual and familiar negro quarrel*. . . .[emphasis added][6]

The notion that these stereotypical portrayals were realistic was commonplace. Carl Wittke, an early historian of minstrelsy, speaks of "Jim Crow" Rice, a popular white ministrel performer, as having "unusual powers as a delineator of Negro character."[7] These caricatures, so enjoyed by whites, moved from the stage to the pages of popular fiction and, eventually, to radio, movies, and TV.

Twain wrote his laudatory remarks about minstrelsy in 1906, just four years before his death. Like many other authors, he was apparently influenced by this tradition throughout his life, even as he argued for more humane conditions for Black Americans and Africans.

Twain's own career as a stage performer gave him a close tie with minstrelsy. Stage performances were a major source of income and status for Twain, and these performances were often based on "readings" of his works, a "lecture" style that was extremely popular at that time. Twain counseled a friend: "Try 'Readings.' They are all the rage now."[8]

Twain's performances point up his willingness to shape his message to his audience. On winning audience approval, Twain himself said: "No man will dare more than I to get it."[9] Following one performance, a Chicago critic wrote: "There is nothing in his lectures, for he very properly sacrifices everything to make his audience roar, and they do."[10]

It is not surprising to find that episodes in *Huck Finn* which read like skits in a minstrel show were probably written after most of the novel was completed, and at a time when Twain was planning a return to the stage with a new tour. These episodes — "King Sollermun," "Balum's Ass," "how a Frenchman doan' talk like a man," Jim's "rescue" by Huck and Tom Sawyer—would fit neatly into a Twain-style lecture tour, and it seems quite likely that they were created with the taste of theater audiences in mind.[11]

The novel's concluding farcical scenes—in which Huck and Tom concoct a nonsensical plan to help Jim, the runaway slave—insured the book's success on and off the stage. As Twain wrote his wife about reading these rescue scenes: "It is the biggest card I've got in my whole repertoire. I always thought so. It went abooming. . . ."[12]

The depiction of Blacks in *Huck Finn* matches those of numerous minstrel plays in which Black characters are portrayed as addlebrained, boastful, superstitious, childish and lazy. These depictions are not used to poke fun at white attitudes about Black people; Jim is portrayed as a kindly comic who *does* act foolishly.

Early in the story, for example, Tom Sawyer moves Jim's hat to a nearby tree branch while he is sleeping. When Jim wakes he claims that witches put him in a trance and rode him over the state; he then elaborates this story several times until he finally claims that witches rode him all over the world and his back was "all over saddleboils."

Throughout the book, Jim is presented as foolish and gullible, given to exaggeration. After Jim and Huck get lost in the fog, an event Jim "painted . . . up considerable," Huck tells Jim their frightening experience was only a dream. Jim believes him, even when he sees evidence that the experience was real:

> He had got the dream fixed so strong in his head that he couldn't seem to shake it loose and get the facts back into its place again right away.[13]

Twain has already established that Huck fulfills the role of a youthful, "unreliable" narrator; however, these comments about Jim *seem* accurate because they are backed up by Jim's own befuddled statements and actions. For example, Jim exclaims: "Is I *me,* or who *is* I? Is I heah, or what *is* I? Now dat's what I wants to know."

Similarly, when the Duke and Dauphin come aboard the raft, Huck sees that they are "lowdown humbugs and frauds," but says it "warn't no use to tell Jim," who is childishly proud to serve royalty.

Chapter eight is like a whole series of minstrel routines. First Jim explains how he speculated in stock, but the stock — a cow — died. Then he invested in a banking operation run by a Black swindler and lost more money. He gives his last dime to "Balum's Ass; one er dem chuckleheads, you know. But he's lucky, dey say . . . ." Balum's Ass gives the dime to the church when he hears a preacher say "whoever give to de po' len' to de Lord, en boun' to git his money back a hund'd times."

The closing chapters serve a thematic purpose as Twain strengthens his attacks on the violence and hypocrisy of adult "civilization." Jim is a convenient instrument in the concluding burlesque, but his docile behavior reinforces his role as a dimwit — and hence as an audience pleaser. Jim could have walked away from his confinement many times, but he acts only under the direction of the white children — the implications being that he so dotes on the children that he will sacrifice his survival to their games, that he is helpless without white assistance and that he can think only on a child's level.

The farcical rescue scenes point up the unequal nature of the Huck/Jim relationship, but it is not the only time that Twain treats Huck and Jim as less than equal partners. For example, Huck makes no effort to find Jim after the raft is run down by a steamboat and the two are separated. He doesn't grieve over Jim's apparent death and doesn't express any relief when the two are reunited, although Jim nearly cries because he is so glad to see Huck alive.

Literary critics calling Jim the novel's one and only noble adult are usually focusing on Jim's kindness toward Huck and Tom. With that image in mind, critics credit Twain with a broadly liberal perspective, but in fact, the "sympathy" that *Huck Finn* evokes for Jim is part of what minstrelsy is all about. "Stage Negroes" were shaped by their creators, according to Alan Green, so that they *would* be viewed sympathetically. Who would not feel affection for a "permanently visible and permanently inferior clown who posed no threat and desired nothing more than laughter and applause at his imbecile antics?"[14] Blacks had to be a source of hilarity for whites, says Green, in order for whites to cease feeling guilt and anxiety.

It's true that Jim is admirable because he is not an inveterate schemer, like most of the other people in the book. Jim also often makes more sense than other characters. For instance, when he argues with Huck about how Frenchmen talk, Jim is the more logical. But this debate "plays" like the dialogue in a minstrel show because Jim has the information base of a child (*i.e.*, Jim believes English to be the world's only language).

When Twain was working on *The Adventures of Tom Sawyer* in 1874, he wrote noted author and editor William Dean Howells, his literary advisor, about his technique: "I amend dialect stuff by talking and talking and *talking* it till it sounds right."[15] The "right" sound, however, was the sound of a white person playing a "stage Negro" — a sound that fitted white expectations. The mock Black "dialect" in *Huck Finn* turns the humor into caricature and makes Jim's every appearance stereotypical. Jim's language is largely made up of either so-called nonstandard words or so-called "eye dialect" — words that look peculiar in print, as when "wuz" replaces "was." This eye dialect reinforces the notion that a character is stupid rather than merely poorly educated.

When Huck and Jim are both satirized in the chapter on having "a general good time," the language tends to isolate Jim as a fool. Huck reads from books salvaged from a sinking steamboat and we see the highly nonsensical result of his learning experiences in a country school. Jim's garbled impression of the Scriptures is similarly revealed, and there is a nice give-and-take between the two vagabonds throughout the whole scene. But while we can easily laugh at Huck's very human confusion in this episode, it is more difficult to see the human side of Jim because of the exaggerated dialect. For example, Jim says:

> A harem's a bo'd'n-house, I reck'n. Mos' likely dey has rackety times in de nussery. En I reck'n de wives quarrels considerable; en dat 'crease de racket. Yet dey say Sollermun de wises' man dat ever liv'. I doan' take no stock in dat. Bekase why would a wise man want to live in de mids' er sich a blimblammin' all de time?[16]

Jim's attempt to escape slavery contributes a strong element of suspense in the early part of the novel, and Twain has an opportunity to comment on that institution. To a certain degree Twain offers a comic/serious protest against slavery, although we must remember that this issue had been decided by the Civil War some twenty years earlier. There are some brilliantly ironic stabs at slavery, but the plot line that focuses on Jim's escape is scuttled when the Duke/Dauphin burlesque takes over. This plot change occurs at the very moment Jim and Huck might have escaped in a newly acquired canoe. Instead, Huck goes in search of strawberries and then performs one of the most illogical acts in the story: he brings the false Duke and Dauphin to the raft he and Jim are living on. If the original plot line had remained important, good-hearted Huck *might* have sympathized with the desperate con men and he *might* have rowed them to some safer location, but it is hard to believe that he would suddenly contradict all his efforts to keep Jim out of sight.

Twain scholar Henry Nash Smith argues that the escape plan is aborted because Huck and Jim are virtually the captives of the Duke and Dauphin.[17] The text does not support this thesis, however, since Huck and Jim ignore several opportunities to follow through with their original plan while the Duke and Dauphin are working their confidence tricks on the river towns.

When Tom Sawyer reenters the story Huck helps him carry out the farcical futile escape plan. Because Jim's escape is not actually a high priority, Tom and Huck play at heroics based upon Tom's favorite adventure stories, affording Twain an opportunity to satirize such tales. When the boys actually release Jim, armed slavehunters are on the premises and the "rescue" has no chance of success. "The unhappy truth about the ending," writes Leo Marx in *The American Scholar,"* . . . is that the author, having revealed the tawdry nature of the culture of the great valley, yielded to its essential complacency."[18]

Jim is, in fact, finally free because his owner dies and frees him in her will. Thus his liberator turns out to be a slaveholder, the very sort, writes Leo Marx, "whose inhumanity first made the attempted escape necessary."[19]

The fact that Huck decides to "go to hell" rather than turn Jim in — to make, in other words, an eternal sacrifice for Jim — is often treated by critics as a superb evocation of antislavery sentiment. But to reach this interpretation, readers must not only ignore the characterization of Jim; they must also arbitrarily withdraw their attention from Twain's thematic and narrative compromises throughout the last fifth of the novel. Since Huck's concern for Jim all but disappears in the farcical "rescue" sequence, and since it is finally a slaveholder who is presented as the true rescuer, the "going to hell" pronouncement seems more closely related to Twain's many satirical commentaries on religion than to an overriding interest in the slave question. (In the incomplete novel "Tom Sawyer's Conspiracy," Twain uses Tom and Huck brilliantly as a means of debunking religion, while Jim is again a minstrel side-kick).

Because *Huck Finn* is very contradictory as an antislavery work, it is important for readers, and for teachers especially, to examine the larger context of the "freedom" theme. This means pinpointing the text's cultural biases — the white supremacist beliefs which infuse the novel and which are not difficult to discover in a close reading. Notions of racial and cultural superiority appear in *Huck Finn* in the various ways that Twain undercuts Jim's humanity: in the minstrel routines with Huck as the "straight man," in the generalities about Blacks as unreliable, primitive and slow witted, in the absence of appropriate adult/child roles, in Jim's vulnerability to juvenile trickery, and in the burlesqued speech pattern.

One of the most controversial aspects of *Huck Finn* is Twain's use of the term "nigger." As with every detail of the novel, the term needs to be examined in relation to its context. Huck uses "nigger" as it was used by white people to ridicule Blacks. When Huck says, "It was fifteen minutes before I could work myself up to go and humble myself to a nigger," he is rising slightly above his cultural conditioning by making an apology, but at the same time the reader sees him caught up in that bigoted culture by his use of a label that whites understood as pejorative.

A serious problem arises, however, in the fact that Jim refers to himself and other Blacks as "niggers," but the self-effacement inherent in his use of this term is not presented as a Black survival tactic. If Twain did not recognize the Black American use of such language as part of the "mask" worn to disarm whites, he was, like Huck, caught unwittingly in the bigoted system that he could not always transcend. If he understood this strategy, but left out any hint of this awareness in order to please a white audience, then he compromised his literary integrity.

These are necessary distinctions for sophisticated adult readers, but most young readers cannot be expected to make such distinctions. Children cannot usually respond to such loaded words with detachment and historical perspective. Whatever the purpose and effect of the term "nigger" for Twain's original white audience, its appearance in a classroom today tends to reinforce racism, inducing embarrassment and anger for Blacks and feelings of superiority and/or acts of harassment by whites.

It is important here to note Twain's use of irony. Some statements which seem blatantly racist are the most highly ironic. For instance, when Huck responds to Aunt Sally's query about an accident, "Anybody hurt?" with the statement, "No'm. Killed a nigger," a double layer of irony strengthens Twain's commentary. Aunt Sally replies, "Well, it's lucky; because sometimes people do get hurt," and the reader can easily discern the social conditioning behind Huck's denial of Black humanity, as well as the extraordinary indifference that makes Aunt Sally's idea of "luck" a bitterly ironic indictment of slavery. Similarly, one of the most potent comments on slavery occurs when Jim threatens to steal his own children and Huck responds:

> Here was this nigger which I had as good as helped to run away, coming right out flat footed and saying he would steal his children—children that belonged to a man I didn't even know; a man that hadn't ever done me no harm.[20]

These ironic, "topsy-turvy" features are perhaps the easiest to teach in an English class.

When looking at *Huck Finn,* it is important to consider Twain's upbringing and milieu. Twain himself emphasized the importance of early "training." Significantly, he lamented the fact that his mother would never abandon her support of slavery, but he defended her by saying, "Manifestly, training and association can accomplish strange miracles."²¹ Huck himself emphasizes the importance of how people are "brung up." Tom was not "brung up" to free a "nigger" unless that slave was already legally free; the Dauphin was not "brung up" to deliver lines from Shakespeare properly; and kings, says Huck, "are a mighty ornery lot. It's the way they're raised." While Twain was in some respects a renegade, he was also "brung up" in a period in which opposition to slavery was a controversial position, and in which sensitivity to other issues of racial injustice was severely limited. In his autobiography, he writes:

> I was not aware that there was anything wrong about [slavery in my schoolboy days]. . . . No one arraigned it in my hearing; the local papers said nothing against it; the local pulpit taught us that God approved it; if the slaves themselves had any aversion to slavery they were wise and said nothing.²²

When Twain first went to New York in his late teens, he was apparently shocked by the sight of Blacks who were not slaves and wrote his mother:

> I reckon I had better black my face, for in these Eastern States niggers are considerably better than white people.²³

Several years later, when the Civil War broke out, Twain's sympathies were with the South, and he enlisted in the Confederate Army. His decision to quit after two weeks of soldiering seems to have had more to do with a new job opportunity out West than with any change of heart about the justice of the Confederate cause.²⁴

Slavery aside, Twain's writings include many statements about Black Americans which reflect the prevailing white racist attitudes of the nineteenth century. In his autobiography, he mentions Uncle Dan'l, a slave on his uncle's farm, as the "real Jim." Uncle Dan'l, says Twain, was patient, friendly, and loyal, "traits which were his birthright."²⁵ In *Huck Finn,* the racial bias of the statement that Jim was "white inside" is so extreme that it seems ironical. Yet, when Jim is commended as an "uncommon nigger," this is not unlike Twain's praise of his own butler as no "commonplace coon."²⁶ (William Dean Howells provides some insight on Twain's attitudes in this regard when he writes that Twain preferred Black or Asian butlers "because he said he could not bear to order a white man about"²⁷.)

Twain amused colleagues by using the same caricatured speech he ascribed to Jim. He wrote his publisher:

> I's gwyne to sen' you di stuff jis' as she stan', now; an'
> you an' Misto Howls kin weed out enuff o' dem 93,000
> words fer to crowd de book down to *one* book; or you kin
> shove in enuff er dat ole Contrib-Club truck fer to swell her
> up en bust her in two an' make *two* books outen her. . . . I
> don't want none er dat rot what is in de small envolups to go
> in, 'cepp'n jis' what Misto Howls *say* shel go in.[28]

Those claiming that Twain became a staunch advocate of social
justice for Blacks usually cite his essay titled, "The United States
of Lyncherdom," written in 1901. However, Twain decided not to
publish this antilynching essay in the *North American Review,* as he
originally intended, because "I shouldn't have even half a friend
left down there [in the South], after it issued from the press."[29]
Instead, he chose to bury his indignation by placing the manuscript
with papers he designated for posthumous publication.

Moreover, the essay's content, not Twain's timidity, is the
important problem. It reveals Twain's deep-seated prejudice rather
than his "de-southernization," which it is said to represent.
Twain condemns lynching primarily because it is not due process,
but he ignores the principle of due process in his discussion of a
particular case. His arguments are based upon an unsupported
presumption of Black guilt. He writes: "I will not dwell upon the
provocation which moved the [lynchers] to those crimes. . . ; the
only question is, *does the assassin take the law into his own
hands?*" And, in arguing that lynching is not a deterrent to crime,
Twain supports the very myth that the KKK promulgated to justify
its attacks—that Blacks threatened white women. He writes:

> . . . one much talked-of outrage and murder committed by a
> negro will upset the disturbed intellects of several other
> negroes and produce a series of the very tragedies the com-
> munity would so strenuously wish to prevent; . . . in a word,
> the lynchers are themselves the worst enemies of their
> women.[30]

Like many of his white contemporaries, Twain clearly had ambivalent attitudes about Blacks. On the one hand, we see his efforts
to help Black college students financially, to aid a Black college, to
publicly support the reputation of Black leader Frederick Douglass
and to speak out boldly and progressively (*e.g.,* there is a
"reparation due," said Twain, "from every white to every black
man"[31]). Yet he could not shake off some persistent white
supremacist notions. In *Huck Finn,* Twain's ambivalence is
recorded in the degrading minstrel elements on the one hand and in

the antislavery theme on the other. (We must remember that the period following the Civil War and the abolition of slavery was one of intense racial conflict in this country as repressive forces sought to reinstate the "benefits" of slavery. Repressive "Jim Crow" laws, exploitative practices, terrorist activities designed to deprive Blacks of their voting and other civil rights—all were part of the climate in which Twain lived and wrote. These historical realities should be included in any classroom discussions of the work.)

Twain specialists have not generally provided much help to those concerned about the book's biases. For instance, Charles Neider, in his Introduction to *The Selected Letters of Mark Twain,* notes the offensive racism of Twain's frontier humor, but this does not prevent him from calling Twain the "Lincoln of our literature" and the "Shakespeare of our humor."[32] Perspective has quite a lot to do with what is classified as comic, and there are basic questions that cannot be passed over. Funny to whom? Funny at whose expense?

In *The Grotesque Essence: Plays from the American Minstrel Stage,* Gary Engle refers to minstrelsy as cruel, grotesque, monstrous and racist, and says it caricatures Blacks as "lazy, ignorant, illiterate, hedonistic, vain, often immoral, fatalistic and gauche." But, in spite of this, he calls Jim a "sympathetically drawn version of the minstrel clown."[33] Engle justifies minstrelsy by claiming that it purged the "American common man" of insecurity and blessed him with the "laughter of affirmation"—"By laughing at a fool, a nation can safely and beneficially laugh at itself."[34] Clearly, he is viewing the nation as a white society exclusively.

It is unfortunate that in extolling a work of literature, most critics feel they must endorse it in its entirety and, in effect, support its biases. Not surprisingly, Black author Ralph Ellison is one of the few commentators who has been critical of the minstrel tradition in Twain's works. It is Jim's stereotypical minstrel mask, notes Ellison, that makes Huck—not Jim—appear to be the adult on the raft.[35]

Literary historian Donald Gibson made the following statements about teaching *Huck Finn* to high school and college students:

> It should be shown to be a novel whose author was not always capable of resisting the temptation to create laughter through compromising his morality and his art. In short the problem of whether to teach the novel will not exist if it is taught in all its complexity of thought and feeling, and if critics and teachers avoid making the same kinds of compromises Mark Twain made.[36]

"All its complexity" must, of necessity, include the book's racism and its ties to the minstrel tradition. If students learn about this aspect of Twain's work, they will increase their capacity to understand *Huck Finn*.

NOTES

1. Twain's talent for vernacular innovation, regional portraiture, mythic associations and other novelistic features could be discussed here, but they have been commented upon extensively in works by other critics. The problem in Twain scholarship is to bring about some balance between discussions of craft and discussions of content.

2. Gary D. Engle, *The Grotesque Essence: Plays from the American Minstrel Stage* (Baton Rouge: Louisiana State Univ. Press, 1978), xvi–xvii, xix–xx.

3. Alan W. C. Green, "'Jim Crow,' 'Zip Coon': The Northern Origins of Negro Minstrelsy," *The Massachusetts Review* 11 (Spring, 1970), 394.

4. In the partially completed novel "Tom Sawyer's Conspiracy," Tom Sawyer goes to his aunt's garret to find "our old nigger-show things" and plan a "nigger" disguise. Blacking-up kits, as well as performance manuals containing sample skits and lyrics, were widely sold to the general public.

5. Mark Twain, *Mark Twain in Eruption: Hitherto Unpublished Pages About Men and Events,* ed. Bernard De Voto (New York: Harper, 1922), 110, 115.

6. Ibid., 113.

7. Carl Wittke, *Tambo and Bones: A History of the American Minstrel Stage* (New York: Greenwood reprint, 1968; original published in 1930), 25.

8. Paul Fatout, *Mark Twain on the Lecture Circuit* (Bloomington: Indiana Univ. Press, 1960; reprinted, Gloucester, Mass.: Peter Smith, 1966), 190.

9. Justin Kaplan, *Mark Twain and His World* (New York: Simon and Schuster, 1974), 69. In the first lectures in 1866, Twain used a mixture of what Kaplan calls delightful "statistics, anecdotes, edification and amusement, humorous reflection delivered after a delicately timed pause, something that passed

for moral philosophy, and passages of gorgeous word painting." In 1884, Twain adopted the format Charles Dickens used in public readings. His style became a blend of telling and acting episodes from his books (Kaplan, 68, 128).

10. Fatout, 106.

11. The approximate times when different parts of the novel were written are discussed in Walter Blair's "When Was *Huckleberry Finn* Written?" (*American Literature* [March, 1958], 1–25); in David Carkeet's "The Dialects in *Huckleberry Finn*" (*American Literature* [November, 1979], 315–32); in Franklin R. Rogers' *Mark Twain's Burlesque Patterns* (Dallas: Southern Methodist Univ. Press, 1960, 139–40); in Michael Patrick Hearn's *The Annotated Huckleberry Finn* (New York: Potter, 1981), 111.

12. Rogers, 148.

13. Samuel Longhorne Clemens (Mark Twain), *Adventures of Huckleberry Finn: An Authoritative Text, Backgrounds and Sources, Criticism,* 2nd edition by Sculley Bradley, Richard Croom Beatty, E. Hudson Long, Thomas Cooley (New York: W. W. Norton, 1977), 71–72.

14. Green, 394.

15. Charles Neider, ed., *The Selected Letters of Mark Twain* (New York: Harper & Row, 1982), 84.

16. Clemens, 65. The dialect in a typical minstrel play reads as follows: "It 'pears dat de Lawd, after he done made Adam and Eve, sot 'em in de Garden ob Edem, dat de Lawd he Tol'em bofe dat dar was a sartain tree and dat dey musn't eat none of eet's fruit. . . ." (William Courtright's *The Complete Minstrel Guide,* Chicago: The Dramatic Publishing Co., 1901, 83).

17. Henry Nash Smith, *Mark Twain: The Development of a Writer* (Cambridge: The Belknap Press of Harvard Univ. Press, 1962), 113–37.

18. Leo Marx, "Mr. Eliot, Mr. Trilling, and *Huckleberry Finn,*" *The American Scholar,* 22, no. 4 (Autumn, 1953), 433.

19. Ibid.

20. Clemens, 74.

21. Charles Neider, ed.,*The Autobiography of Mark Twain: Including Chapters Now Published for the First Time* (New York: Harper & Row, 1959), 30.

22. Ibid., 6.

23. James M. Cox, *Mark Twain: The Fate of Humor* (Princeton: Princeton Univ. Press, 1966), 7.

24. Twain scholar John C. Gerber has explained how Twain tried to justify his withdrawal from the Confederate Army in an essay Twain wrote in 1885 entitled,"The Private History of the Campaign That Failed." Twain introduced fictional content into his explanation that would help him pacify his Southern critics. (See *Mark Twain: Selected Criticism,* ed. by Arthur L. Scott, Dallas: Southern Methodist Univ. Press, 1967, 281–82).

25. Neider, *Autobiography of Mark Twain,* 5–6.

26. Arthur G. Pettit, *Mark Twain and the South* (Lexington: Univ. of Kentucky Press, 1974), 104.

27. William Dean Howells, *My Mark Twain* (New York: Harper, 1910), 34.

28. Pettit, 128.

29. Kaplan, 194.

30. Maxwell Geismar, ed., *Mark Twain and the Three R's: Religion, Revolution—and Related Matters* (Indianapolis/New York: Bobbs-Merrill, 1973),p. 34.

31. Edward Wagenknecht, *Mark Twain: The Man and His Work,* 3rd edition (Norman: Univ. of Oklahoma Press, 1967), 222.

32. Neider, *Selected Letters,* 2, 5.

33. Engle, xxvi.

34. Engle, xxvi, xxviii.

35. Ralph Ellison, "Change the Joke and Slip the Yoke," *Partisan Review* 25, no. 2 (Spring, 1958), 215, 222.

36. Donald Gibson, "Mark Twain's Jim in the Classroom," *English Journal* 57, no. 2 (February, 1968), 202.

Is *Huckleberry Finn* Racist?
How Burlesque Humor Operates

Paul Schmidt

Huckleberry Finn has been attacked as racist. Huck, it is claimed, is a white chauvinist and Jim is a stereotyped chuckleheaded Black. These charges arise in the main from failure to understand the burlesque humor which is the main literary strategy of the novel. The critics without exception misread the deadpan of Huck and Jim as the mark of their idiocy. As in most vernacular American humor, Huck and Jim *pose* as simple-minded backwoods hayseeds in order to take in the presumably refined and superior genteel. It is these Protestant slave-holders who are the ultimate target of Huck's burlesque. An analysis of Clemens' humor in the novel reinforces Bernard DeVoto's claim that this is the great novel to come out of the Civil War. It is great because it strikes a powerful blow for Black and white fraternity and equality, great because of the intensely real drama of Jim's escape from slavery, great because it mounts a profound criticism of upper class slave-holding culture.

In what follows I make three points. First, burlesque humor is the collision of high with low and the reversal of their ostensible values: high becomes low, and low becomes high. Second, the moral strength of Huckleberry's and Jim's attack on WASP culture lies in their solidarity with the working class community, Black and white. And third, the novel is flawed with serious inconsistency when Tom Sawyer takes over.

The function of comedy and laughter in human evolution is ridding us of obstruction and hindrance to our development. It is

This essay has been printed in part in *Outlook* 24 (July 1986) and is published with permission of the author and the publishers of *Outlook*.

Paul Schmidt is Professor Emeritus at the California College of Arts and Crafts in Oakland and was Fulbright Professor of American Literature in Turnovo, Bulgaria, and in Leningrad, USSR.

critical. We laugh off, as we say, awkwardness and childishness, stupidity and absentmindedness.

At thirteen Huckleberry is more man than boy, and his humor engages issues of significance. It is neither the bright sayings of children, nor Don Quixote tilting at windmills. He takes on the racism and religious hypocrisy of American Mississippi Valley society, and the demagoguery of bourgeois republican pretensions, the hollow claims of democracy and plenty in a class-divided society. Certainly he uses the boy pose to carry it off and to protect himself, but the pose is a mask behind which his laughter demolishes the Mississippi Valley gentility.

Property is often Huckleberry's target. He and Jim are floating down the Mississippi on the raft at night so they won't be caught. He says,

> Every night, now, I used to slip ashore, towards ten o'clock, at some little village, and buy ten or fifteen cents' worth of meal or bacon or other stuff to eat; and sometimes I lifted a chicken that warn't roosting comfortable, and took him along. Pap always said, take a chicken when you get a chance, because if you don't want him yourself you can easy find somebody that does, and a good deed ain't ever forgot. I never see pap when he didn't want the chicken himself, but that is what he used to say, anyway.[1]

It is not surprising to find Huck a thief; thieving is a necessity if he and Jim are to eat. Nor is it out of character to hear Pap back up Huck's stealing, but Pap's pose as a boy scout authority—"a good deed ain't ever forgot"—is splendid. Huck continues,

> Mornings, before daylight, I slipped into corn fields and bor-rowed a watermelon, or a mushmelon, or a punkin, or some new corn, or things of that kind. Pap always said it warn't no harm to borrow things, if you was meaning to pay them back, sometime; but the widow said it warn't anything but a soft name for stealing, and no decent body would do it.

A collision of authorities: the Widow, the genteel, the "quality," as Huck usually describes them, vs. Pap, lumpen proletariat, lower if not working class, "white trash" in the vernacular.

And now Jim and Huck enter the discussion.

> Jim said he reckoned the widow was partly right and pap was partly right; so the best way would be for us to pick out two or three things from the list and say we wouldn't borrow them any more—then he reckoned it wouldn't be no harm to

borrow the others. So we talked it over all one night, drifting along down the river, trying to make up our minds whether to drop the watermelons, or the cantelopes, or the mushmelons, or what. But towards daylight we got it all settled satisfactory, and concluded to drop crabapples and p'simmons. We warn't feeling just right, before that, but it was all comfortable now. I was glad the way it come out, too, because crabapples ain't ever good, and the p'simmons wouldn't be ripe for two or three months yet.

On the face of it this discussion of how to decide the issue of Pap's vs. the Widow's moral judgment is so transparently idiotic that it marks not only Huck but Jim too as a mindless child. Exactly. It is the obvious idiocy of conscious clowns. Huck and Jim, idly drifting down the great Mississippi at night, while away the time playing out the burlesque roles of vaudeville comedy, comic set-ups to the Widow's straight. Like Charlie Chaplin they assume the stupidity which the propertied genteel project on the uneducated lower class. It's as if Huck and Jim were to say to the Widow, "Ah, you think we haven't the intelligence to tell right from wrong? We'll show you what it is to be a dumbbell and a dodo! And we'll show you *who* is credulous and ignorant!" They play their roles with the unsmiling deadpan which is required to take in the Widow—and us if we go along with her—and thereby laugh her off. Humor and comedy, as I remarked, rid us of some encumbrance; in this case we laugh off the genteel misjudgment of the lower classes. We laugh *with* Huck and Jim, not *at* them; the comic butt we laugh at is the Widow.

If we suppose, as Huck's critics do, that he and Jim are chuckle-headed idiots, then we are taken in by their humor just as the Widow and the Judge are: we become, with them, the butt of the humor. To recapitulate: the bourgeois genteel figure, the Widow, accuses the lower class type, Huck or Jim, of gross ignorance of the difference between stealing and borrowing. Whereupon Huck and Jim put on the ignorance and lack of moral refinement of which they are accused; they act it out with a dead-pan in order to take in the widow and her notion that, yes, they are vulgar ignoramuses; no, they not only fail to distinguish between stealing and borrowing but they are also unaware of what a convenient solution they come to in deciding not to steal crabapples and persimmons they wouldn't eat. The U.S. Western tall tale almost invariably plays this joke on the genteel tenderfoot. *We Always Lie to Strangers* is the title of Vance Randolph's collection of Ozark mountain folk tales. Huck and Jim exaggerate the idiocy of which the Widow accuses them, make it taller and taller until finally the pose is so egregious it collapses into laughter at the Widow's expense. She is the comic butt for believing Huck and Jim are lower class dolts, and we laugh her off and her genteel pretensions at superiority.

That this play may seem elaborate and sophisticated for a thirteen-year-old boy and a Black slave is due to a typical underestimation of the working class and laughter. Burlesque is as natural as daylight to ordinary folk everywhere. They have an abiding love of laughter and much dexterity in the practice of the rituals of comedy.

One may well ask where this leaves the moral issue. Is it good or bad to steal? Huck's morality is, as usual, bedrock, and as usual, not expressed explicitly. There is a higher law than property — brotherhood. Huck's and Jim's morality put the Widow's and Miss Watson's Christian piety to shame. And the triumph of the novel is its realism: we believe in Huck and Jim as ordinary working people, alive as you and me.

Huck burlesques and laughs off the heart and soul of American leisure class culture. He turns his caustic wit on Christian conscience on page one and throughout the novel. He burlesques the American republican reform movement, specifically temperance. He burlesques the literary romanticism of the graveyard poets descended from Gray's "Elegy." He burlesques the commodity fetishism which inspires bourgeois home decoration. Finally he gives a scorching account of what Marx called the "idiocy of rural life" in the towns along the banks of the Mississippi, their hysterical credulity at a Protestant revival meeting, the spineless ease with which they are swept up into a mob lynching, their meanness and their sadism. In doing so he demolishes the romantic ideal of back to nature, the primitivism which we take in with our mother's milk, and the idyl of the backwoods yeoman.

Swindling, thieving, murder. Wherever Huckleberry puts in to shore he finds nothing but ugly violence. Perhaps the ugliest is the murder in an Arkansas village of the town drunk, Boggs, a stupid and ranting but nevertheless harmless old fellow, by the town's Southern aristocrat, Colonel Sherburn. Sherburn shoots him in cold blood because Boggs has been cursing him out in public for swindling him. The medical attention Boggs gets is of a superstitious crudeness which fits the rest of the town.

> They laid him on the floor [Huck says], and put one large Bible under his head, and opened another one and spread it on his breast. . . . He made about a dozen long gasps, his breast

> lifting the Bible up when he drawed in his breath, and letting
> it down again when he breathed it out—and after that he laid
> still; he was dead.[2]

This searching rejection of the rural ideal, of a return to nature, is
conscious in Huck. It is part and parcel of his adequacy to
whatever bourgeois slave society confronts him with. He is the
comic on top of his run-ins with slave-hunting sheriffs, feuding
slaveholders, and a father with the d.t.'s—in the fullest sense, then,
a hero. And as such, the diametric opposite of the lonely,
alienated, wounded hero of romanticism. He is not the heir of
Hamlet, nor Melville's Ishmael; nor are Hemingway's Frederick
Henry and Salinger's *Catcher in the Rye* his proper descendants.
His great distinction is to be altogether outside the established
tradition of romantic individualism and alienation.

If Huckleberry and Jim are not alienated, what is the source of
their power? From what community do they draw this intrepid
strength to stand up to the bourgeois quality? They belong to the
community of men who work the boats on the Mississippi, the
sailors, raftsmen, keelboatmen, roustabouts, and pilots of what in
Mark Twain's time was the main artery of shipping.

Huck's solidarity with workmen on the River is most vivid in a
chapter which Clemens wrote for *Huckleberry Finn* and took out on
the advice of his publisher, Charles Webster, and his friend
William Dean Howells.[3] That chapter tells of Huck's swimming to
a "huge raft" they meet up with floating down the River.
Arrived at the raft he watches the deck crew of thirteen hands
gathered around the campfire in the middle of the big craft. He
has already told us that "It *amounted* to something being a
raftsman on such a craft as that." Huck hides where he can
watch them dance the break-down and listen to them singing and
telling stories. They are drinking together, a lively roisterous
"rough-looking lot." Pre-TV entertainment cultivates community,
at least for working people, and one is reminded that that's what
art is. Work songs are to get the crew together so they can work
together.[4]

As a member of this community and sensing its strength flowing
in his veins, the riverman becomes a paragon of strength. One of
the raftsmen who calls himself the Pet Child of Calamity is drunk
with this power. He jumps up in the air three times, cracks his
heels together every time and crows in the traditional ecstatic Wild
West ritual of the half-hoss, half-alligator Salt River Roarer:

> Whoo-oop! I'm the old original iron-jawed, brass-mounted,
> copper-bellied corpse-maker from the wilds of Arkansas!—Look

at me! I'm the man they call Sudden Death and General Desolation! . . . Look at me! I take nineteen alligators and a bar'l of whiskey for breakfast when I'm in robust health, and a bushel of rattlesnakes and a dead body when I'm ailing! I split the everlasting rocks with my glance, and I squench the thunder when I speak! Whoo-oop! Stand back and give me room according to my strength! Blood's my natural drink, and the wails of the dying is music to my ear! Cast your eye on me, gentlemen! — and lay low and hold your breath, for I'm bout to turn myself loose!

This ode in praise of his power as a raftsman has the epic and mythic impersonality of the folk tales of the rivermen and their demigod keelboatman, Mike Fink. Exaggeration is functional here, both to the burlesque strategy of the tall tale and to a community potency which transcends the individual.

What Huckleberry and Mark Twain respond to in these ritual claims, so inappropriate to the isolated individual (a moment later when the Pet Child is forced into an actual fight he fails miserably), is indeed a celebration of community. Like Pablo Neruda, Huck is "fully empowered" by their strength. The raftsmen and Jim are the only ones along the Mississippi who speak his language, the only ones he can't lie to — they catch him up in a split second.[5] In Huck's serene strength, his infinite capacity to take whatever this vicious violent fake world of the Mississippi Valley dishes out to him and be on top of it, he is the diametric opposite of the castrated and suffering heroes of Hemingway, the infinitely introspective Ancient Mariners of the inner world, those Lost Generations. It is this sense of working class strength and solidarity which gives the burlesques of Huckleberry and Jim their moral foundation and conviction.

Of course the most important source of Huck's power and potency is his community and identification with the Blacks, with Jim. We misjudge Huck if we cast him out for using the word "nigger." True, it marks most writers off as racist bigots looking down on Blacks. But not Huckleberry. He is down there at the bottom of society, laughing at the pretensions of those who affect superiority. *Black like me* is his natural but heroic understanding of his case.

The image of Huck and Jim naked and drifting down the River on the raft is powerful; it is a hymn to the salvation they have achieved.

Sometimes [Huck says] we'd have that whole river all to ourselves for the longest time. . . . It's lovely to live on a raft.

> We had the sky, up there, all speckled with stars, and we used to lay on our backs and look up at them, and discuss about whether they was made or only just happened—Jim he allowed they was made, but I allowed they happened; I judged it would have took too long to *make* so many.[6]

This may be a contemplative burlesque of astronomical observation, but the poetry of a magnificent view of the universe takes over.

> Jim [Huck continues] said the moon could a *laid* them; well, that looked kind of reasonable, so I didn't say nothing against it, because I've seen a frog lay most as many, so of course it could be done. We used to watch the stars that fell, too, and see them streak down. Jim allowed they'd got spoiled and was hove out of the nest.

Huck and Jim figure the universe as a warm barnyard, as some great brooding hen in a fertile spree of laying the millions of stars. The world is peaceful, contented, luxuriantly expansive. It reflects the inner calm and poise of these two. They have no illusions about the vicious world of the quality which exploits Jim as a slave and Huck as a potential slave-holder. Their serenity comes from accepting their place at the very bottom of society. They have, as Karl Marx said, "nothing to lose but their chains." The property-less can afford, Thoreau points out, to live what is essential.

Passages like Huck's description of the night sky make clear what Hemingway means when he says, "All modern American literature comes from one book by Mark Twain called *Huckleberry Finn.*"[7] Unfortunately the novel is not all of a piece. Hemingway goes on, "If you read it you must stop where . . . Jim is stolen from the boys. That is the real end. The rest is just cheating." Both the opening and closing chapters are seriously marred by Tom Sawyer's taking over and directing the action.[8] Tom *is* racist. He is conventional and respectable and what Huck calls "quality." His boyish games have, as Huck himself recognizes on occasions, "all the marks of a Sunday school." He plays practical jokes on Jim, and through his conventional eyes we see Jim in chapter two as a superstitious fellow who is proud of having been, as he supposes, visited by witches.[9] Once Jim makes a break for freedom he becomes heroic, a strong-hearted intelligent man. Huck's attempts after that to continue playing Tom Sawyer practical jokes on him backfire. If any education of Huck takes place in the course of the novel, it is his learning that the man he instinctively allies himself with when he says "they're after *us*" is not going to tolerate any childish games and that he, Huckleberry, can no longer be a boy. They are both men and have to face and outwit the violence and rapacity of bourgeois Christian law and order. Jim has dignity beyond any white man in the book. When Huck tries to make a joke of Jim's interpreting their separation by the fog, Jim insists that Huck treat his feelings with the consideration and respect they deserve, and establishes his, Jim's, superiority to Huck's childish joke. Huck rises to the occasion and apologizes. They are established again as full equals. Jim is sensitive and open in his affectionate feelings for Huck (contemporary academic criticism plumbs its usual depths by smirking at Jim's calling Huck "honey" as homosexuality). One of the most touching scenes in the novel is Jim's sorrowful discovery that his baby girl, Elizabeth, is deaf and dumb. He says that he shouts behind her, and

> *She never budge!* Oh, Huck, I bust out a-cryin; an grab her up in my arms, en say, "Oh, de po' little thing! de Lord God Almighty forgive po' ole Jim, kaze he never gwyne to fogive hisself as long's he live!"

Jim is strong, capable, decisive. His decision to make a break for freedom is heroic. He is the heir of the freedom which the Black folk hero, Brer Rabbit, fights for. As a portrait of a Black he deserves comparison with the magnificent Frederick Douglass.[10] Douglass was a personal friend of Clemens.

The apology which T. S. Eliot makes for the ending of the novel is that it returns us to the level of its beginning. That will hardly wash. Tom Sawyer takes on freeing Jim as a game, for he knows, as Huck and Jim do not know, that Jim has already been freed by Miss Watson. Tom's Alexander Dumas hijinks make the last chapters of the novel what Bernard DeVoto calls "the most chilling descent in all literature."[11] Jim in captivity on the Phelps farm under Tom's direction keeps a journal on a shirt with his blood, digs meaningless tunnels, and docilely follows Tom's Sundayschool Boyscout plots and his racist point of view. Jim couldn't, the novel tells us,

> see no sense in the most of it, but he allowed we [Tom and Huck] was white folks and knowed better than him; so he was satisfied, and said he would do it all just as Tom said.[12]

The ending makes hash of all the brilliant and profound satire on bourgeois culture and religion. The slaveholding Christian, Miss Watson, is whitewashed. Huck falls into Tom's treachery. He observes about Jim when he insists on calling the doctor to take care of Tom's gunshot wounds that he knows Jim "was white inside." When Mrs. Phelps asks Huck if anyone was hurt in the steamboat accident, Huck makes the most abysmally racist reply, "No'm. Killed a nigger." One may argue that Huck's use of the term elsewhere is natural and inevitable in his speech, but here it denies the very humanity of Blacks.

The book is not, then, a consistent whole. What comic masterpiece is? Chaucer, Cervantes, Rabelais, all are flawed and fragmented in their greatness. Only in the twentieth century do geniuses like Charlie Chaplin and Bertolt Brecht and Jaroslav Hasek sustain large comic designs. Perhaps the burlesque detonation of bourgeois presumption on the working class is too explosive for Mark Twain to carry through to conclusion; Tom Sawyer was a way of weaseling out. Theodore Dreiser points out a strong dualism in what he calls "Mark, the Double Twain." There is, I agree, a division between his solidarity with the working riverboatmen and his uneasy membership in the bourgeois genteel.

But in the last analysis we cannot let Tom Sawyer destroy the miraculous achievements of this novel. It lies altogether outside the bourgeois literary traditions of individualism and romanticism. I rub my eyes at the notion that a nineteenth century humorist should be class-conscious, that he should conduct such a profound satirical attack on the individualism which is the gospel of capitalism. Perhaps I am reading this into Huck's laughter? The offered alternatives make bright sayings of children out of this great folk hero, or twentieth century *weltschmerz*. Excuse me, I think I do him more justice.

Huckleberry Finn is flawed then, but it still richly deserves its place in the canon of world literature. Its accomplishment is nothing short of miraculous, a work of genius, and one which heartens, enlightens, and empowers the struggle in our country and the world for Black and white equality and for economic equality—a struggle led by working class whites like Huck and working class Blacks like Jim.

NOTES

1. Mark Twain, *Adventures of Huckleberry Finn*, edited by Henry Nash Smith (Boston: 1958), 56.
2. Ibid., 121.

3. Ibid., 247.

4. Clemens knew the riverboat community intimately. He was a licensed pilot on the Mississippi passenger boats and belonged to the Pilots' Association, a trade union, which shored up his authority as a pilot. "A pilot, in those days, was," he says, "the only unfettered and entirely independent human being that lived in the earth." (Mark Twain, *Life on the Mississippi,* illustrated by Thomas Hart Benton, edited by Willis Wager [N.Y.: Heritage Press, 1944], 90.)

5. *Huckleberry Finn,* Appendix A, 257–58.

6. Ibid., 100.

7. *Green Hills of Africa* (New York: Scribner, 1935), 22.

8. Specifically chapters 2, 3, 32 through the end of the book and passages such as boarding the wrecked steamboat where Huck invokes Tom Sawyer's inspiration.

9. Jim's superstition is not always pure childishness and simpleminded. It forecasts the character of Huck's story. When he uses the flight of birds to forecast the coming of a storm we feel that folk wisdom is the basis of his observation.

10. Frederick Douglass, *My Bondage and My Freedom,* with an introduction by Philip S. Foner (New York: Dover Publications, 1969).

11. Bernard A. DeVoto, *Mark Twain's America* (Chautauqua, N.Y.: 1933.)

12. *Huckleberry Finn,* 208.

Japanese Americans in Books or in Reality? Three Writers for Young Adults Who Tell a Different Story

Harue Palomino

As a children's librarian in California during the '60s, '70s, and the '80s, my work was directly involved with reading and reviewing newly published children's books, and thus I could follow the trend in children's books which inevitably follows or accompanies great social and political movements which sweep the country. With the Civil Rights movement in the '60s came a trickle, then a flow, of children's books by Black authors, some good, some poor, but in this process an astonishing array of extremely fine Black writers emerged. Black children from preschool and elementary school years to young Black students in high schools and colleges could find their past heritage with roots in Africa, stories of Black family life on southern plantations from generation to generation, as well as stories on urban life, and in this process find their identity reflected in these books, whereas up until then there were hardly any books that Black children could identify with positively.

But what about the Asian Americans? Specifically, since I am a Nisei (a second generation Japanese), I ask, what are today's Japanese American children and young people finding in the large young people's collections in public libraries and schools about themselves and the country of their origin? And what sort of books about the Japanese Americans are young people of other races being exposed to? There are a few preschool books emphasizing

Harue Palomino, a retired children's librarian, compiled an authoritative bibliography, *The Japanese And The Japanese Americans: A Critical Bibliography*. She is a member of the National Jane Addams Children's Book Award Committee and participated in the conference of Asian-American writers in Honolulu in 1979 the quaint customs of the "transplanted" people of Japan, or of a model Japanese American girl growing up in a comfortable middle class family, apparently undergoing little or no generational conflict. Exceptions are books by Taro Yashima, but they are mostly about young children in Japan.

In the fiction and nonfiction sections, there is an absolute dearth of books for young people showing with honesty and truth the real experiences of the Japanese people who had immigrated from Japan and had established their families on the soil of Hawaii and on the West Coast of the United States.

My interest aroused, in view of the fact that Black children's authors had made some breakthrough into the large commercial publishing houses of the East (granted, there was a large receptive audience for such books following the Civil Rights Movement), I set about systematically to read and record any and all books for young people that dealt with Japan or the Japanese American experience. This eventually led to the compilation of a critical bibliography on the Japanese and the Japanese Americans. The books that I included in this bibliography, mostly books on Japan since I could find little material on the Japanese American experience, were judged not only for literary quality, authenticity, accuracy of information and appeal to children, but were also examined and judged to see if they were demeaning or condescending, or whether racial stereotypes were reinforced. Here I emphasize that the number of books *not* included in the bibliography far exceeded the number of books included in the bibliography, which highlights the sad state of affairs in the publishing field for this ethnic group.

Why was there such a dearth of good books on the Japanese American experience, I wondered, that come to terms with the immigrant experience, that tell of the horrendous conditions in which the Isseis worked, of the conflicts between the old culture that they had brought from Japan and the present culture in which they lived, and of the consequent impact upon their children? Surely there must be some record of these experiences, I thought.

I found my answer after attending a conference of Asian American writers. Yes, there were such books, I discovered, great working class novels and plays and poems by powerful writers whose works should be part of the literature collection of every high school and college curriculum. But these writers were hardly known, I myself had never heard of them, and they were ignored by the establishment press with all its attendant publicity outlets. Their works had been published either independently or by struggling small presses. Toshio Mori, one of the greatest Japanese

American writers from the West Coast, wrote for fifty years, after a full day working in a nursery, with hardly any recognition, and even now one of his best works, *Woman From Hiroshima,* has only recently been brought back into print.

It is my purpose in this article to discuss these works containing the essence of Japanese working class experiences in this country. These are important works for young adult Japanese Americans searching for their past history and identity.

I will start with the examination of Toshio Mori's *Woman From Hiroshima,* a story told by a grandmother to her grandchildren about her life in America.

This is a lively, humorous, deeply moving account of an Issei woman's unquenchable thirst for life as she makes the fateful decision to leave Japan to join her husband in San Francisco in the early 1900s. From a warm, close, family relationship in a small tightly knit village in Japan, she experiences culture shock as she arrives in San Francisco, a big western city, with international cuisine, western dress, and unfamiliar housing conditions. She adjusts to these changes, a zest for new experiences overcoming initial resistance, but soon she comes across an incident that is totally out of her realm of experience. Walking with her husband on the streets of San Francisco, unable to understand the English language, she encounters some angry people. "Why do they look that way at us?" she asks her husband.

> "They do not like us," he replies.
> "But we haven't done anything to them," I protested, "We haven't even met them before."
> "You do not understand," your grandpa said gently. "They do not like us for what we are."
> "They do not like us for what we are? What do you mean?"
> "They don't like Japanese," was the reply.[1]

This is beyond the realm of her comprehension. More horrible experiences follow when their home is pelted with an avalanche of rocks, and doors and windows are smashed. She enters into a deep depression but slowly recovers.

> Yes, children, (she says) my wound slowly healed. It took time. I raised my head one day. Strange, this spirit. Life's imperfections did not bother me so much after that. I laughed and taunted life. "What! Are you trying to defeat me?" I cried to myself. "Well, it's going to take you a lifetime to triumph and then you cannot be too sure."[2]

Here is no weak submissive Japanese housewife, but a sturdy earthy woman of the soil.

She and her husband gravitate towards the other Issei men in the area who were mostly single (women could not be called over from Japan until cash for their steerage passage was raised).

> And until then our men lived hard. These men made money by hard labor — back-breaking jobs in the hot sun and cold spell. They worked in the railroad gangs. They cleared the woods for rich farm lands. They toiled in the mines, on the farms. They became dishwashers, laundrymen, butlers, gardeners, small shopkeepers. Your grandpa began as a farmhand in San Jose. [3]

Eventually they save enough to buy a bathhouse in San Francisco.

Henceforth, we see this strong, life-giving woman raise a family, help her husband in the garden nursery business in San Leandro, California, overcome the sudden shock of widowhood, and lastly, go through the traumatic experience of incarceration at Topaz. And always, in spite of more great tragedies — the death of one son in the 442nd unit in Europe (the much celebrated Japanese American regiment that helped turn the tide in fascist Italy and in occupied France) and the paralysis of a second son in the same regiment — the indomitable spirit of the woman lives on.

Lawson Inada, a well-known Japanese American writer and critic, says of Toshio Mori: He is "a true folk artist in the finest sense of the term — one who conveys our very soul."[4]

Next we come to a gifted young Japanese American poet and playwright, Momoko Iko, who brings the working class Japanese American experience to contemporary times. Her play, *The Gold Watch,* was presented in the fall of 1976 on the PBS Visions series and was one of two entries, along with *Roots,* to be accepted at the 1977 Monte Carlo International T. V. Festival. But it is her powerful narrative essay *And There Are Stories, There Are Stories* that I will discuss here. Using street language in rhythmic cadences interspersed with Japanese words she begins:

> It ain't the end, babes, it's the beginning
>
> 1940 — of Issei parents, born premature and put on the oven door . . .
>
> 1943 — At night, trying to sleep, I saw and felt and knew concentration camped grown up anger and tension and fights and quiet fucking
>
> 1945 — Circling the clover leaf streets of philadelphia. . . .
>
> And on to Chicago, Where I started school . . .

Hey, hey, do your eyes goes that way, cause your mama
had you sideways. . . . Hey, hey, pressed against the
schoolyard's iron fence and then running, away from, Hey,
hey, Jap girl, jap girl, come back and play, to home and big
sister, who told me: Some people just don't know any better,
just don't listen to them. You're just as good as anyone else
and to *MAMA,* who was always coming home from work carrying 2 full and heavy shopping bags full of the ripe peaches
and crunchy apples . . . *MAMA* just cradled me, cause hurt
little kids need cradling, not a lot of palaver . . . [5]

AND THE STORIES
At 78, Papa, one of three Issei, who from Addison Street
near Wrigley Field to Soldier's Field . . . 53 blocks marched
for Martin Luther King . . . and oh I was proud . . . Cause we
buddhaheads who hadn't forgotten our buddhahead past . . . we
ain't bleeding hearts, We are just buddhaheads who haven't
forgotten our buddhahead pasts . . . that's all. We
buddhaheads, we are selfish as all hell and we just figure if
we let you fuck over black folks, the next folks you will be
concentratin on, again, is us. It is just the instinct for self-
preservation. Isn't that right, papa? Isn't that the reason you
marched with Dr. King.
So ca? Maybe . . . Dr. King, he, good man, that's all . . . [6]

And I call me a writing artist now.
I call me Amerasian . . .
And Mama would be so happy
And Papa, too.
I am finally among my own . . .
Hey, you sure come on white.
Don't you believe in yellow . . .[7]

This narrative essay is great writing—not to be missed. It has a
special appeal for young Sansei and Yonsei (third and fourth generation Japanese) who grew up during the Civil Rights and Vietnam
eras and to whom Momoko Iko is a contemporary. They will
identify with her experiences in grade school and high school
where she stands up to and will not accept second class
citizenship, of her interracial love in college for a tall Texan where
she again stands on her integrity by not accepting his racial bigotry
towards the Blacks. "What was that Robert Frost said: 'Two
roads diverged in a yellow wood and sorry I could not travel both
and be one traveler.' "[8]

Lastly we come to an outstanding Japanese American writer who has made a significant contribution towards preserving the working class Japanese American heritage of Hawaii. Whereas *Woman From Hiroshima* is about an Issei woman in San Francisco and Oakland, Milton Murayama's *All I Asking For Is My Body* is about a Nisei (2nd generation Japanese) growing up in Hawaii in the '30s and '40s. Here the reader is transported, not into the shallow superficial outward calm and peace of a middle class Japanese family, but into a dynamic unrepressed working class family full of conflicting values and ideals. Or, as Kiyo, the narrator of this book observes:

> You couldn't tell because every family was a walled city, and you never knew unless you were inside. And if you were on the inside you never talked stink about the family, but kept up the family face.[9]

Murayama takes you inside such a family.

After an early childhood spent near the ocean in Pepelau, Hawaii, where Kiyo's father is a fisherman, hard times force the ever-growing family to a plantation town in the mountains called Kahana.

> There were many different races in Pepelau, but Kahana had about one hundred Japanese families, about two hundred Filipino men, about seven Portuguese and Spanish families, and only two *haoles* (Caucasians). Mr. Boyle was the principal of the Kahana Grade School, and Mr. Nelson was the overseer of Kahana. . . . It was a company town with identical company houses and outhouses, and it was set up like a pyramid. At the tip was Mr. Nelson, then the Portuguese, Spanish and Nisei *lunas* in their nicer-looking homes, then the identical wooden houses of Japanese Camp, then the more run-down Filipino Camp.[10]

Tosh, the eldest son and older brother of Kiyo, quits school in the ninth grade to work on the sugar plantation to help pay off the family debt. In a bitter argument with his mother he says:

> "How come you bear more children than you can send to school?"
>
> "You *ni ga haru* (too big for your breeches). You've worked only three months and you're talking big. Look at Minoru Tanaka, Hideo Shimada, Kenji Watanabe, Toru Minami, they've been working for their parents for over ten years, and they never complain," mother said.
>
> "They're dumb, that's why. They don't want to go to

school. With me it's different. I like school."
"Every child must repay his parents."
"How much? How long?"
"Your father helped grandfather for twelve years without a word of complaint."[11]

Tosh is outspoken, is critical of his family's (to him) false sense of honor and insistence on filial duties and never hesitates to argue against them, even to the point of invoking hot-tempered violence in his father. After a particularly violent argument, when Tosh storms out of the house, Kiyo is sent out in the evening by his worried mother to fetch Tosh.

"I sick and tired getting hit all the time," he (Tosh) muttered. "From nowon I goin' dish it out too. You doan know how much he been beat me up when I was a kid. He always called me a crybaby. I was no *samurai,* I had no *gaman* (patience), no *enryo* (holding back). But shit, thass the only way I can fight him. If I start holding back, I play right into his hands. Hard work, patience, holding back, waiting your turn, all that crap, they all fit together to keep you down."[12]

His parents turn from the eldest son and seize on Kiyo, the second son, to fulfill their expectations, which by now include a debt of six thousand dollars that they are honor bound to pay. Kiyo is an even-tempered likable boy, caught in the conflict between his brother and his parents, feeling the burdens placed on the family through his parents' rigid adherence to old-world customs and yet compassionate towards them. This is mainly the story of Kiyo, his childhood friends and activities, his adolescence, and of his struggle to rise above the oppressive influence of the plantation system. It is of a boy and his brother who tenaciously fight to rise above it, unlike the majority of the boys they knew who gave in and lost all hope. And the reason they were able to rise above it, as Murayama shows in his book, was because they did not accept the stereotypical behavior that had been drummed into them by the plantation system and the forces of society.

And Tosh never stopped crabbing . . . "You see the dumb Bulaheads, they like it for their sons to be dumb. They like them to obey. They consider you a better man if you said yes all the time."
"The plantation the same way," I said.
"Yeah, we gotta fight two battles all the time."[13]

Since I too was born in Hawaii of immigrant parents I could identify closely with this book. I too wandered with childhood friends in a town similar to Pepelau, gathering *opihis* off the lava rocks near the sea, or climbing cherry trees laden with sweet fruit. And I also experienced the time of reckoning during adolescence when the future gaped empty—marriage for girls after high school, or plantation work or clerking in a *haole*-run business for the boys.

All the wonderful island humor is caught in this book, the beauty of the islands as well as the squalor of the plantation camps. The pidgin dialect used here is true to form and is an important part of this book, for it was this language that bridged the gap between generations and among the different races while we were growing up. This is an important work, useful as a sociological study, a slice of life that has all but vanished in the islands, and one that young people will enjoy, for all the joys and innocence, the heartaches and despair of growing up are embodied here.

It might be pertinent to note at this time that I came across Momoko Iko's work in a periodical, and Milton Murayama's *All I Asking For Is My Body* is self-published.

No article on Japanese American literature would be complete without taking into account the many books on the Concentration Camp experience (when the Japanese Americans were incarcerated during World War II in barbed wire camps throughout the west by Executive Order no. 9066, issued on February 19, 1942), but this in itself will require lengthy analysis. However, I have included in the list of *Recommended Reading* some books I regard as significant.

It is my hope that the works discussed here will open up new avenues of approach to Japanese American literature, for all three of these powerful writers wrote about ordinary people, of families struggling to stay alive, of laborers and shopkeepers, of fishermen and gardeners, with illuminating insights, never caving in to outside pressures to make their works more popular by emphasizing the false or the exotic, or by reinforcing popular stereotypes of model Asians, or by the use of standard English which takes away the flavor of the ethnic group. These books will give young adult Japanese Americans or Japanese Americans approaching adolescence a sense of continuity with the past and a realization of their ethnic worth.

Again, I would like to emphasize that these are working class novels and poetry, written by working class authors, about all the ordinary people who had passed intimately through their lives.

NOTES

1. Toshio Mori, *Woman From Hiroshima* (San Francisco: Isthmus Press, 1978), 13.
2. Ibid., 15.
3. Ibid., 16.
4. Ibid., back cover.
5. Momoko Iko, "And There Are Stories, There Are Stories," *The Greenfield Review: Special Asian American Writers Issue*, 6, nos. 1 & 2 (Spring 1977), 39.
6. Ibid., 43–44.
7. Ibid., 45.
8. Ibid., 43.
9. Milton Murayama, *All I Asking For Is My Body* (San Francisco: Supa Press, 1975), 46.
10. Ibid., 28.
11. Ibid.
12. Ibid., 46.
13. Ibid., 68.

RECOMMENDED READING

Aiiieeeee! An Anthology of Asian American Writers. Edited by Frank Chin, Jefferey Paul Chan, Lawson Fusao Inada, Shawn Hsu Wong. New York: Anchor Press/Doubleday, 1975.

Ayumi: A Japanese American Anthology. Edited by Janice Mirikitani. San Francisco: Japanese American Anthology Committee, 1980.

"Asian Americans in Children's Books." *Interracial Books For Children Bulletin* 7, nos. 2, 3 (1976).

Greenfield Review (Special Asian American Writers Issue) 6, nos. 1, 2 (Spring 1977).

Iko, Momoko. "And There Are Stories, There Are Stories." *Greenfield Review* 6, nos. 1, 2 (Spring 1977): 39–46.

Mori, Toshio. *The Chauvinist And Other Stories*. Los Angeles: Asian American Studies Center, UCLA, 1979.

———. *Yokohama, California.* Introduction by William Saroyan. Caldwell, Idaho: The Caxton Printers, 1949. Reissued by Univ. of Washington Press, 1985.

———. *Woman From Hiroshima.* San Francisco: Isthmus Press, 1978.

Murayama, Milton. *All I Asking For Is My Body.* San Francisco: Supa Press, 1975.

Okada, John. *No-No Boy.* San Francisco: CARP Publishing Co., 1957. Reissued by Univ. of Washington Press, 1984.

Okubo, Mine. *Citizen 13660.* New York: Arno Press, 1978.

Takashima, Shizuye. *A Child In Prison Camp.* Montreal: Tundra Books, 1971.

———. *Nisei Daughter, 1953.* Seattle: Univ. of Washington Press, 1984.

Weglyn, Michi. *Years of Infamy: The Untold Story of American Concentration Camps.* New York: William Morrow, 1976.

"Are Indians Nicer Now?": What Children Learn From Books About Native North Americans

Magda Lewis

My focus in this essay is on the issue of cultural bias against the Native peoples of North America as these biases are presented to very young children by way of the children's picture book.[1] Further, it will be shown that the appropriation of knowledge that serves the dominating group's political, economic, and cultural interests becomes general and taken-for-granted knowledge and is reflected in the status quo.

The books I have chosen to look at were selected more or less at random from an elementary school library and a moderately sized public library which houses among its collection a special Native-Canadian Section.[2] My deliberate intention was not to do a historical survey, or a survey of a genre, or indeed to follow any rationalized approach to choosing the representative books. Rather, my intention was to imagine how a student in a primary grade (Kindergarten to Grade 3) in a large urban, predominantly white middle/upper middle class public school might go about choosing books in order to do a class assignment on "Indians." What I will try to show is how, given a random selection of a limited number of books, the construction of a version of Native reality is accomplished for non-Native children. The possibility for a comparative analysis is provided by the fact that there is a small, but apparently growing, selection of books authored by individuals of Native descent. All of these were found in the public library. However, due to limited space I shall not be taking up any of these

Magda Lewis is a doctoral candidate at the Ontario Institute for Studies in Education, and is working on a feminist critique of the social construction of national identity and coauthoring a book on feminist theory and critical pedagogy/cultural studies.

books in this paper.[3]

My son Geoffrey has just turned five years old. On the evening that I brought home my bundle of books, his eyes grew large and interested. He immediately appropriated the books, retired to a quiet corner and began looking through them. After some time, having leafed through all of the books, he emerged from his quiet place and asked soberly, "Are Indians nicer now?" The message so clearly given through the visual representations in these books was obvious to him and did not fail to make its impact. What this message is, is the focus of analysis for the remainder of this essay.

What is typical of the style of most of the books I found is that the pictures tended to be presented as snapshots. The text tended mostly to refer to the picture descriptively but made no attempt at connecting one picture to the next or indeed to locate the picture in a larger context. Hence the overall effect was one of disjointedness as the images were decontextualized and made to appear unconnected to a wider, reasonable, and sufficient cultural base. Generally, the books did not sufficiently explain the Native peoples' culturally based behavior, behavior which, therefore, tended to seem arbitrary, irrational, and "quaint." This approach mitigates against the reader's ability to penetrate the culture with a reasonable amount of understanding.

The images presented in these books work successfully on two levels. For very young readers, the disjointed and decontextualized visual impact is immediate and implies a way of seeing the world. In the absence of counter images, the young child begins to assimilate this point of view and assumes it to be a direct representation of reality, much the same as she assumes family photographs to be a direct representation of reality. For older readers who have already had experience with this kind of imagery and who, therefore, bring a stock of preconceived notions to the text, these images work to reinforce those very notions. The individual, in projecting her "knowledge" onto the image, has its "truth" reaffirmed through the dialectic process: the image feeds the common understanding which in turn, in part, defines the image. Hence, it is clear that, in order for the images to make any sense at all, they depend to a large extent on what the reader already brings to the content. A good example of this process is provided by the title page of a book called *The North American Indians* by Ernest Berke. We are provided here with a picture of a lone Native man. He is typically naked on his upper torso. He is wearing elaborate ornamentation. There are three feathers in his hair at variously skewed angles. On his lower torso he is wearing buckskin, fringed leggings and there is a small blanket loosely strapped around his waist. On his belt there is a large knife in an ornamented case. He is wearing moccasins and in his hand he is holding a pipe. He is sitting "Indian style" (note how the stereotypical images have invaded the very language used to describe them) on a buffalo skin blanket on which there is laid out an ornamental item — rather prominently placed. His head is at a 45 degree angle turned toward the sky. There is a small fire set in front of him from which the smoke is rising straight up in the air in a thin, wispy shaft. His horse, also adorned with feathers and what appears to be a shield, grazes nearby. The man and his horse are alone on top of what appears to be a small hill, the terrain of which is very rough and rocky and looks hard and inhospitable. There are a few scrub bushes about. The man has a sullen look on his face, his mouth is downturned and his eyes are half closed. The fact that this picture appears on the title page is particularly interesting because there is no explanatory text that accompanies it. However, the picture is so heavily laden with stereotypical images that although we have no idea of what this man is doing or why, we almost seem to "know."

What has been presented here is a myth, in Barthes' sense of that word,[4] specifically in that the images of the Native peoples are overlaid by a socially determined understanding of the meaning of these images. Hence, for example, when we see the Native man, with his horse and pipe on the barren hill, his head turned toward the sky, we also see the "loner," the "mysterious," the "sinister," the "religious": someone who is doing strange, yet strangely familiar, things. These are often repeated images of the Native peoples — images that reinforce our particular understanding of them. The images we see in these books are images that are laden with predetermined meaning and hence present themselves as statements of fact. Indeed, the hegemonic process has worked to its full potential here as the particular point of view of the dominant group; their ideological penetration into the warp and weft of the social fabric has so infused our common understanding and everyday knowledge that its validity and source are never questioned. In the process, Native reality is reified as their activities are abstracted from any sensible context.

What is totally lost in these books as a result of this approach is that first, they make it practically impossible for the child to become aware of the fact that a culture, foreign though it may be to the reader, has a reasonable and sufficient base which dictates certain acceptable behavior (acceptable within the parameters of that culture). And second, they conceal from the child the fact that it is necessary to have an understanding of different cultures from this perspective so that her knowledge of these differences does not feed bias but rather enables her to understand the possibility of approaching life situations from different perspectives. Inasmuch as there is on the one hand a proliferation of this type of children's material and on the other hand a suppression of the culture of the oppressed, it therefore appears that the agenda of the dominant culture is precisely the denial of such an understanding in order that their superiority, through cultural and therefore economic and political means, may be maintained. In other words, in order that the invader's treatment of the Native people, both through physical and cultural abuse and extermination, may be justified, in their own minds and historically in the minds of their children, these books serve as a vehicle for Dehumanization of the Native in the eyes of non-Native children and for Mystification of the Native in the eyes of Native children. The fact that, until only very recently, there have not been any significant publications offering perspectives that could effectively counter the standard images of Native peoples attests to the success of these processes: Both the dominator and the dominated have internalized the desired effects of dehumanization and mystification respectively.[5] In what follows I shall examine in specific detail how this is done.

The most blatantly biased and misrepresentative book, and the one which set the tone for the entire collection, was a most strikingly "effective," large, "childsized," book by Ernest called *The North American Indians.* This book serves as a useful representative volume around which to focus the analysis of the other books for two reasons. First, it is the sort of book, a version of which every library has a copy, that I shall call the travelogue or photo album approach. It is effective precisely because of the repetitive images that are reinforced page after page, largely out of context and devoid of historical perspective. Its sheer brilliant colorfulness, the heavy, solid texture of the pages, the glossy and visually forceful images of the pictures have the effect of compelling the reader to look at it, and leaf through it, pressing its message upon her.

The cover of Berke's *Indians,* which serves as an introduction to the book, is a striking and colorful collage of perhaps a dozen Native people, of indeterminate origin, engaged in the stereotypical "War Dance." It must be noted that nowhere in the text is the idea ever articulated of what a "War Dance" is, how and when it was used or how it connected to the wider social and cultural practices of Native people. Yet there is not one to whom I have shown this picture who could not identify it immediately as a "*War Dance.*" It is, therefore, most telling that these images which have been perpetuated about Native cultural practices have so invaded our understanding and awareness of these cultures that the visual clichés are accepted as knowledge. That the author chose this image for his cover, moreover, immediately locates the Native people as a warring people. In fact, as will become obvious, the perpetuation of the idea of the warlike nature of Native people is a central theme throughout many of the books I looked at.

On the front cover of this book, then, the overall image is that of feathers, "war paint" and frenzy. We see hair flying, weapons flashing, and drums being beaten. We can almost hear the "whooping" as we look at the wide open "chanting" mouths and the intense "crazed" faces. A frightening picture indeed for a five-year-old—if this is what Native people look like, he surely doesn't want to meet one.

This image is repeated again in a picture titled "An Iroquois War Party." Here the men, eight to a canoe, are described as stripped, painted, and crafty. They glide out of the fog, "toward an enemy Indian village or a white man's settlement." The white man's settlement, interestingly, is not described as an enemy settlement. However, the text goes on to say that "crafty Iroquois such as these terrorized the entire Northeast during the years of the French and Indian wars." Here again the text and the visual images work successfully to reinforce each other. Visually the child sees, emerging from the fog, canoes manned by fierce-looking individuals, most of whom are hunched over—much as an animal would be when he readies to spring in attack. The fog imagery gives these figures a mysterious ghost-like quality. The text makes no suggestion as to the historical circumstances surrounding these Native "attacks." The omission of such a historical perspective speaks seriously to the Native Peoples' place in the social structure.

Depicting the Native peoples as aggressors, particularly if it can be demonstrated that they are so by nature and that "warring" is a fact of their cultural reality, conquering them, "domesticating" them, and subordinating them becomes a legitimate activity for those who need to justify their dominance and economic and political power over this minority group. The question, therefore, of whether this is an accurate depiction of history is not only counterproductive to this process but in a real sense is irrelevant.

"Hegemony," says Gitlin, "is the suffusing of the society by ideology [those assumptions, procedures, rules of discourse which are taken for granted], by rendering their preeminence natural, justifiable, and beneficial" (1982, p. 206). That this was important in 1963 when Berke's *Indians* was published and that this is still important over twenty years later when this and other books of its ilk stand mostly unchallenged (by counter presentations) on school and public library shelves, gives a strong indication that Native rights and the challenge to the lack of such rights is an issue which is not current but which sits close to the surface of the socially arbitrated racial relations—what Gitlin calls organized consent.

This one-sided version of history is repeated again in a picture entitled "Osceola's Defiance." The text reads as follows: "In 1834 the United States tried to force the Seminoles to move to the Oklahoma Indian Reservations. Osceola, one of their greatest chiefs, sliced the treaty to ribbons, starting a bloody seven-year war that cost the United States Government millions of dollars and the lives of hundreds of soldiers" (*Indians,* p. 16). That many Native people also died is not mentioned. The issue surrounding the removal of native people onto reservations, the land deals made and broken (still contentious issues among Native and European inhabitants of North America), or even an explanation of what Native reservations are, how they function, what purpose they are meant to serve, and why it was important to the European settlers—and the European population even today—that the Native people accept their removal to these reservations passively, is nowhere mentioned. The picture shows a defiant Native man, knife drawn, piercing a document. The soldier is indignant and surprised. That this "act of defiance" was not what caused the "bloody wars" but rather that these wars were the result of the presumptions under which the Europeans attempted to settle the "New World" is not in the best interest of the ruling and dominant groups to articulate. In this regard an interesting discussion could be had as to the culturally determined definitions of war—how acts of war are constituted, how winning in war is constituted, how honor of the "soldier" in war is constituted, how inter-relationships among people may change or stay the same during times of war and times of peace. These are only a few of the questions, the answers to which would be helpful in understanding how the Native population and the European population may have differed or concurred on what was going on during the time of the "Indian Wars." Answers to these questions may even point to why the Native inhabitants were so easily defeated in many instances and why the "Indian Wars" in fact cover only a very short time in the history of the settlement of the "New World" (Wright 1975).

The emphasis on warring, this time fused with religious ritual, is demonstrated in the picture entitled "The Evening War Prayer," (*Indians*, p. 28), showing the chief asking the aid of the gods the evening before his war party departs. The chief is standing alone, in the typical hunched stance, on a windswept hill, wrapped in a blanket, beating a drum. In fact the tendency to describe not only religious but a great deal of Native behavior in the context of warring and fighting is a constant and recurring theme throughout many of the books. Consider this description of life on the plains for example: "The Indians of the Plains were buffalo hunters and horsemen. They lived active lives following the herds, stealing horses from each other, dancing, and making war" (*Indians*, p. 2). Similarly in a small book, *Plains Indians,* in describing some (unexplained) game the text reads: "The Indians enjoyed games that were good practice for hunting, or fighting, such as racing, archery, or wrestling on horseback" (p. 25).

Tough Enough's Indians capitalizes ruthlessly on this distorted version of Native history and culture. In this book, as in most, our focus is first drawn to the front cover where the five Tatum children are shown dressed in fringed buckskin, headbands, and feathers, peering out into the distance from under their hands which shade their eyes. They all have sullen though not grotesque faces. It is interesting that the substance of the images in this book is not unlike those found in Berke's *Indians* with the exception that these are non-Native children "playing" Indian. While the caricatures are more whimsical and "child-like," the message remains the same. The "whooping wardance" image is repeated as the story begins with: "Beanie Tatum and his brothers and sisters were playing Indians" (p. 5). The picture that accompanies this text shows the five children "dancing" around in a circle. Again they are all hunched over, they each have a leg up in the air, they wear headbands and animal masks, they have rattles and tomahawks in their hands. "All of them were hopping and bouncing and skipping and stamping" (p. 5). As the story progresses, the sisters Annie Mae and Serena attach chicken feathers to their horse Sass and their dog Tough Enough. The ensuing commotion brings Beanie who upon seeing the two struggling animals says: "Injuns didn't go fussin' up their critters that-a-way. . . . They didn't have time. They were too busy huntin' and beatin' drums and scalpin' other Injuns and white folks, cuttin' their skin and hair right off, somethin' terrible, and burnin' 'em up at the stakes" (p. 12). Somehow the message on the fly-leaf of this book, that this was a day when the Tatum children "learned a lot about people," is lost in the discourse. While the book attempts to recover some measure of humanity for Native people as the story progresses, it is neither adequate nor effective enough to overcome these initial images so firmly established in the early pages. Quite aside from the false and distorted information provided in this lengthy exchange, one wonders what purpose the authors thought they were serving by providing such a colorful, detailed and gruesome description in a book intended for the enjoyment of young children. The white author of *Indians* indulges equally his lust for fantasizing and thereby participating vicariously in the aggressive, romantic, nomadic images of the Native that he himself, in fact, created. As seductive daydreams, these images, then, turn on themselves and feed their creator. They feed his need for escapism, not only at a benign level but also at a very destructive level. And all this is done at the expense of the Native people.

In *Tough Enough's Indians,* the children, having been lost in the woods with a forest fire raging nearby, find themselves face to face with a Cherokee family upon whose cabin they have stumbled. The children are terrified and Beanie says to himself as he gazes up at the Grandfather whose face is described as "seamed and leathery": "He's mean-lookin.' He's mean inside and outside. If I touched him with my tongue he'd taste bitter" (p. 41). As they go inside the cabin and begin to make friends with the Native children, Mr. Climbing Bear, the Grandfather, begins to sharpen his knife on a whetstone. The text continues: "Beanie looked at Annie Mae's long golden hair, at Serena's long brown braids. He shivered. But then he told himself, 'Injuns don't go around scalpin' folks, not nowadays they don't. It was just old-timey Injuns did all that scalpin.' " This method of visual and textual representations, which fail to sufficiently articulate historical time or geographical location, which decontextualize and, therefore, focus on some specific behavior, magnifying it out of proportion to the total and complex cultural, social, and historical activities, results in the intermingling, exchanging, and fusing of fact with fiction until it becomes impossible to tell one apart from the other. Whether these books represent fiction or nonfiction, therefore, is not a question that can be answered as easily and as thoughtlessly as it would at first appear.

Even defeat is turned back on the Native people in "The Smoke Screen" illustration in Berke's *Indians*. The attending text reads: "From time to time treacherous raids by U.S. soldiers resulted in the massacre of many Indian women, children and old people." While the viciousness of the invader's attack is acknowledged, it is the Native people who are pictured escaping under the cover of smoke, having set the plains on fire. By not providing adequate explanation the author turns their defeat and retreat into a final act of aggression and destruction, rather than a reasonable strategy for escape. Hence the emphasis on warring and at the same time the omission of any honest historical context or any suggestion that the conflict, besides having to do with property invasion, obviously had a great deal to do with a clash of cultures—as it still does today—is repeated over and over again.

As a final example, the repeated reference to the Battle of the Little Bighorn serves as a useful summing up point. Projecting an image of the Native peoples as aggressive, warring, and ruthless is used to justify the aggression and ruthlessness directed toward them. At the same time this same image is used as an effective tool to quiet their potential thinking about Native rights and their relationship to a political, economic, and social system that has grossly ignored their existential reality. Through such quieting they become participants in what Freire calls the "Culture of Silence," unable to emerge as critical knowing subjects for whom the world also emerges as an objective reality susceptible of change. The effectiveness of this silencing is demonstrated in no insignificant way by the fact that Berke's *Indians,* among others, is a book that appeared on the Ontario government's Ministry of Education circular of recommended books for school libraries—the recommendation having come from a panel that included a number of Native consultants. For obvious reasons, then, this process serves the needs of the dominant group well.

Back in Berke's *Indians,* the text reads: "The most famous battle between the Plains Indians and the U.S. Army took place in 1876 at the Little Bighorn River in Montana. Lieutenant Colonel George Custer led his troops into a Sioux Indian camp on the riverbank. Custer planned to move the Indians off their land, but the Sioux resisted. Many soldiers, including Custer, were killed in the fight. All over the plains similar battles were fought and men and women died needlessly" (p. 40). The fact that these deaths are described as "needless" seems to imply that the Native resistance to the invasion ought not to have happened.

Nowhere, throughout the majority of the books I looked at, does one get a sense of the validity of the Native culture, the invasion of this culture by the white settlers or that physical retaliation is not an unusual or unprecedented response to such invasion. Although care must be taken with children to explain possible alternative models of problem solving—even when these problems involve such serious things as the large scale appropriation of a people through cultural invasion, to present such a one-sided historical perspective does harm both to the Native child's and the white child's valid understanding of the historical significance and importance of her particular and distinct culture.

The flip-side of "The Native as Warrior" is "The White Man as Superhero." In Berke's *Indians* the picture entitled "When War Cries Rang" (p. 8) is particularly interesting when it is juxtaposed to the picture called "A Desperate Situation" (p. 62). On page sixty-two we see a Native man taking on a huge bear in combat. The "lone hunter" battles the "six-hundred-pound grizzly" says the text. The Native man has only a small knife and his bow and arrow. Yet in the picture on page eight, three such men seem to be quite easily managed by the lone pioneer whom the "hawk-eyed" and "wolf-hearted," "hostile Indians" have come to invade. One Native is lying on the ground holding his bloodied face, the second is just falling over from the blow of the butt of the white man's gun, and the third is about to be attacked. All three of the Native men have tomahawks. These, however, appear useless to them. White man as superhero is reinforced again in the genre of Superman and a whole host of T.V. and comic book invincibles. This image is again repeated in "One Down," (*Indians,* p. 36) where we are presented with a picture under which the caption reads, "Cheyenne warriors retreat in confusion at seeing one of their number knocked down. The white men [notice the constant reference to Indian *warriors* but white *men*] armed with powerful rifles, make their stand a couple of hundred yards away."

Significantly the vast majority of the images in these books are premised on a notion of Native people as individuals from a distant past rather than as a current reality. The fact that they are written in the past tense and the fact that the images are almost always contextualized in a typical noncurrent setting implies a distant past which has no relationship to the present. Typical of this is the book *Plains Indians*. The last page of this book shows a group of Native people being removed on horseback and in wagons to the Indian reservations. The text reads, "The Indians were finally defeated in 1890 at Wounded Knee. They were herded onto reservations on land that white people did not want. With no buffalo to hunt, their lives became dependent on the government. They lost their freedom, and their whole way of life on the plains they loved" (p. 28). And so it ended. What is striking about the picture that accompanies this text is that the season that is depicted is winter. Throughout the rest of the book – and indeed throughout all of the books in this selection – summer is the season that is most typically shown. Indeed, most often the pictures convey the image of parched heat and an inhospitable terrain. Here, however, at the end of the book, at the end of the "freedom and a way of life," at the end of the "Indian Wars," at the final defeat, the finality is reinforced by the visual imagery – that of winter and the last of the four seasons when everything "dies." Symbolically then we are readied for the new spring, a new era when battle will no longer have to be waged with the Native people, when the pioneer of Berke's *Indians* can go on with his planting and tilling without fear of being attacked by "lurking, hostile Indians" (p. 8).

That these images of the vanished "Indian" permeate the cultural fabric of the child's social context is emphasized by the fact that Native images are at once everywhere and nowhere. *Everywhere:* children's nursery rhymes; advertising; and common language (e.g., acting like a bunch of wild Indians). The logo for Mutual of Omaha personifies this use of the Native image. It consists of a head wearing a feathered headdress covering the eyes. Below it is a bulbous nose and below that a down-turned mouth. What makes this logo particularly interesting is that the image is not only rigidly stereotypical and immediately recognizable as that of an "Indian" but it is difficult to imagine what religious/ cultural artifact of any other group in North America could be used so blatantly, be so immediately recognized by the wide majority of the population and go so routinely unchallenged. In the context of the present paper, children's nursery rhymes are particularly relevant in that they are littered with Native images. The one that addresses itself specifically to the vanishing Indian, however, is the familiar "one little, two little, three little Indians." As the rhyme proceeds up to ten little Indians, the countdown starts in the other direction until it stops at "one little Indian boy." They are all gone but one. One can almost see the "little Indian boys" jumping out from behind trees, where they had been "lurking" and being "popped off" by the ever ready, vigilant white man. This is no mere fanciful extrapolation, overdone analytic zeal, or stretching an analogy. As Hartmut Lutz points out, there were economic, political, and ideological reasons for mythologizing the white man as superhero and the Native people as the evil that lurks behind every tree and which, therefore, had to be eliminated. Indeed, parallel images in Germany support the notion of the need for the dominating group to legitimize their power by making the ever present enemy invisible but still ever present. To justify the Super-hero, as in Spiderman, how ever often the "enemy"—the forces of evil—is defeated, it keeps coming back. And so the vigil is kept up, the rhyme goes on and the books keep being reprinted. Lutz confirms: "Since in [Germany] no immediate economic interests called for the extermination of the Native Americans, no ideological justification was needed for the murder of Indians such as was developed and propagated by the English colonialists or the Americans in their literature. Although the colonial imperialism of the German empire was given ideological support in correspondingly racist children's literature on Africa and Asia, no political situation ever called for anti-Native American literature. There was no place for the song 'Ten Little Indians,' which thus became 'Zehn Kleine Negerlein,' [Ten Little Negroes]" (Lutz 1979, pp. 17–18). *Nowhere:* these images have become so much a part of everyday discourse and everyday references that they most often no longer (if they ever did) appear to be curious or strange or ridiculous. Racism is the dialectical relation between these two poles: Everywhere and Nowhere. Racism grows out of those hegemonic forces that on the one hand strive to make the dominated group invisible while at the same time make them a central thread in the fabric of social, political, and particularly economic structures.

In "Bad Medicine" (*Indians,* p. 37) the picture shows a group of defeated "warriors" as they head back to camp after an unsuccessful "raid." They look demoralized, "scrawny," and weak. One wonders why men such as these were ever sent to battle in the first place. The whole picture—ground, cliffs, sky, and men—is tinted with a deep red hue; the men practically blend into the landscape. It is interesting, therefore, that even though the book is constant with its references to Native attacks, raids, and slaughter of the white man, nowhere do we have a picture showing European settlers in a defeated posture. There is obviously no such bias toward not showing Native people in this way. Hence the superiority of the white man's image is maintained. Even in defeat, such as the description of the battle of the Little Bighorn in Wellman's *Indian Wars and Warriors: West,* the image of the white man's superiority is reiterated. In this book, the vehement denial that Custer perhaps committed suicide on the one hand, and on the other, the assertion that he in fact "fell on the field of battle, brave to the last" portrays an image of the white man that is echoed in a small book entitled *The Indian Princess*. In this story, the white captain is described as " . . . a true soldier of fortune, brave as a lion, with fair skin, blue eyes and a bushy yellow beard" (p. 5).

The genre, "White Man as Superhero," reaches its ultimate manifestation when it is connected in the child's mind with the "knight in shining armor." This is exactly the message in *The Indian Princess* where the explorers have just come ashore from their ships bearing "the red cross of St. George on their white sails," and "the armor of their officers shone in the sun" (p. 4). Contrast this with the description of the Native people (in the same book) when John Smith was captured and taken to the Native village to see Powhatan. When he entered the house, "Smith blinked in the reek of the smoke and of the bear's grease with which the Indians dressed their hair and skins." But unlike the perpetually "hunched" Indians, "in spite of his fear he stood up straight and held his head up high" (p. 15).

This same contrasting image is echoed in a contemporary story about a Native boy who lives on an Indian reservation: *Alphonse Has an Accident*. When he gets burnt in a game he and his friend play, which consists of throwing a lighted match into empty oil drums, Alphonse is taken to the hospital in the city. When he awakens in the hospital room, the text continues: "Alphonse had never seen such a nice room all white, and everything so shiny and sparkly" (p. 13). When he sees the nurse, "Alphonse just stared at her. He had never seen anyone so beautiful. The nurse had hair just like the angels in Father Bernard's church window" (p. 11). (She was blonde.) These vividly contrasting images of the white people's world and the Native people's world go a long way toward structuring the social relations between these groups in such a way that the legitimacy of the former precludes the legitimacy of the latter.

The connection between Native people and animals is yet another constant image that contributes to the child's understanding of the Native as inferior, incapable, and unseen. The hegemonic process connects in this image at many levels not the least of which is the white, urban child's relationship to animals both in the urban and rural context. Hence the full force of the constant comparisons between Native people and animals and the analogies, both textual and visual, drawn between their behavior can be understood from this perspective. This is particularly so when, at the same time, those Native cultural practices that depend on the material conditions embedded in a reciprocal relationship between nature and everyday life in the Native village are never addressed.

The repeated reference to the Native people as "hawks" and "wolves" provides an image of stealth, unpredictability, and cunning. First, that these animals often do their hunting under the cover of darkness suggests a cunning that even very young children cannot help but connect to the image of the Native people presented here. And, second, because children's literature is stocked with references to the "Big Bad Wolf," the association is doubly sinister. The description of the white man, on the other hand, as a lion (as is the case in *The Indian Princess*) immediately connects in the child's mind with the "King of Beasts." Statements such as, "like the animals they hunted, the Ojibwa could see far into a thicket and hear even a twig snap," (*Indians,* p. 13) are neither value-free nor inconsequential. The portrayal of Native people as animals (and equally portraying animals as Native people, which many children's books do) denies them their full humanity. It is the worst kind of mystification, which not only contradicts their culture, style of life, social, economic, and political reality, but also denies their very existence as fully human beings. The effect of such portrayals is fully comprehended when it is used not only to justify any kind of offensive and aggressive behavior directed against them, but in fact to contribute to the notion of their nonexistence, hence requiring no political, economic, or social accounting to be taken of their domination.

It is one of the myths and certainly one of the easy rationalizations for harnessing the labor power of one segment of the population by another segment of the population, to claim that those who are thus subjugated do not mind or even prefer their positions of service. The history of the Black races, the history of the working classes, the history of women and certainly the history of Native people are circumscribed by such justifications. Again Berke's *Indians* serves as a good starting point for exploring these images. In a picture called "The End of the Portage" (p. 13), showing a French fur trader and his Native guides and porters, the fur trader is carrying a gun and a knife. The Natives are carrying the canoes and large packs on their backs. However, there is no suggestion as to the negotiations or the conditions under which these relationships were formed between the white men and the Native people.

On the contrary, in a bizarre little book called *Granny and the*

Indians, the negotiations and circumstances under which the Native people become "willing servants" is all too clear. This book deserves a much closer examination than is possible to accomplish here at this time as it provides a litany of stereotypes and distorted and dehumanizing images that require comment. However, in this writing I shall limit myself to the construction of "native as willing servant." As the story opens, Granny, with large determined steps, is heading off toward the woods. Her encounter with a bear is no problem—Superhero Granny "whacked the bear across the nose" with the butt of her gun. There is a befeathered head peering out from behind the bushes as "eyes, Indian eyes, watched Granny." When she sees a rabbit in a trap, Granny removes it to her basket and goes home to make stew. Again, "eyes, Indian eyes, watched her," this time from behind a tree. The next day, when Granny goes berry picking, a big fish leaps out of the river and lands in her basket. The ever present Indian peering out from behind the tree has become " . . . eyes, those *angry* Indian eyes watching her" (italics added). When Granny sees a big fat turkey up in the tree, she aims her gun, although it is not loaded, and pulls the trigger. The turkey falls out of the tree with an arrow in it to which her only response is, "Well do tell!" As Granny sits at her dinner table eating the turkey, there are several Native people looking in her window, eyes squinched, mouths downturned and feathers in place. Their faces without exception are grotesque. But "Granny didn't see those eyes, those angry Indian eyes looking at her."

The next page shows the Native people conferring as to what to do about Granny who is "taking our food." One suggestion is "we could shoot her." But the "chief" does not think that this is a good idea because the people from the town would shoot them in turn. Granny's problems begin when her cabin catches fire. Granny's solution to her problem, however, is not to move to town, or build another cabin. Instead she heads for the Native settlement and announces, "My house has burned down. . . . I'm moving in with you." She moves into their long house, and with the declaration, "This place is a mess! . . . I'll have to fix that," she goes about "cleaning" and rearranging. When the chief implores her to "go home" she answers, "I am home." Lutz's analysis of the imperialist agenda is confirmed at this point as it comes through with full force. This brings us finally to the Native as Willing Servant in the solution that the Native people have devised as a way of dealing with Granny Guntry. They build her a new cabin and when Granny offers to come and cook for them every day so she "won't have to worry about meat for my stew pot," the Native people decide to supply her with meat instead, which they leave daily by the door in a basket.

On the last page we see Granny, with a sly smile on her face saying, "I could have done a lot for those Indians. I'll tell them so when I see them." But of course she never does see the Native people again. Whether this final statement from Granny locates the Native people, as they so often are located, as helpless, irrational, incapable, incompetent, and child-like and hence needing Granny Guntry (or the Department of Native Affairs) to look after them; or whether the imagery and message connect more closely to the Vanished Native, who while he no longer needs to be taken account of still somehow participates, and contributes to procuring "meat for our stew pot," is difficult to decide. Nonetheless, "to the extent that a minority of individuals [Granny], in whose hands rests the control of power and therefore capital, is able . . . to define [and prescribe] the very quality of life of the majority [the Native people in this story] whose only bartering power lies in the sale of their labor [whatever the negotiated currency], the controlling interests hold unprecedented possibilities for manipulating the economic, political, and social context for the realization of their own goals" (Lewis 1977, p. 15). What role text and trade books play in this process is clarified by Anyon: "If school knowledge is examined as a social product, it suggests a great deal about the society that produces and uses it. It reveals which groups have power and demonstrates that the view of these groups is expressed and legitimized in the school curriculum. It can also identify social groups that are not empowered by the economic and social patterns in a society and do not have their views, activities, and priorities represented in the school curriculum" (1979, p. 328). In *Granny and the Indians,* it is clear who belongs to which group.

The Indian Princess falls prey to this same image. In this well known story of Pocahontas, the young Indian girl saved John Smith's life only to be kidnapped on board the British ship and held in ransom for food. She is eventually taken to England where "she was to show that the 'savages' could be civilized" (p. 28). Her "dignified behavior" made her famous throughout London. However, on the last page we are told that since the "Indians had no real resistance to the diseases of Europe" Pocahontas and all her Indian servants (who wore full paint and feathers) soon died. Again there is no sense of conflict or of resistance but only a willingness to be subjugated. Further, that there is something inappropriate about being showcased as the "savages from

America" and being required to dress in religious and ceremonial attire is never questioned. The selective silences echo throughout these books for children. The commodification of a people, not only the sweat of their brow but also their culture, their religion and their emotional, social and psychological life are unproblematically paraded across the pages of these books. Although it is not impossible to use such books and stories for stimulating discussion and for bringing even quite young children to an awareness of the problems inherent in presenting Native history and culture in this way, the sheer authority of colorful, well presented books, and the general unavailability of counter images presented in books of equal quality makes this task rather difficult for the teacher or librarian.

The clichés, in fact, are legion. I have touched here only on the four major themes that permeate the images and that serve as the child's predominant source of knowledge about Native history and culture. Other themes could just as easily have been chosen and they would have yielded equally rich material for discussion. What I have tried to show in this short paper is that these images of Native people are not confined to one book but rather that this version of Native history and culture has a consistency in children's picture books which the child cannot escape. Given the social, political, and economic context within which the publishing industry functions, it is perhaps not surprising that the books, both from the school library and from the public library, were so blatant in their biases and represented often and with noticeable impact the view of the dominant culture. In general, as can be seen, the culturally biased view of the Native peoples is the familiar one often represented through other popular media such as television, consumer items and service industries catering to the tourist trade. These various and wide-ranging vehicles for the dissemination of the popular culture work in remarkable concert to bring forth the accepted version of Native reality.

Although the literature from the public library contained some of the books found at the school library as well as many not found there, there was a small selection of materials that were more subtle in their biases, as well as a small collection of materials that presented a rather different understanding of Native history and culture.[6] Analysis of this material is included in a longer version of this paper. Whether these in fact succeed in showing Native people in a more positive light is not altogether clear since the social, political, and economic forces that created the necessity for presenting a particular view of Native people has not changed substantially over the past one hundred years. Nonetheless these books are a welcome development as they present quite significant counter images to those described above. It seems to me that picture books for children, with regard to bias, ought to serve at least two distinct, but not unrelated, purposes. For the non-Native child, the images presented ought to locate the minority groups in such a sensible and acceptable cultural milieu that the understanding of the characteristics of these cultures locate them as complete and reasonable responses to the life situations of each specific group. For the Native child, these images must provide this same understanding, but beyond it they must also provide a basis from which to counter the realities of bias and prejudice. Because of these apparently divergent interests it is sometimes assumed by both Native and non-Native teachers that it is not possible to present the same images and content to Native and non-Native children. Those who would argue against presenting the same images to Native and non-Native children do so on the premise that Native children must be reimmersed in a Native framework in order to be able to understand the Native culture which they have to a large degree lost. Conversely, then, it is contended that it makes no sense to require of non-Native children the same level of immersion into a commitment to the culture, as would be required to Native children, just as it would make no sense to require them to immerse themselves in Judaism or Christianity or Buddhism if these do not represent their ancestry. Nonetheless, the results of such an examination, as in this paper, clearly points to the conclusion that "To the extent that the needs of the social, economic, and political institutions take precedence over the needs of the individuals who are involved in them, society demands that the function of education should be to integrate individuals into accepting, either consciously or unconsciously, the human relationships inherent in the system. Education, therefore, is used as a manipulative device whereby individuals are prepared to adjust to the world in its context of social, political, and economic relations, while systematically denying them the possibility to critically perceive these relations and to critically respond to them" (Lewis 1977, p. 110). But it must not be forgotten that at the same time, as Anyon says: "The school curriculum as a major contributor to social attitudes can be used to change those attitudes. To argue that ideologies influence behavior is to accord real power to symbols and symbolic forms in education. Just as the public school curriculum has hereto supported patterns of power and domination, so can it be used to foster autonomy and social change" (1979, p. 385). It is on this terrain that the struggle for social justice must be contested.

NOTES

1. I wish to acknowledge Roger Simon for his support and useful criticisms of an earlier draft of this paper; and also Joel Taxel for his welcome comments.
2. In my efforts to trace how books eventually make their way to a library shelf I spoke to several people in bookstores; the reference library for all Canadian books published in the last decade; the Writers' Union of Canada; Book and Periodical Development Council; the Freelance Editors' Association of Canada; and some school and public librarians. While these contacts were all undocumented telephone or personal conversations, the general consensus of my discussions with them seemed to be that anything a publisher thinks will sell will get published. The decisions are made based on general and subjective judgments as to what the buying public will or will not accept. With regard to discussions about censorship it was generally felt that if counter positions needed to be presented, it would be incumbent upon someone to write a book from this different perspective and have it published. Whether this is in fact possible, given the vagaries of the economics governing the publishing industry, was not addressed by the respondents to my questions. [See my comments in footnote twenty-five in the *Introduction.* – Ed.]
3. Some of this work has been undertaken in a longer version of this paper.
4. "Myth does not deny things, on the contrary, its function is to talk about them; simply it purifies them, it makes them innocent, it gives them a natural and eternal justification, it gives them a clarity which is not that of an explanation but that of a statement of fact. If I *state the fact* of French imperiality without explaining it, I am very near to finding that it is natural and goes *without saying:* 1 am assured" (Barthes 1982, p. 143).
5. What is surprising about many of these books is the copyright dates – these are not books of the era of *Little Black Sambo.* The least recent book I looked at was published in 1960 – except for a single reference to a book published in 1959 – and the others published far more recently than that.
6. I have marked these books with an * in the Book List. For a perspective on the debate as to whether Native authorship is important – indeed essential for presenting culturally and historically unbiased materials in children's literature, the

following two articles should be looked at: Byler (1974, pp. 36–39) and Rockwood (1982, pp. 1–5).

BOOK LIST

*Armstrong, Jeannette C. *Enwhisteetkwa: Walk In Water.* Okanagan Indian Curriculum Project, Penticton, 1982.

Berke, Ernest. *The North American Indian.* New York: Doubleday and Company, 1963.

Border, Rosemary. *The Indian Princess.* London: MacDonal Educational Limited, 1978.

Carroll, Ruth and Latrobe. *Tough Enough's Indians.* New York: Henry Z. Walck Inc., 1960.

*Dewdney, Selwyn. *The Hungry Time.* Toronto: James Lorimer and Co., Publishers, 1980.

*Dolby, Lois, and Jeannette McCrie. *The New Baby.* Winnipeg: Peguis Publishers, n.d.

Football, Virginia. *Tsequa and the Chief's Son.* Dogrib Legends, Programme Development Division, Department of Education, Northwest Territories, 1974.

*Fox, Mary Lou. *Why the Beaver Has a Broad Trail.* Manitoulin Island, Ont.: Ojibwe Cultural Foundation, 1974.

*– – –. *How the Bees Got Their Stingers.* Manitoulin Island, Ont.: Ojibwe Cultural Foundation, 1977.

Friskey, Margaret. *Indian Two Feet and His Horse.* Chicago: Children's Press, 1959.

– – –. *Indian Two Feet and His Eagle Feather.* Chicago: Children's Press, 1961.

Hamilton, Mary. *The Sky Caribou.* Toronto: Peter Martin Associates, 1980.

Hiebert, Susan. *Alphonse Has an Accident.* Winnipeg: Peguis Publishers, 1974.

Parish, Peggy. *Granny and the Indians.* New York: Macmillan, 1969.

Pluckrose, Henry. *Plains Indians.* Toronto: Gloucester Press, 1980.

Russell, Don. *Sioux Buffalo Hunters.* New York: Meredith Press, 1962.

Stuart, Gene S. *Three Little Indians.* National Geographic Society, 1974.

Wellman, Paul I. *Indian Wars and Warriors: West.* Boston: Houghton Mifflin Company, 1959.

WORKS CITED

Anyon, Jean. "Ideology and United States History Textbooks." *Harvard Educational Review* 49, no. 3 (August 1979).
– – –. "Social Class and School Knowledge." *Curriculum Inquiry* 11, no.1 (1981). Toronto: Ontario Institute for Studies in Education.
– – –. "Social Class and the Hidden Curriculum of Work." *Journal of Education* (Boston) 162, no. 1 (Winter 1980).
Apple, M. W. *Ideology and Curriculum.* London: Routledge and Kegan Paul, 1979.
Barthes, Roland. *Mythologies.* Toronto: Granada Publishing, 1982.
Byler, Mary Gloyne. "The Image of American Indians Projected by Non-Indian Writers." *School Library Journal* (Feb. 1974).
Council on Interracial Books for Children. *Unlearning "Indian Stereotypes."* New York: 1977.
Derman-Sparks, Louise, et al. "Children, Race, and Racism: How Race Awareness Develops." *Interracial Books for Children Bulletin* 11, nos. 3 and 4 (1980).
Falcon, Nieves. "The Oppressive Function of Values, Concepts, and Images in Children's Books." In *The Slant of the Pen: Racism in Children's Books,* edited by Roy Preiswick. Geneva: World Council of Churches, 1980.
Giroux, Henry. *Ideology, Culture, and the Process of Schooling.* London: Falmer Press, 1981
– – –. *Theory and Resistance in Education.* Massachusetts: Bergin and Garvey Publishers, Inc., 1983.
Gitlin, Todd. "Television's Screens: Hegemony in Transition." In *Cultural and Economic Reproduction in Education,* edited by Michael Apple. London: Routledge and Kegan Paul, 1982.
Lewis, Magda. *Some Implications of Paulo Freire's Philosophical and Pedagogical Approach for Canadian Education.* Master's Thesis. Univ. of Toronto, 1977.
Lutz, Hartmut. "The Image of the American Indian in German Literature." *Interracial Books for Children Bulletin* 10, nos. 1 and 2 (1979): 17–18.
– – –. "Indians Through German vs. U.S. Eyes." *Interracial Books for Children Bulletin* 12, no. 1 (1981): 3–8.
Rockwood, Joyce. "Can Novelists Portray Other Cultures Fairly." *The Advocate* (Univ. of Georgia) 2, no. 1 (Fall 1982): 1–5.
Seale, Doris. "Bibliographies About Native Americans – A Mixed

Blessing." *Interracial Books for Children Bulletin* 12, no. 3 (1981): 11–15.

Taxel, Joel. "Justice and Cultural Conflict: Racism, Sexism, and Instructional Materials." *Interchange* 9, no. 1 (1978–79).

———. "The Outsiders of the American Revolution: The Selective Tradition in Children's Fiction." *Interchange* 12, nos. 2–3 (1981).

Wexler, Philip. "Structure, Text, and Subject: A Critical Sociology of School Knowledge." In *Cultural and Economic Reproduction in Education,* edited by Michael Apple. London: Routledge and Kegan Paul, 1982.

Williams, Raymond. *Marxism and Literature.* Oxford: Oxford Univ. Press, 1977.

Willis, Paul. *Learning to Labor.* New York: Columbia Univ. Press, 1977.

Wright, Will. *Sixguns and Society: A Structural Study of the Western.* Berkeley: Univ. of California Press, 1975.

Part 5. Whose History?

The American Revolution in Children's Books: Issues of Race and Class

Joel Taxel

The American Revolution is taught in every U.S. school, and the colonists' struggle to attain "liberty and freedom" is impressed upon every child. Given the stress placed upon this aspect of U.S. history, it is instructive to see what other messages children get when they read about the Revolution.

This article examines the messages about race and class that appear in thirty-two children's novels about the Revolution. It should be noted at the outset that this piece looks only at the portrayal of Blacks, although the books' messages about Native Americans also merit examination. Also deserving of analysis but not covered in this piece is the portrayal of women in these books.

The sample consists of books recommended by selection tools (Wilson's *Children's Catalog*, Brodart's *Elementary School Library Collection*, etc.), which school and public librarians frequently consult before purchasing books. Thus, the sample contains the books which young readers are most likely to read on the subject. In addition, because the books were published over a seventy-seven year period (1899–1976), it is possible to trace attitudinal changes over those years. An understanding of how race and class are treated in this sample is important because of the subject matter – a revolution fought to advance human liberty and freedom. The fact

Reprinted from *Interracial Books for Children Bulletin*, 12, nos. 7/8 (1982): 3–9 by permission of the publisher.

Joel Taxel is Assistant Professor, Department of Language Education, University of Georgia. Dr. Taxel is the editor of the new children's literature journal, *The New Advocate*.

that almost all of the authors exhibit race and class bias even as they repeat the impassioned, ideologically charged language used to justify the Revolution, points up some of the contradictory and still unresolved facets in our national legacy and our social agenda.

The racial stereotyping in the books under scrutiny (see list at end of article) is appalling. In fact, it is not until *When the World's on Fire,* published in 1973 and chronologically the twenty-eighth book in this thirty-two book sample, that one finds a Black character who is not a slave or servant (although there were in fact many free people) or who does not share some or all of the characteristics of the Sambo stereotype. Blacks are described as "bug-eyed," "apish," cowering, and superstitious with "flashing" smiles.[1] While some authors display considerable paternalism toward Blacks (e.g., Perkins and Hawthorne), others seem to take active and conscious delight in derogating Black characters. One reads of "little monkey niggers" (Boyd, pp. 142–145, 176), "little black monkeys" and "little black imps" (Gray, pp. 106, 197), and "Sambo" (Hawthorne, p. 93).

One soon realizes how oblivious most writers have been to what has been termed the "central paradox of American history"—the fact that the Revolutionary movement for liberty and independence occurred at the very time slavery was being institutionalized in many colonies. Most writers failed to see the irony inherent in depicting white characters who are both slaveholders and champions of freedom, liberty, and independence. In *Meggy MacIntosh,* for example, Scottish-born Meggy must choose between Scottish Highlanders who remain loyal to King George and those "fighting for freedom and their homes" (p. 261). Meggy, of course, chooses those whose "battle cry is 'liberty or death'." But she is never shown to consider the compatibility of these goals with the fact that "everybody had a nigger servant[2] just for himself" (p. 72).

Rising Thunder offers a similar situation. A character ill-disposed to submit to "oppression and injustice" waxes eloquent on "the struggle for freedom" and "the right to be a man amid equals" (p. 5), yet he is himself a slaveholder.[3] At one point the author appears ready to confront this contradiction when she notes that many important families were bankrupt due, in part, to the fact that many slaves "had run off to join the British, having been promised freedom as a reward." We then learn that these slaves found "freedom of a sort" when smallpox "swept the Blacks like a great scythe into their graves" (pp. 209–210). This point is discussed no further, and it would appear that divine retribution had been visited on these helpless souls for having had the audacity to covet the very thing their masters were fighting and dying to secure.

There are other instances where authors come face to face with this contradiction only to back down. In *Silver for General Washington,* twelve-year-old Gilbert Emmett returns to his home in occupied Philadelphia hoping to smuggle out the family silver in order to contribute it to the impoverished American army. He is greeted by Ezra, the faithful family slave, who has not only been steadfastly guarding the family house, but has also devised a scheme to remove the silver. Referring to a local innkeeper who will assist them, Ezra notes that he is an "honest man" who is "workin in secret against the pesky Britishers, jes like everybody else who wants to be free" (p. 178). Whether Ezra and his wife Martha are to remain slaves after this freedom is won and the entire question of the status and role of Blacks in the struggle are issues the author never addresses.

In *Rebel Siege,* Kinross McKenzie meets York, a Black slave, near an army encampment. Asked what it is like to be a slave, York replies that he is well fed, well treated, and grateful he doesn't have to go fight "no Tories, an' get shot like so many white gen'man Is seen ca'ied to this house. But," York wistfully concludes, "I guess it would be nice not to be owned" (p. 205). The sympathetic protagonist, however, never again inquires about York's thought and feelings. This scene suggests the author's discomfort with the issue, but it is by no means certain that he fully appreciates the irony of a slave fighting for whites' liberty. Consider the following statement made by Kin's father only one page before our first glimpse of slaves "toiling in the fields":

> . . . *Here the common man has been assessed at what he is worth, an' not at what some accident of birth seems to make him worth.* This is an army o' common men, goin' forth to fight what they know is tyranny. (p. 201, emphasis added)

Apparently, it did not occur to the author that race is also an "accident of birth" that should not be considered when assessing an individual's worth.

Battle Lanterns provides the most dramatic case in which the blessings of liberty are seen to apply only to whites. The double standard is made clear by Bill Barlow, the novel's hero, who fights with those who believe that "liberty is the only thing in the world worth fighting for to the death," yet he is able to accept "Negro slavery as a matter of fact" (pp. 10, 81). Bill and a group of slaves, including a Black man named Luke, are taken to a West Indian island where they are all enslaved. Despite protestations that he is "free and white" (p. 69) and can't be made a slave, Bill is forced to labor against his will. Thanks to Luke, Bill survives the ordeal and learns some painful truths about freedom and liberty. He and Luke make a miraculous escape and return to fight with Francis Marion's forces.

The remarkable thing about this episode is the way Luke ultimately attains his freedom. One might have supposed that Luke would have automatically been freed because of his actions, the ideals of the struggle and the function this island ordeal serves in the novel. Instead, there is a complicated, legalistic explanation concluding that Luke can be freed *only* because he has become Bill's property as a result of the fortunes of war. These legalisms are scrupulously observed by men who, at that very moment, had conveniently cast aside the legal authority of the Crown that had governed the colonies for well over a century.

This discussion becomes more readily comprehensible when seen in the context of the author's racial attitudes. Early in the novel, the author laments the fact that the conflict is between "men of one's own race" (p. 5). Later, Francis Marion speaks of "race suicide" and laments "Anglo-Saxons slaughtering each other when they should be standing together against the rest of the world" (p. 24). The author's racial attitudes become quite clear at the conclusion of the book when Luke explains why he has decided to return to Africa: "Dat de place for a black man. De lawd put black folkes in Africa an' white folkes some udder place like yo' plant rice in de water an' cohn on dry lan'. Yo' mix 'em an' yo git a crop ob trouble" (p. 258).

The first book in the sample to mention the paradox under discussion is Rebecca Caudill's *Tree of Freedom,* a 1949 book detailing the war's impact on a family settling in Kentucky in the spring of 1780. Stephanie Venable, the novel's protagonist, carries with her the seed of an apple tree, itself the fruit of a tree her Huguenot grandmother, Marguerite de Monchard, had brought from France. This "tree of freedom" symbolizes the continuity between the past and current struggles for freedom, since the Huguenots themselves had fled Europe "because they refused to forsake their religion and make slaves of their consciences." Much to Marguerite's dismay, many of the same "liberty loving" Huguenots "began enslaving others as soon as they found a refuge in [the] new world" (p. 87). The de Monchards, however, are so appalled by slavery that they use their entire fortune to buy and free as many slaves as they can. Their money and friends gone, and having made a dent on the institution of slavery "so little a body couldn't see it even with a spy glass trained on it" (p. 89), the de Monchards flee Charleston painfully aware of the bitter, costly fruit Marguerite's tree of freedom had borne.

Tree of Freedom is also the first book in the sample that contains an explicit denunciation of slavery and states the need to guard against making "any deal with slavery of any sort" (p. 142). Earlier books, as we have seen, not only avoid the issue, but treat treat Blacks so stereotypically that their exclusion from participation in the great issues of the day seems to be a logical outgrowth of their "obvious inferiority." Furthermore, they seem so contented with their place and appear to be so well treated that, given their limited potential, they really needn't ask for more!

The pejorative view of Blacks presented in these early books is consistent with both the societal attitudes of the periods in which they were written and the roles to which Blacks were consigned. Segregation was still in effect and overt discrimination received important ideological support from diverse sectors of society, including historians.[4] For example, U. B. Phillip's view of the "peculiar institution" of slavery as a benign and benevolent institution designed to bring the blessings of civilization to an "inert and backward" people continued to hold sway, although his position was not unchallenged.[5] The point here is that the books were consistent with and served to reinforce the blatantly racist ideology pervading U.S. society.

It is also interesting at this point to note that there was far more consciousness of the questions raised by a growing slave presence at the time of the Revolution than these authors would have us believe. The issue here is not simply one of damning authors who worked in a markedly different social and historical context. The important point is that at the time of the Revolution many whites and certainly most Blacks *were* highly conscious of the paradox posed by slavery and freedom and that the failure of so many of the books in the sample to even mention the issue indicates that these authors reflect their own perspective far more than historical reality.

In one of the landmark studies in the historiography of the Revolution, J. Franklin Jameson asked a series of questions which go to the heart of the issue under consideration:

> How could men who were engaged in a great and inspiring struggle for liberty fail to perceive the inconsistency between their professions and endeavors in that contest and their actions

with respect to their bondsmen? How could they fail to see the application of their doctrines respecting the rights of man to the black men who were held among them in bondage far more reprehensible than that to which they indignantly proclaimed themselves to have been subjected by the King of Great Britain?[6]

In answer, Jameson notes that the colonists *did* see the disparity between their rhetoric and their actions in regard to Blacks. Indeed, he points out that "there is no lack of evidence that, in the American world of that time, the analogy between freedom for whites and freedom for Blacks was seen."[7] To illustrate this point, Jameson quotes from a letter by Patrick Henry, whose fiery words on behalf of freedom are among the best remembered of an era noted for its impassioned rhetoric:

Is it not amazing that at a time when the rights of humanity are defined and understood with precision, in a country above all fond of liberty, that in such an age and in such a country we find men professing a religion, the most humane, mild, gentle and generous, adopting a principle as repugnant to humanity as it is inconsistent with the Bible and destructive of liberty? . . . Would anyone believe I am a master of slaves of my own purchase. *I am drawn along by the general inconvenience of living without them. I will not, I cannot justify it.* However culpable my conduct, I will so far pay my devoir to virtue, as to own the excellence and rectitude of her precepts, and lament my want of conformity to them. (Henry, quoted by Jameson, p. 22; emphasis added)

In fact, although Jefferson's attempt to include a passage denouncing slavery in the Declaration of Independence was defeated, there was significant support for abolition in the colonies. Nevertheless, an overwhelming majority of books in this sample ignored this, making it seem as though the issue of freedom for Blacks and the questions it raised were never entertained either by the white majority or Blacks themselves. The latter point is especially important because these novels also leave the reader with the distinct impression that Blacks were unconcerned and did little to advance their own freedom.[8] Such a belief has, in fact, provided important ideological support for the paternalistic white belief that Blacks are, and have been, incapable of thinking and fending for themselves; it constitutes an important component of the stereotype of the carefree, indolent Black.

If those writing prior to the publication of *Tree of Freedom* were part of a society dominated by the ideologies of white supremacy and Black inferiority, later authors wrote during an era when these ideas came under assault. This is especially true of the sixties and the seventies, when the civil rights movement dominated public consciousness. Given this, it is surprising how little influence the movement had on the books in the sample.

Of the books published after *Tree of Freedom*, those written by Beers, Cavanna, Fast, Fritz, Lawson, Savery, Snow, and Wibberly contain not a single Black character. Several books—*Who Comes to King's Mountain?*, *My Brother Sam is Dead* and two titles by Finlayson—do contain minor Black characters fighting for the American cause, but the authors never give any indication of why they chose to do so given the whites' at best ambiguous attitude about slavery.

While more recent books are free of the vicious stereotyping characteristic of earlier titles, the absence of Black characters and the lack of discussion of the "Black issue" suggest that the authors were still unable or unwilling to deal with the contradictions posed by the Black presence. No longer able to simply dismiss Blacks because of their "inferiority," recent authors instead avoid the issue, either by eliminating Black characters altogether or by casting them in secondary roles. This dismissal of the Black issue can be explained, in large part, by the conception which the authors have of the Revolution, one which sees it as being almost exclusively concerned with the issue of independence from Britain. As I have demonstrated elsewhere,[9] this focus on the issue of "home rule" fails to consider the internal aspects of the Revolution and the impact it had on the status of "outsider" groups such as Blacks, women, Native Americans, and lower-class whites.

The only book in the sample that demonstrates concern with such outsiders and confronts the myth of Black apathy is Sally Edwards' *When the World's on Fire*. This is also the only book with a Black protagonist. Edwards paints a poignant picture of the tragic situation so many Blacks confronted during the Revolution. Could they trust either the British or the Americans, both of whom understood the vital role Black soldiers could play and who, therefore, made promises they either couldn't or wouldn't keep? Recognizing this dilemma, the unforgettable Maum Kate angrily states that:

> The Americans promise freedom, if only we will ride and fight with them in the swamps. The Americans babble about liberty—yet it is only their own liberty they dream of, not

ours. And the British, the most civilized of men, promise freedom only to enslave the slaves. We lose either way. (p. 101)[10]

Maum Kate's greatest rage is, however, voiced as she speaks of the Declaration of Independence:

> What beautiful words the white men write—life, liberty and the pursuit of happiness. Four men from Charleston signed that declaration. Yet their slaves are still slaves, serving at tables, toiling in the fields. (p. 101)

Although Maum Kate "does not blame all white people for slavery" (p. 102), there is little notice given to those whites who saw the tragedy and paradox posed by the Black dilemma and struggled to attain liberty and justice for all. Edwards' narrative is instead directed at showing Blacks engaged in bold and successful action on behalf of their own freedom. Again, it is the fiery Maum Kate who gets to the heart of the matter when she delivers the most decisive—in fact, the only—affirmation of Black humanity and strength to be found in all of these books:

> We are too easily fooled by so much talk of liberty. Yet we have our own strength, our own spirit. And someday this spirit will shine so brightly the sun will seem a feeble candle. (p. 102)

Despite having something refreshingly "new" to say about the Revolution, *When the World's on Fire* was permitted to go out of print after only two printings, a fact that might lead one to infer that the novel was simply too iconoclastic, too "out of sync" with the commonly held conception of the Revolution to remain in print.

Later authors, who *must* have been aware of the paradox, chose to avoid the issue. Blacks, however, are not the only group shown to be excluded from the promises of the Revolution.[11] This is also true of those who constituted the faceless mob or "rabble" that is often mentioned but rarely discussed in these novels.

Because authors rarely speak explicitly in terms of class, it is far more difficult to analyze the role played by social class in these novels than is the case with race. Thus, information about social class must be inferred from dress, manner of speech, overall living conditions, etc., rather than from direct attribution. Nevertheless, it is possible to arrive at some fairly explicit conclusions that reinforce the belief that cultural artifacts tend to reflect the dominant group's perspective.

Such a thesis is borne out most strikingly by the extent to which the novels' protagonists are drawn from the middle and especially the upper classes of society. Many of these upper-class champions of liberty are rarely shown to be sympathetic to those less fortunate than they, and they often disparage those below them on the social scale. Furthermore, those lower-class characters we do meet are often depicted as being uncouth, overly zealous and prone to violence! See, for example, the way Beers, Boyd, Crownfield, Collier and Collier, Finlayson, Ford and Fritz depict certain groups, including the "Liberty Boys."

The earlier books in the sample are especially dominated by characters who come from wealthy families owning large estates and slaves. Squire Meredith in *Janice Meredith,* for example, owns a 20,000-acre estate and is a man of great power and prominence in his community. Likewise, John Fraser in *Drums* is "above the common rank," holds several key positions in his community, owns several slaves, and wants his son to be a gentleman of learning as well as birth (p. 3). The Abbotts in *Continental Dollar* are a family of considerable means and have many "dependent servants," while the Priestlys in *American Twins of the Revolution* have a large estate with barns and "servants' " quarters one-half mile from the spacious family residence. Reba Stanhope in *Freedom's Daughter* lives among the "prosperous and influential class" in Philadelphia (p. 3), as do the Emmetts in *Silver for General Washington,* who have two slaves, a fashionable house and enough silver to make a dent in the mounting debt being incurred by the Continental army. The Jouetts in *Rising Thunder* own a prosperous tavern, race horses, and fields worked by slaves. Even the impoverished Johnny Tremain in *Johnny Tremain* is an heir to the considerable fortune of the Lyte family. Meggy MacIntosh in *Meggy MacIntosh,* though orphaned and without means of support, is from an upper-class family that was ruined when her father sided with Prince Charles in the Scottish Revolution. Despite her precarious position, Meggy owns jewelry and uses it to purchase an indentured servant. In a similar vein, *Battle Lanterns'* Bill Barlow, though penniless throughout the novel, searches and eventually finds a buried treasure bequeathed to him by his merchant father.

This pattern also holds for later books in the sample. If we exclude books set in the frontier settlements where class was less important, more ambiguous and difficult to define, we have only two protagonists—Harry Warrilow in *Redcoat in Boston* and Annie McGee in *When the World's on Fire*—who are from the poor, propertyless, dispossessed classes of society. Annie, the protagonist, is a slave, while Harry is a British soldier who enlisted in England after being orphaned and near starvation. Thus, there is not a single leading character in the sample who is an American-born, lower-class white. There are some secondary characters who fit this description; but, in contrast to the protagonists, they are often depicted as being shoddy, untrustworthy and, at times, even worse. Other characters, like the blacksmith Isaac Huntoon in *Freedom's Daughter,* are seen as good and well meaning if somewhat lacking in intelligence and judgment. When Sargeant Jasper, in *Battle Lanterns,* turns down a sword of honor and a commission in reward for his heroism, he is lauded as a "hero and a sensible man." Jasper had reasoned that he passed "well enough with the boys, but effen I had a c'mission I'd have to keep higher company" (pp. 32–33).

The crucial point here is that the leading characters — those readers invariably identify with — are drawn almost exclusively from the dominant classes. Furthermore, where lower-class characters are depicted, they are usually seen in a less than positive light if they are white and vilified if they are Black.

Interestingly, the few times when the issue of class is explicitly discussed, it is in a context designed to illustrate either the difference in American attitudes toward class or, more precisely, that class in the European sense of the term is not really relevant to life in the colonies. Differences between British and American attitudes toward class are rather clearly illustrated by Johnny Tremain's friendship with Lieutenant Strange of the British army. This friendship provides Johnny with puzzling encounters with British class consciousness. While the young officer is "proud and class-conscious enough when they met indoors," once they are both in the saddle for their riding lessons, "they were equals" (p. 201). Johnny becomes quite attached to the Lieutenant but is disturbed by the officer's attitudes: "Indoors he was rigidly a British soldier and a 'gentleman' and Johnny an inferior. This shifting about puzzled Johnny. It did not seem to puzzle the British officer at all" (p. 203).

Rebecca Ransome in *Rebecca's War* is similarly bewildered when Fitch, a servant, refuses to sit down and join her for a cup of tea because "it is not suitable that we should eat at the same table." Thinking that he means that such an action would constitute "consorting with the enemy," Rebecca is surprised to learn that Fitch's refusal actually stems from a conviction that it would be improper if she, "the young lady of the house," should share a table with a servant. "Rebecca, who had been eating at the same table with Ursula [an indentured servant] and her predecessors for fourteen years, couldn't make head or tail of that. The English did have some curious ideas about things" (p. 92).

The irrelevance of the European idea of inherited class position is suggested in several other books. Early in the *Green Cockade,* the author notes that Squire Stonebridge and his wife had "little financial wealth" but were "rich in imagination, health, and courage." In "Old England they would have been middle class by inheritance." However, in the forests of New England, "class was established by brain and muscle," and the Squire "looked up to no one" (p. 14). The subsequent discussion serves to point out that while the colonists considered themselves loyal subjects of the King, the tradition the King represented meant much less to them than it had to their ancestors. Indeed, central to the author's concept of the Revolution is the belief that men and women who "of their own initiative . . . fought and worked for their homes" should not be subject to the rule of those thousands of miles away. This discussion makes clear the importance that contrasting visions of society played in leading men like Squire Stonebridge to believe that "they could manage their affairs if, for some reason, all monarchs went out of business" (pp. 13–14). This position does, however, conflict with the Squire's later insistence that his wife ride a horse with a pillion, as "befitted one of her station" (p. 59).

The absence of a clearly defined hereditary class is also alluded to in *Redcoat in Boston.* On a "deserted patrol" outside of Boston, the British soldier Harry Warrilow overhears a lieutenant's comment that he'd seen nothing all day that could be called "a gentleman's seat." Harry mumbles to himself that "he'd not seen anything that could be called a hovel, either" (p. 65), a reference to the sharp contrast in the living conditions of English peasants and lords. This point is made even more strongly later in the novel when Harry considers "buying out" of the army and heading West. Once again, Harry contrasts conditions in the colonies to those in England:

> England was full of men who had farmed all their lives and couldn't point to an acre of soil that belonged to them. But here, with all the wilderness to fill, even a Northampton sweep could search out a choice bit, build a cabin [and] clear some ground. (p. 229)

Despite a paucity of specific information provided about social class, it is clear that the books present the Revolution from the perspective of the dominant classes in colonial society. Although several books point out that colonial America provided unprecedented opportunity for personal advancement, they stop short of explicitly pointing out that this greater freedom was restricted to whites, and even then, not to all whites. And, of course, none mention that this "advancement" was achieved at the expense of Native peoples who were either killed or dispossessed.

The books also ignore the existence of growing unemployment and urban unrest among those classes who ultimately provided so much of the support for the colonial cause. Many books like *Freedom's Daughter, Crystal Cornerstone, Early Thunder* and *Redcoat in Boston* negatively portray the often violent actions of the urban "mobs" without placing these actions in any context. *John Treegate's Musket* is, in fact, the only book to provide an explanation for the mob's discontent and behavior (pp. 86, 183). There is, however, no major character from this group, so the discussion of their plight *(e.g.,* persistent and rising unemployment in Boston) tends to form the background of this book rather than its substance. By always presenting an upper- and middle-class perspective, these books tend to imply a universality for these particular experiences, when, in fact, other groups had markedly different perceptions of and involvement with the issues.

In an essay that attempts to see the Revolution "from the bottom up," Jesse Lemisch notes that social scientists have persisted in drawing conclusions about entire societies "on the basis of examinations of the minority on the top." He points out that such an approach has "distorted our view and, sometimes, cut us off from past reality." Therefore, Lemisch notes, we tend to view "our earliest history . . . as a period of consensus and classlessness in part because our historians have chosen to see it that way."[12] By focusing almost exclusively on the perspectives of those who dominated colonial America and by ignoring the life conditions and roles played by those both white and Black on the bottom of society in fermenting the Revolution, the books in the sample serve to reinforce the image of America as a classless society free of deeply rooted conflict. Furthermore, what conflict we do see is usually depicted as stemming from a lack of judgment and restraint on the part of those possessing an insufficient regard for the rights, feelings, and property of others.

While it is undoubtedly true that Revolutionary America promised freedom, it is also true that significant segments of society were excluded from this promise.[13] Because the experiences of this significant segment are either derogated, minimized or eliminated altogether, these books tend to give a rather distorted and biased view of the Revolution – and of colonial society.

The books also present some ambiguous and contradictory messages. The most significant of these is the identification and legitimation of hierarchical relations in the formal structure of the novel, which is then denied at the level of content when the Revolution is explained as an historical event (i.e., as a struggle for freedom and liberty for all). The extent to which young readers become aware of this contradiction needs investigation beyond the scope of this paper. Nevertheless, it does seem likely that such a contradiction is seen by only the most mature readers, and the fact that the novels repeat the perspective of middle- to upper-class whites may lead readers to conclude that such experiences were far more common than they, in fact, were. The books may be said to contribute to the acceptance of what has been termed "the legend of equality of opportunity and the idea of [the U.S. as] a classless society."[14] These myths provide crucial ideological support to a social system which can hardly be said to provide equal opportunities to all of its members.

The authors of these materials have consistently omitted – and often slandered – the points of view of social groups whose history, not coincidentally, has been marked by powerlessness and oppression. A basic claim made here is that the treatment of Blacks, women, and lower-class groups in curricular materials not only reflects this powerlessness but may also encourage ideologies and attitudes that provide important support to, and justification of, racism, sexism, and the inequitable distribution of social and economic power and resources. Clearly, writing, incorporating and transmitting the history of *all* people must be seen as one of the great challenges confronting us today.

NOTES

1. For a discussion of how Charles Waddell Chesnutt, a militant nineteenth century Black author, dealt with the Sambo stereotype, see my article entitled "Charles Waddell Chesnutt's Sambo: Myth and Reality" in *Negro American Literature Forum* 9 (1975), 105–108.
2. "Servant" is a commonly used euphemism for slave in the books.

3. When Jack prepares to return to active duty, he remarks matter-of-factly to his father that he'll have little trouble managing without him as the "crops are doing fine and the niggers are all in good condition" (p. 186).

4. J. W. Blassingame, while noting efforts of young scholars in the 1960's to find a "usable Black past," referred to this movement as "a dramatic shift from the conspiracy of silence, vituperation and misrepresentation of historians bent on preserving white supremacy." See "The Afro-Americans: From Mythology to Reality" in *The Reinterpretation of American History and Culture* (Washington, D.C.: NCSS, 1973).

5. See, for example, H. Aptheker's *American Negro Slave Revolts* (New York: Columbia Univ. Press, 1943) and K. Stampp's *The Peculiar Institution: Slavery in the Ante-Bellum South* (New York: Knopf, 1956).

6. J. F. Jameson, *The American Revolution Considered as a Social Movement* (Princeton, N.J.: Princeton Univ. Press, 1940), 21.

7. Ibid.

8. This is precisely the point made by *Rifles for Washington* when one of the characters is said to be "moved . . . to perpetual amusement" by the numbers and appearance of the slaves left alone at work in the fields. "The cage door's open," Andy says, "again and again" (p. 298). Andy's amusement stems from the fact that these slaves do not flee.

In *Battle Lanterns,* the hero, Bill Barlow, is reunited with the Black slave, Luke, on a remote section of the island where they are both held in bondage. Although Luke is older and physically stronger than Bill, he sees Bill's arrival as a sign from God. Luke, seemingly incapable of fending for himself, says "he gwane fotch us outen of Egyp' yet" (p. 187).

In *The American Revolution: Explorations in the History of American Radicalism* (DeKalb, Ill.: Northern Illinois Univ. Press, 1976), A. F. Young notes that of the approximately 500,000 Blacks in the colonies, "a very small minority took up arms for, or aided the patriot cause, a much larger group . . . aided the British and the largest number of all voted with their feet against either side, that is, they fled to freedom under whatever circumstances they could" (p. 452).

9. J. Taxel, *The Depiction of the American Revolution in Children's Fiction: A Study in the Sociology of School Knowledge* (PhD. diss., Univ. of Wisconsin, Madison, 1980).

10. In the epilogue, the author notes that in the year 1783, the year of the final British defeat, English merchants received 1,700,000 pounds of sterling for the sale of American slaves. She also points out that despite promises of freedom made to Blacks by the Americans, "with few exceptions, the Patriot slaves were returned, voluntarily and otherwise, to their former masters" (pp. 123–124).

11. A similar case could be made for the way in which Native Americans and women are treated in the novels. See, for example, F. Jennings, "The Indian's Revolution" in A. Young, ed., *The American Revolution: Explorations in the History of American Radicalism* (DeKalb, Ill.: Northern Illinois Univ. Press, 1976) and J. H. Wilson, "The Illusion of Change: Women in the American Revolution" in the same work.

12. J. Lemisch, "The American Revolution Seen from the Bottom Up" in B. Bernstein, ed., *Towards a New Past: Dissenting Essays in American History* (New York: Vintage Books, 1969), 5.

13. Lemisch (see above), for example, notes that "increasingly colonial Boston was less a place of equality and opportunity, more a place of social stratification. Throughout American property qualifications excluded more and more people from voting until a Jacksonian Revolution was necessary to overthrow what had become a very limited middle-class 'democracy' indeed" (p. 8). Property qualifications to vote are not mentioned in any book in the sample.

14. R. Thursfeld, "Developing the Ability to Think" in the seventeenth *NCSS Yearbook* (Washington, D.C.: NCSS, 1947).

BOOKS EXAMINED IN THIS STUDY

Allen, M.P. *Battle Lanterns.* Longmans, Green & Co., 1949.

Allen, M.P. *Green Cockade.* Longmans, Green & Co., 1942.

Altsheler, J. *The Scouts of the Valley.* Appleton-Century Crofts, 1911.

Beatty, J., and P. Beatty. *Who Comes to King's Mountain?* William Morrow & Co., 1975.

Beers, L. *The Crystal Cornerstone.* Harper & Row, 1953.

Boyd, J. *Drums.* Charles Scribner's Sons, 1925.

Caudill, R. *Tree of Freedom.* Viking, 1949.

Cavanna, B. *Ruffles and Drums.* William Morrow & Co., 1975.

Collier, J. L., and C. Collier. *My Brother Sam Is Dead.* Scholastic Book Co., 1974.

Crownfield, G. *Freedom's Daughter.* E.P. Dutton, 1930.

Edmonds, W. D. *Wilderness Clearing.* Dodd, Mead & Co., 1944.

Edwards, S. *When the World's on Fire.* Coward, McCann & Geoghegan, 1973.

Fast, H. *April Morning.* Bantam Books, 1961.

Finlayson, A. *Rebecca's War.* Frederick Warne & Co., 1972.

Finlayson, A. *Redcoat in Boston.* Frederick Warne & Co., 1971.

Forbes, E. *Johnny Tremain.* Dell, 1943.

Ford, P. L. *Janice Meredith.* Dodd, Mead & Co., 1899.

Fritz, J. *Early Thunder.* Coward, McCann & Geoghegan, 1967.

Gray, E. *Meggy MacIntosh.* Viking, 1930.

Hawthorne, H. *Rising Thunder.* Longmans, Green & Co., 1937.

Kjelgaard, J. *Rebel Siege.* Random House, 1943.

Knipe, E.B., and A. A. Knipe. *A Continental Dollar.* The Century Co., 1923.

Lawson, R. *Mr. Revere and I.* Dell, 1953.

Meadowcroft, E. *Silver for General Washington.* Thomas Y. Crowell, 1944.

Nolan, J. C. *Treason at the Point.* Julian Messner Inc., 1944.

Perkins, L. F. *American Twins of the Revolution.* Houghton Mifflin, 1926.

Savery, C. *The Reb and the Redcoats.* Longmans, Green & Co., 1961.

Singmaster, E. *Rifles for Washington.* Houghton Mifflin, 1938.

Skinner, C. L. *Silent Scot, Frontier Scout.* Macmillan, 1925.

Snow, R. *Freelon Starbird.* Houghton Mifflin, 1976.

Wibberly, L. *Peter Treegate's Musket.* Ariel Books, 1959.

Why Would a Child Want to Read about That? The Holocaust Period in Children's Literature

Ursula F. Sherman

To forget what we know would not be human. To remember (it) is to think of what being human means. The Holocaust was a measure of man's dimensions. One can think of the power of evil it demonstrated—and of those people who treated others as less than human, as bacteria. Or of the power of good—and of those people who held out a hand to others.

By nature, man is neither good nor evil. He has both possibilities. And the freedom to realize the one or the other. . . . Indifference is the greatest sin. . . . It can become as powerful as an action. Not to do something against evil is to participate in the evil.[1]

These words from the postscript of Milton Meltzer's *Never to Forget: The Jews of the Holocaust,* answer complex questions with a straightforward conclusion, give us an acceptable rationale for writing about this event for children. But using these words as guides, there is still a need to be more specific. What must be included in this literature to do the period justice? Compassion for the victims is but one part, and Auschwitz is not all there is. Readers need to be moved into the victims' shoes, for a brief time, but they must also learn that these people, children as well as adults, did not meekly go to their own destruction. The

Ursula Sherman is a Lecturer on Children's Literature and Library Work with Children, University of California, Berkeley, and a Children's Library Consultant. She was a researcher and translator at the Nüremberg Trials.

enormous difficulties and risks in opposing the Nazi system, and resistance itself, have to be understood. The Holocaust needs to be explained in historical and human terms, including the roots and persistence of anti–Semitism. Any discussion of the systematic plan to destroy the Jews of Europe must also honor the rescuers and inspire active compassion. (Samuel Oliner, director of the Altruistic Personality Project at California's Humboldt State University, estimates that there were perhaps 200,000 non-Jewish rescuers who risked their lives.)

The most difficult prospect for a children's writer struggling with this subject may well be the need to deal with the reality of evil. Children's literature, excepting folklore, rarely deals with this. Only recently has contemporary fiction mentioned the existence of "bad" adults, such as the rapist or the child abuser. Occasionally, in historical novels, evil people and deeds are described. But to bring such truths forward into this century, and see such deeds not as isolated events but as part of a systematic plan for human extermination, forces writers into the shame-faced admission that our world is not automatically good, and that grown-ups are not consistently decent and trustworthy.

In the United States, who reads this literature? Aside from those children whose families were involved in World War II, in addition to children of parents touched by the Holocaust itself, the questions raised by this event are of such universal impact that all young people can find in this literature meaning for their lives. The period, which many adults find difficult to discuss face to face with a child, can be described in a once-removed setting, a book. Issues of war and peace, the history preceding World War II, anti–Semitism and racism, courage, fear, survival against great odds, they are all here. In these books readers confront, in ways appropriate to their age, understanding and need, the ultimate decisions humans may be forced to make: to help another at personal risk, to flee, to take a stand, to oppose authority, to make decisions about life and death. This literature also becomes a celebration of the sturdiness of children, of their ability to survive and rebound, despite extraordinary adversity.

There are so many titles dealing with Holocaust themes, that only a few can be selected, as examples, from mainstream American publishers. A selective list of additional titles is appended.

In these books, intended mainly for personal reading rather than for education, it is possible to be honest, and not deal in generalities. In Milton Meltzer's *Never to Forget,* quoted earlier, the truth is revealed in quotations from letters, journal entries, eyewitness statements, reminiscences, news stories and similar material, with the editor's commentary to illuminate and clarify.

In *Anne Frank: the Diary of a Young Girl,* the most beloved and long-lived children's title to emerge from the period—and the best known book of history American children read—young people share Anne's life in the Secret Annex. They read it, year after year, with a kind of passion. They understand and empathize with Anne's adolescent growing pains, the difficulties of living in hiding, the tensions of sharing close quarters with sometimes unpleasant adults, the ongoing differences with parents. Because every reader knows Anne's fate while reading this personal journal, the impact is intensified. The emergence of Anne herself, this very likable, hopeful and typical teenager, gives this title its greatest strength.

Another nonfiction title, appealing to adults as well, is Joffo's *Bag of Marbles,* a French autobiographical work in translation, unfortunately out of print. Told by the younger of two brothers, ten and twelve, when they escaped from German-occupied France to the Southern Petainist half, it describes hair-breadth escapes and lucky accidents. The fact that the boys' father, at the age of seven, made a similar flight from Tsarist Russia to escape being caught by military recruiters, adds a shocking historical perspective. Although the tale is almost totally straight adventure, a gallop through a fearful time with the heroes' survival at the end, it also illustrates one particular aspect of the Nazis' systematic eradication of the Jews. It honors the risks taken by the rescuers, and points to the scarcity of survivors.

Maurice and Joseph have been in SS custody for three weeks, interrogated over and over, each one separately retelling the story they had agreed on before their arrest. Once more, they are in the interrogation room. Joseph explains:[2]

> ". . . They hadn't dropped our case at all, and it knocked me for a loop. They had a world war on their hands; they were retreating before the Russians and Americans; they were fighting at the four corners of the globe; and yet they could still use men and time to find out whether two kids were Jewish or not—and spend three weeks doing it."

A bit later, "the most stubborn, the most witty priest in the whole Alpes-Maritmes Province . . . the priest most bent on snatching Jews from the clutches of the Germans" rescues them with fake baptismal certificates.

Then Joffo continues: "more often than not, one's life hangs by a thread: but that year, for us, there wasn't even a thread—only the fact that we had been arrested on a Friday, that we had come to the Hotel Excelsior when the quota for the weekly train had already been filled, and there was time for the Germans, with their administrative obsession, to set up a file folder headed, Re: Joffo, Maurice and Joseph. Few were as lucky as we were."

A Pocketful of Seeds by Marilyn Sachs, a novel based on actual events, is another work dealing with the complexities of a child's survival in Petainist France, with much attention paid to the feelings and fears of Nicole Nieman, who grows from eight to thirteen in the story. She is alternately brash, loving, jealous, seeking friendships and wishing her most admired classmate would not call her a dirty Jew. (This Lucie, we learn later, is the daughter of Socialist Italian refugees.) Nicole's parents argue about flight to Switzerland—her father fears that they will be shot on the way. The reader knows the real dangers, and because she can't push the whole family across the Swiss border herself, she too is trapped. The reader follows Nicole the day she returns from school and finds an empty, ransacked apartment, with parents and little sister gone. Nicole rides her bicycle from one friend or acquaintance to the next, seeking shelter, and is finally taken in by Mlle. Legrand, her school principal, a Petain supporter. Some of Nicole's schoolmates say that the principal's gesture is due to the Germans' imminent defeat and possible charges of collaboration against her, and this adds another layer to the complexities of human motives.

Sachs deals with universal concerns in a moving passage. Nicole is offended by the laughter of a man whose children disappeared and tells her mother:[3]

> "How can he laugh and go to the movies, when his wife died, and his children are lost? If we were lost you and Papa wouldn't laugh, and you wouldn't go to the movies. You'd look for us."
>
> . . . "Listen Nicole, M. Bonnet is looking for his children, and he is grieving. . . . He is grieving but he has hope that he will find them again. He has lost a great deal, but if human beings can hold on to hope they can live through the worst of times!"
>
> "But you and Papa would look for us. You wouldn't laugh."
>
> "Papa and I would look for you as long as we had any

strength left in our bodies, and we would hope for as long as we're alive that we would find you."
"And you wouldn't laugh."
"I think we would. People who don't laugh are dead."

This kind of thinking is more easily expressed in fiction than nonfiction, with the exception of Anne Frank's diary, perhaps, where Anne can be so very honest.

The sturdiness and practicality of Nicole's mother (she and the father sell sweaters in France's outdoor markets) is in marked contrast to the household of nine-year-old Anna and her twelve-year-old brother Max in Judith Kerr's *When Hitler Stole Pink Rabbit.* Anna's father is a well-known writer and her mother an accomplished pianist, there is a resident cook and Heimpi, the maid and nurse. The father's writings force the family to flee to Switzerland, in a tense border crossing where the children for the first time cope without the resourceful and dependable Heimpi. They learn to become refugees. Mama learns to cook and to knit, and the family moves again, first to France, then to England. The affluence and security of Anna's early childhood changes to lean times, simple birthday presents, messages about the death of friends and Nazi violence, back home. Anna admits her preference for the more independent and exciting life she leads now, despite its deprivations.

But this is still peripheral. To be a refugee in England, to be caught by the Nazis in France, this is not yet life in the very center of the whirlwind. Can writers go there and still reach children?

Friedrich, a novel by Hans Peter Richter, was published in Germany in 1961 and in the United States in 1970. Set in a German town, the friendship between two boys, one the son of an unemployed worker and the grandson of a patriarchal anti–Semitic grandfather, the other the son of a Jewish postal employee, is destroyed as the Nazi system separates out the Jews. Herr Resch, the landlord who in 1929 wrecks a snowman built by the Jewish Friedrich and his mother, is an air-raid warden in 1942.[4]

A Sergeant says: "have you gone out of your mind? You can't send the boy out of a shelter in this raid?"
"Do you know who that is? . . . That's a Jew!"
" . . . Let the boy stay!" came from all sides.
"Who do you think you are?" Herr Resch screamed. "How dare you mix in my affairs? Who is air-raid warden here, you or I? You follow my orders, is that understood? Otherwise I'll report you."

. . . Mother cried against Father's shoulder.
"Do pull yourself together!" begged Father. "You'll endanger us all otherwise."

Friedrich is found dead outside the shelter, after the raid.

In very brief chapters and spare language, this novel describes the social and political conditions in Germany as perceived by Friedrich's friend. This title has its counterpart in Richter's other book about the same period, *I Was There,* where the events are seen through the eyes of a Hitler Youth. To read both books in sequence creates a particularly vivid portrait of time and place, as the political and social process which engendered dehumanization as a system is unfolded.

Another look at the Nazi universe, autobiographical this time, occurs in Ilse Koehn's *Mischling, Second Degree,* the survival story of Ilse. She has Socialist anti–Nazi parents, a gentle, educated middle class Jewish grandmother on her father's side, and a fierce peasant of a grandmother on her mother's. This grandmother, who has seen wars and bad times come and go (an adult reader senses that her genes remember the Thirty Years' War), is intent on growing, preserving, and scrounging enough food so that at least her immediate family – grandfather and Ilse and her mother – will survive. Ilse's parents divorce to insure Ilse's safety. The child, unaware that she is a quarter Jewish, participates in Nazi Youth activities (just don't become a leader, say her parents). With her class, she is evacuated to Czechoslovakia during the air raids and wonders why the Czechs don't like them. Later she returns to Berlin before the Russians arrive. Here again is a sturdy youngster, learning survival skills, with a devoted network of people to keep her safe, and a network of Nazis intent on destroying her. But there are limits to her rescuers' compassion. Although one of Ilse's young neighbors keeps saying that his Nazi father is going to kill the whole family before the Russians' arrival, no one reaches out to save the life of that child.

We can get still closer, nearer to the Concentration Camp universe.

We are in Warsaw with Joseph Ziemian's *Cigarette Sellers of Three Crosses Square.* This is the true story of a group of Jewish boys and girls who escaped the Warsaw Ghetto in 1942 and survive in Aryan Warsaw by begging, stealing, trading, and selling cigarettes, while ever hunting for safe places to spend the nights. The writer was in his twenties when he met the children, ranging from seven to fourteen years. His notes form the basis of the book. Although labeled young adult, this is essentially a story for adults about children. The German title is far more appealing: *Just Don't Call Me Moshe, My Name is Stasiek.*

There are scenes where the children plead for shelter with offers of food or money, encounters with the ever-present blackmailers, and escalating and violent competition as the Polish children, equally hungry, threaten those suspected of being Jews. The tale moves like a documentary film, but the viewer never gets close because he is only permitted to observe. The most touching character is little Bolus, age seven, too Jewish-looking for his and the other children's safety (Ziemian and the Jewish Resistance try to find him shelter), who first appears in a huge fur coat dragging the ground. It is tied with string, and in a 1942 photograph all that can be seen of the child are two inches of face and the hands. Bolus makes his living singing in the streetcars with a five-year-old Polish girl. In this book, the photos translate the events into a searing truth. On the front cover appear five boys, looking both tough and vulnerable. On the inside there are pictures of most of the children, from 1942 Warsaw. But they are followed by later photographs: Bolus, in 1962, as an Israeli officer, handsome, tall, totally unlike the seven-year-old waif in the too-big fur coat. And photos of the others who survived, looking mature, capable, no longer victims. The pictures carry their own message.

Occasionally, a conversation dramatizes the situation, but only an adult has enough information to flesh out the words. Once, while some of the boys are singing in one courtyard for the coins that the tenants throw down to them, they meet two other boys, eleven and nine, singing in the adjacent yard.[5]

> "We're alone," said Toothy. "Mum and Dad died in hospital from typhus and our sister was taken to Treblinka. . . . A Pole on Grochowska lets my brother sleep in his house and I climb over the railings into Skaryszewski Park and sleep between the chairs on the orchestra stand."

There are other titles about survival in Poland that may be more appealing to young but mature readers. Yuri Suhl's *On the Other Side of the Gate,* for instance, describes how a young Jewish couple first decide to have a baby, an act of foolhardy affirmation, and then smuggle it out of the Warsaw Ghetto. In Jack Kuper's *Child of the Holocaust,* blond nine-year-old Jankele becomes a Polish farm boy and survives the Nazi occupation, in constant danger from anti-Semitic Poles, blackmailers, and suspicious farmers.

The ultimate survival novel of that time and place is Suhl's

Uncle Misha's Partisans, retelling actual events so unusual that at least two other writers have turned them into novels (Romain Gary's ironic *European Education,* first published in France in 1945, and Gertrude Samuels' documentary *Mottele,* both written for adult readers). Yuri Suhl has succeeded in portraying twelve-year-old Motele, who pretends to be a Ukrainian street musician after his parents and sister are murdered by the Germans. He not only becomes a Jewish partisan with the famed Uncle Misha's group, and a hero, but he also has adolescent dreams about love and growing up. After he joins the partisans, his violin gets him a job at a German Officers' Mess. He memorizes their insignia and keeps count for his reports, remembers and grieves for his dead sister as he plays his music, abhors his made-to-measure German uniform, pretends he doesn't understand German, and plays with the children of his Ukrainian landlady, a good woman whose husband has been deported to Germany as slave labor. The reader shares Motele/Mitek's life, thoughts, and feelings. The worst time comes when he rehearses the Nazi Party anthem, the *Horst Wessel Lied,* with the old German pianist, his civilian boss.[6]

They were alone in the large hall, he, the old man, and the life-size figure of Hitler staring down at them from the wall. It was the Führer's favorite song that the old man wanted him to play to perfection. Motele turned his back on that wall, as if blotting the Führer out of his range of vision would make it easier for him to go through the ordeal. But as he was nearing the dreaded stanza the fingers of his right hand stiffened, clutching rather than holding the bow, and he bore down so heavily on the word *Judenblut* that what came out of the instrument was a scratchy, jarring sound. . . .

The old man stopped playing, shook his head disconsolately, then turned to Motele, and in a tone of uncontrolled anger said: "What the devil got into you, Mitek? You play complicated pieces by Brahms, Mozart, and Paderewski without a single false note and you bog down over a simple melody like the 'Horst Wessel'! And twice over the same phrase! What is it about this phrase that throws you?" He leaned forward to his sheet music and, locating the phrase, recited out loud, " '*Und wenn das Judenblut vom Messer spritzt/Sodann geht's nochmal so gut . . .*' Do you know the meaning of those words, Mitek?"

Motele shook his head.

"I thought so!" said the pianist. "Here, let me translate them for you," and he began reading in Ukrainian: "When

Jewish blood spurts from the knife then things go twice as well. . . . That's all there's to it, Mitek," he said, in the same casual tone he had read the translation. "Now let's take it all over again from the beginning."

During his last weeks with the officers, Motele smuggles explosives into an unused room, and finally blows up the whole house. As he races through the town amid blasts, he remembers his sister: "Basha! Basha! Can you hear it?" On his way to the forest in the partisans' wagon, he takes a last look at the burning Officers' House. "That's some candle you lit there," Yoshke said, pulling Motele close to him. "A *yahrtzeit* candle for our dead," one of the partisans added.

End of book. The young reader is permitted to hope that Motele survived the war, while in the adult titles he is killed in a later incident. And Suhl has captured the elation of a job well done, the high adventure and the enormous dangers, the satisfaction of revenge as well as the grief, and our hero is still a young boy with a child's feelings and dreams.

So many titles, and the reader has not yet entered an extermination camp. Although Moskin's *I Am Rosemarie* describes Bergen-Belsen concentration camp, the heroine sees it from the privileged position of a prisoner holding a Latin American passport, and her view is considerably filtered. Few mainstream publishers bring the full horror before young people's eyes. Meltzer's *Never to Forget* does it through eyewitness quotes. *I Never Saw Another Butterfly,* a well-known collection of art and poetry by the children of Camp Terezin, the Nazi "show camp," is a tribute to the dedicated teachers who enabled the children to express what was in their hearts. A very special book, it is most accessible to young readers through teachers.

Can there, should there be, a juvenile novel about the ultimate horror, degradation and destruction human beings were subjected to? A writer would have to have the literary talents of a Dante and the artistic genius of a Hieronymus Bosch to do justice to the subject. Chester Aaron, an American writer for children who helped liberate Buchenwald, attempts to picture the concentration camp reality in *Gideon.* Smuggling and trading scenes, similar to those in the *Cigarette Sellers,* are described, but as fiction. Fourteen-year-old Gideon participates in the Warsaw Ghetto uprising, and his subsequent actions and survival at Treblinka are determined by his father's words:[7]

"The important thing, Gideon, is to survive. In any way, at any cost, survive. By surviving you can not only fight back, you can carry the story of what is happening in this ghetto. The world must know. You and others must tell. You are of no use to our people dead."

The Nazi system of extermination in the "killing" camps is described in full detail. The author uses eyewitness texts as sources. Gideon, who for thirty years hid his Jewish and camp survivor identity from his wife and children, finally writes this book to bear witness. Although it is a powerful telling, it seems to me that if a child is old enough, or interested enough, and needs to know, he or she should read eyewitness reports. To write a concentration camp novel, so that children, or young adults, may be able to read about those facts, seems a contradiction in terms, and nothing is gained by substituting an invention for the truth.

Fifteen titles have served as examples for this journey through the Holocaust times. At least as many more, equally powerful and worthwhile, have been published by American mainstream publishers. Young readers have vicariously been hunted and rescued, they've risked death to help another, known when to run and when to hide. They have learned that it can be proper to disobey orders. For over forty years, adult to adult, writers have struggled with the questions raised by this period. But these times also touched children. There may still exist a kind of old-fashioned shame about uncomfortable realities that makes adults say: not in front of the children! But this has not protected children from the real world. Adult secrecy may have shielded grown-ups from the naive and straightforward questions our young know how to pose, but in the long run our shameful secrets have become known even to children. The more our young know about why the Holocaust happened, and how it took place, the more they, as our future adults, will be prepared to deal with the trends in society that endanger our humanity.

NOTES

1. Meltzer, *Never to Forget: The Jews of the Holocaust,* pp. 191, 192.
2. Joffo, *A Bag of Marbles,* pp. 215, 223, 225.
3. Sachs, *A Pocketful of Seeds,* p. 79.
4. Richter, *Friedrich,* pp. 135, 136.

5. Ziemian, *The Cigarette Sellers of Three Crosses Square*, p. 87.
6. *Uncle Misha's Partisans*, pp. 161–62, 211.
7. *Gideon*, p. 8.

WORKS CITED

Titles noted in the text

Aaron, Chester. *Gideon.* J.B. Lippincott, 1982.
Frank, Anne. *Anne Frank: The Diary of a Young Girl.* Doubleday, 1967.
Gary, Romain. *A European Education.* Simon & Schuster, 1960.
Joffo, Joseph. *A Bag of Marbles.* Houghton Mifflin, 1974.
Kerr, Judith. *When Hitler Stole Pink Rabbit.* Coward, McCann & Geoghan, 1972.
Koehn, Ilse. *Mischling, Second Degree: My Childhood in Nazi Germany.* Greenwillow, 1977.
Kuper, Jack. *Child of the Holocaust.* New American Library, 1967.
Meltzer, Milton. *Never to Forget: The Jews of the Holocaust.* Harper & Row, 1976.
Moskin, Marietta. *I Am Rosemarie.* John Day, 1972.
Richter, Hans Peter. *Friedrich.* Holt, Rinehart & Winston, 1970.
– – –. *I Was There.* Holt, Rinehart & Winston, 1972.
Sachs, Marilyn. *A Pocket Full of Seeds.* Doubleday, 1973.
Samuels, Gertrude. *Mottele: A Partisan Odyssey.* New American Library, 1977.
Suhl, Yuri. *On the Other Side of the Gate.* Watts, 1975.
– – –. *Uncle Misha's Partisans.* Four Winds Press, 1973.
Volavkova, Hana, ed. *I Never Saw Another Butterfly: Children's Drawings and Poems from Terezin Concentration Camp, 1942–1944.* Schocken, 1978.
Ziemian, Joseph. *The Cigarette Sellers of Three Crosses Square.* Lerner, 1975.

Extended List of Titles

Benchley, Nathaniel. *Bright Candles: A Novel of the Danish Resistance.* Harper & Row, 1974.

Bernbaum, Israel. *My Brother's Keeper: The Holocaust Through the Eyes of an Artist.* G. Putnam's Sons, 1985.

Bishop, Claire Huchet. *Twenty and Ten.* Viking, 1952.

Davis, Enid. *A Comprehensive Guide to Children's Literature with a Jewish Theme.* Schocken, 1981.

Forman, James. *The Survivor.* Farrar, Strauss & Giroux, 1976.

Hannam, Charles. *A Boy in that Situation.* Harper & Row, 1977.

Hautzig, Esther. *The Endless Steppe: Growing Up in Siberia.* T. Y. Crowell, 1968.

Jackson, Livia Bitton. *Elli: Coming of Age in the Holocaust.* Times, 1980.

Levitin, Sonia. *Journey to America.* Athencum, 1970.

Meltzer, Milton. *The Jewish Americans: A History in Their Own Words, 1650–1950.* T. Y. Crowell, 1982.

Orgel, Doris. *The Devil in Vienna.* Dial, 1978.

Orlev, Uri. *The Island on Bird Street.* Houghton Mifflin, 1984.

Reiss, Johanna. *The Upstairs Room.* T. Y. Crowell, 1972.

Rossel, Seymour. *The Holocaust.* Watts, 1981.

Siegal, Aranka. *Upon the Head of the Goat.* Farrar, Strauss & Giroux, 1981.

Spanjaard, Barry. *Don't Fence Me In.* B & B Publishers, 1981.

Suhl, Yuri. *They Fought Back: The Story of the Jewish Resistance in Nazi Europe.* Crown, 1967.

Ancient Egypt for Children—Facts, Fiction, and Lies

Beatrice Lumpkin

"Those books don't stay on the shelf too long," the librarian told me, when I inquired about children's books on ancient Egypt. Young readers are fascinated by stories of pyramids and people who so enjoyed life that they mummified their dead in hopes of an afterlife.

But what are children learning about Egypt—facts, fiction, or lies?

How many of us know the facts—that the base of our entire Western civilization came from Africa? It was in ancient Egypt that the so-called Western philosophy, ethics, classical learning and science, even religion, originated. And European scholars acknowledged this gift, which they received via Greece from Egypt, until American slavery and the rise of imperialism changed the writing of history.

As a mathematics teacher I studied the ancient Egyptian contribution to mathematics. The first cipherization of numbers (using symbols instead of tally marks, for example, for ten), a system of fractions that was used up to modern times, geometric formulas including the volume of a truncated pyramid and the area of a curved surface, and formulas for the sum of arithmetic series were among the earliest Egyptian discoveries.

In science, too, there were many Egyptian "firsts" including the first calendar, sun dial, water clock and steam engine, a 365-day year and 24-hour day, and the beginning of medicine as a science. The Egyptians were the teachers of the ancient Greeks. Little wonder, then, that the greatest center of "Hellenistic" science was in Egypt, at Alexandria, at a time when the population

Beatrice Lumpkin is associate professor of mathematics (retired) at Malcolm X College in Chicago.

was native Egyptian and few Greeks had immigrated to that great city.[1]

Western literature, architecture, religion and ethics were also greatly influenced by those of Egypt. In religion, the story of Moses as a baby in the bulrushes is a close analogue of the earlier Egyptian Horus story. (Isis hid Horus in a basket among the reeds of the Nile.) The Christian trinity was a later import from Egypt and is not found in the Old Testament.

Yet one after the other, the classical histories I consulted were negative in their evaluations of the Egyptian contribution. Just two examples suffice to show the extent of prejudice in the standard historiography:

Compared to the Greeks, wrote Morris Kline, "The mathematics of the Egyptians and Babylonians is the scrawling of children just learning how to write, as opposed to great literature."[2]

David E. Smith, whose *History of Mathematics* became a model for many later historians, said of Egyptian mathematics:

> So little was accomplished in the Orient from 1000 B.C. to 300 B.C. . . . the East has always been the East and the West has always been the West. . . . Even the ancients recognized the difference for Quintilian remarks, "From of old there has been the famous division of Attic and Asiatic writers, the former being reckoned succinct and vigorous, the latter inflated and empty."[3]

Although I was shocked, I should not have been surprised, because I had read W. E. B. Du Bois. He replied to Arnold Toynbee's claim that Egyptian civilization was "white" or European, and to other assertions that Egypt was in reality Asian, not African:

> There can be but one explanation for this vagary of nineteenth century science. It was due to the slave trade and Negro slavery. It was due to the fact that the rise and support of capitalism called for rationalization based upon degrading and discrediting the Negroid peoples. It is especially significant that the science of Egyptology arose and flourished at the very time that the cotton kingdom reached its greatest power on the foundation of American Negro slavery.[4]

We may continue to ask why both we and our children are fed such a racially biased story of the origin of our civilization. Why haven't we been taught that the base of our so-called Western civilization was created by the African peoples of Egypt? Why has the Egyptian contribution been downplayed, or if admitted, attributed to a mysterious non-African "white" race?

The reasons are economic and political. Racism is big business. In 1972 Victor Perlo estimated superprofits due to racist differentials in wages, rents, etc. as forty-nine billion dollars. Its political value in dividing working people and allowing the transnational companies to dictate American government policy is incalculable (*Economics of Racism USA*, New York: International, 1975).

Truthful literature on ancient Egypt can go a long way towards refuting racist premises by showing that modern civilization is based on the great achievements of the African people of Egypt. Good children's books could:

1. develop pride in the contributions of the African peoples of Egypt who laid the foundations for our own civilization;

2. build an understanding of historical development, an understanding which helps in all studies;

3. build the self-confidence of female students because many women rose to leadership in Egypt;

Unfortunately, of the thirty-two children's books in this survey, most did not live up to this potential. Many of the books contained excellent material but fell short in some crucial aspects, measured against the following checklist:

Does the book show the following?

1. Egypt is in Africa and the Egyptians are an African people.

2. The high civilization of ancient Egypt was initiated and developed by Egyptians and was not imported from any other continent.

3. Construction gangs for the pyramids, obelisks, and temples were not based on slave labor. Rather they consisted primarily of farmers who worked for an allowance, especially during the flood season when the fields could not be farmed. Farmers had legal rights and could, and did, enter the courts to enforce these rights.

4. The miracle of Egypt was not a passive "gift of the Nile"; rather it was the product of highly centralized, efficient administration and Egyptian science and technology.

5. Many of the first principles of science were developed in ancient Egypt.

6. The relationship of Egypt to Greece was that of teacher to student. Egyptian contributions to Western Civilization did not end with the Greek conquest but continued, on a higher level, at Alexandria and other Egyptian cities well into Roman times.

7. Women enjoyed far more equality in ancient Egypt than in Europe or Asia. Some rights guaranteed ancient Egyptian women are not yet generally established, such as marriage contracts.

How did the books (twenty-three nonfiction and nine fiction) score in the survey? The books were those available on the shelves of the Oak Park, Illinois, Public Library, which had a larger collection on shelf than the Chicago Public Library Juvenile Division.

The African identity of ancient Egypt was specifically mentioned in only two of the books. A third book, of the twenty-three nonfiction books, does mention that Egypt is in Africa, but facial features in the illustrations do not show the people as African. Fully twenty of the twenty-three books omit mention of the African location and identity of Egypt.

In some cases the book illustrations suggest that the Egyptians were really Europeans. Right on the cover of *Gods and Pharaohs* by Geraldine Harris, there is a big spread of a rather Nordic looking, blue-eyed pharaoh! One need only contrast this drawing with the statue of Tutankhamen, in the same pose of royal crook and flail crossed against his chest, to see the contrast between the clearly African features of Tut and the Europeanized version in this book.

The text of *Gods and Pharaohs* does indeed include valuable information. Perhaps the author had no control over the illustrations used by the publisher. Still the impact of art is much greater than the impact of copy for audiences of any age.[5]

Many books show the Egyptians as tanned Greeks, for example, *The Egyptians Knew,* by Pine and Levine. There is not one word identifying Egyptians as Africans, or even locating Egypt in Africa in this otherwise useful book. That is especially unfortunate because this book is one of only three in this survey that was written for the lower grades.[6]

Wilbur Cross' book, *Enchantment of the World—Egypt,* has the opposite problem. Excellent photographs clearly show the African people of Egypt, but the text classifies Egyptians as non-African. Cross states, "Some people from Upper Egyptian areas are very dark skinned, the result of many generations of intermarriage with Nubians and other Africans." This implies that Egyptians are not Africans.[7]

In eight of these books, although nothing is said in the copy, good photographs are reproduced which clearly show the African features of ancient Egyptians. Does this reflect progress in books published since the late 1960s, when the fight to introduce Black Studies won many victories?

Of the eleven nonfiction books published before 1970, only three picture Egyptians as Africans, four as non-Africans, and four omit any reference to art on the identity of the Egyptian people. The figure is somewhat better for the twelve produced since 1970 with six picturing the Egyptians as Africans, two as non-African and four omitting such information.

The second survey question was on the indigenous character of the Egyptian civilization and is closely related to the first question.

The racist version of history, after asserting that the Egyptians were not African, then claims that the culture was imported. The implication is that the Egyptians were not capable of developing so high a civilization.

Anne Millard's *Egypt* repeats this version of history:

> Writing appears fully developed in Egypt, whereas in Mesopotamia a long history of experimentation in this art can be traced, and it has been suggested, therefore, that writing was introduced into Egypt from Mesopotamia.[8]

Millard did not have available the results of the Nubian Salvage Mission which uncovered further proof of the African origins of Egyptian writing and culture. This evidence includes very early hieroglyphs and the existence of generations of predynastic pharaohs in the South of Egypt.[9] Ancient Egyptian was a Hamitic African language and the flora and fauna models used for the hieroglyphs were also African. As Du Bois charged, the theory of an Asian origin of Egyptian language and writing was a racist, not a scientific construct.

T. G. H. James presents the same theory of a foreign origin but also quotes an interesting alternative:

> As Egyptian civilization . . . seemed to appear as if from nowhere, it was proposed that some invading race must have arrived in Egypt. . . . Petrie in 1893 thought that the dynastic race came, not from Asia, but from further south in Africa.[10]

Unfortunately, the search for a source of Egyptian civilization farther south in Africa waited for seventy years, so deep was the prejudice that Africa could not be the source of high civilization. It follows that only five of the twenty-three books surveyed credit Africans for inventing this great African civilization.

How the pyramids were built was our next question. In Payne's *The Pharaohs of Ancient Egypt* we get the same picture, dramatized in some Hollywood spectaculars:

> He could hear the groans of the slaves who had labored under the lash of Cheops's brutal overseers to raise this mighty tomb skyward.[11]

Sondergaard in *My First Geography of the Suez Canal* is even more graphic, claiming the building of a canal cost the lives of 120,000 workers, a scare figure which has no basis in the historical record.[12]

A number of children's books have corrected this error. In *Gods and Pharaohs,* despite its blue-eyed pictures of pharaohs, Harris makes the following correction:

> It is wrong to think that the pyramids were built by gangs of slaves toiling under the lash. The main work force was the general population that had nothing to do for three-four months while the fields were flooded.[13]

It could be added that the work force was also paid, perhaps a form of work relief. Despite the growing realization that the slave-labor picture of ancient Egypt is false, this stereotype persists in children's books.

Was the ancient Egyptian civilization a passive "gift of the Nile"? Of the eight books which deal with Egypt "as the gift of the Nile," only two credit the ingenuity and intelligence of the Egyptian people for the development of this remarkable civilization. Silverberg's *Before the Sphinx* describes the heavy rains which "turned the Nile into a savage monster" requiring a great coordinated effort to turn the calamity of a flood into the blessing of irrigated agriculture.[14]

Payne speaks of the Egyptians being "forced to use their wits" given the challenge of partly predictable floods.[15] The other six which discuss the "gift of the Nile" continue to reverse cause and effect. In *The Nile,* for example, Warren writes, "Because of the river, Egypt became one of the great cradles of world civilization."[16]

The damage done by this viewpoint is often compounded by a belittling comparison to Mesopotamian civilization. Even in Boyer's valuable *History of Mathematics,* we read:

> Geometry may have been a gift of the Nile, as Herodotus believed, but the Egyptians did little with the gift. . . . For more progressive achievements one must look to the more turbulent river valley known as Mesopotamia.[17]

On the fifth survey question, we found that the outstanding contributions of ancient Egypt to mathematics and science were mentioned in only eight of the twenty-three nonfiction books surveyed. The Egyptian 365-day calendar was the forerunner of our own calendar and was the invention most often mentioned in these eight books. It seems a pity that more wasn't done with the scientific aspects of mummification, since this feature of Egyptian culture has a universal appeal for young readers. The use of mathematics is also generally slighted.

On the relationship between Egypt and Greece, most Western authors claim that the classical Greek scholars were mistaken in writing that they had acquired their learning from Egypt. So it is to be expected that children's books published in the U.S. would also deny ancient Egyptians credit for achievements of the Alexandrian school which flourished in Egypt from about 300 B.C. for nearly a thousand years. In 415 A.D. a Christian mob brutally murdered an algebraist and philosopher, the Egyptian woman named Hypatia.

By omitting the achievements of the Alexandrian scholars, some of the most fascinating material in the history of Egypt is lost. Only by denying the Egyptian character of Alexandria, could the children's book, *Before the Sphinx,* say, " . . . in 1090 B.C. Egypt ceased forever to have major importance among nations."[18] In fact, Egyptian culture remained a leading force into the fifth century and came forward again, under Muslim rule, in the ninth century.

One of the pleasures of writing children's books on ancient Egypt is the opportunity to write about the advanced position of women. The equal rights of women to own, inherit, and retain their own property on the dissolution of marriage were all guaranteed by law. Women freely entered the Egyptian courts to enforce their rights. Many women gained wealth and power through their skill as traders. Women were among the most effective rulers of Egypt. The never-to-be-forgotten Hatshepsut even put on the two crowns of Egypt and declared herself King (not Queen) – Pharaoh of all Egypt.

This theme comes across strongly in *Ancient Egypt* by Charles Robinson, revised in 1984 by Lorna Greenberg. Marriage as a partnership with respect for the freedom of the wife and reverence for the mother was the Egyptian way.[19] But in all, only three of the books surveyed include the topic of women's rights.

In summary of the nonfictional children's books on Egypt found on the shelves of the Oak Park, Illinois, Library, these books present a wide variety of facts on Ancient Egypt, but marred by omissions and distortions. Little is said about the African identity of Egypt. Hopefully, many children will look at the features of the pharaohs for themselves and will realize that Egyptians are Africans, even if these books say otherwise.

However, there is less of value in the fiction on Egypt which, incidentally, is almost all for "young adults." Only two of the nine books surveyed were below the junior high school level.[20]

Certainly the author of fiction has more leeway than the writer of nonfiction. But both should respect the facts. Good historical fiction, especially for young readers, should not distort history. If the nine books surveyed are a representative sample of those recommended by the library journals, most novels for young readers fail the test as an instructional medium about Egypt.

Eight of these nine books portray ancient Egypt as a slave society. There is adventure without any insight into the culture of the time, as in *Treasure of Tenakertom.*[21] In this book and in *Honey of the Nile* there is a mistaken emphasis on Akhenaten as the "most important pharaoh" because he replaced the traditional religion with the supposedly monotheistic worship of the Aten.

In reality, Akhenaten did not play a key role in Egyptian history. Nor was his supposed monotheism a progressive development, rather it was a move towards less democracy and greater absolute power for Akhenaten. The fascination with Akhenaten proceeds from the viewpoint of modern, monotheistic Christianity, extrapolated into another time of many gods who were unified under the basic principle of Ma'at, truth, or the right way.

Four of the nine novels include some points of interest. *The Bright and Morning Star* opens with a family traveling to Kemi (Egypt) in the hope that the famous physicians of Egypt can save their sick child. Despite this promising beginning, the rest of the book deals with palace intrigue and provides little insight into ancient Egyptian culture.[22]

In *The Princess Runs Away* there is some description of Egyptian technology such as weaving and making papyrus.[23] *The Egypt Game* was especially interesting because the characters are modern kids who play that they're in Egypt. The hero of the book is a Black child and there is a sense of excitement about their fascination with ancient Egypt.[24]

Scarab for Luck by Meadowcroft is a good story for the middle grades with lots of adventure and lots of information. Unfortunately, it is marred by too many stereotypes. Huge statues are pulled by "four long lines of slaves," "Negroes" are referred to as different from Egyptians, doctors are shown practicing magic but not analyzing the disease scientifically (which Egyptian doctors did do within the limits of the knowledge of the time).

In the fiction surveyed here, my own two books, *Young Genius in Old Egypt* for grades four to six and *Senefer and Hatshepsut—A Novel of Egyptian Genius* for young adults[25] were omitted but not because of a false sense of modesty. These books were published noncommercially, with the DuSable Museum of African American History. To have included them in the survey would have skewed the results. They were written in the hope of meeting the above criteria but have reached only a relatively small number of readers. Thus, their impact remains limited.

There really is no shortcut to the goal of ridding our books of racism. The publishing monopolies will respond only to mass pressure and mass struggles by workers, parents, students, and faculty united to fight racism at all levels.

NOTES

1. George Sarton, *A History of Science* (Cambridge: Harvard, 1959), p. ix.
2. Morris Kline, *Mathematics in Western Culture* (New York: 1953), pp. 9–10.
3. David E. Smith, *History of Mathematics* vol. 1 (New York: Dover, 1951), p.93.
4. W. E. B. Du Bois, *The World and Africa* (New York: Viking, 1947), p. 99.
5. Geraldine Harris, *Gods and Pharaohs from Egyptian Mythology* (Vancouver: Schocken, 1983).
6. Tillie S. Pine and Joseph Levine, *The Egyptians Knew* (New York: McGraw-Hill, 1964).
7. Wilbur Cross, *Enchantment of the World—Egypt* (Chicago: Children's Press, 1982), p. 109.
8. Anne Millard, *Egypt—The Young Archaeologist* (New York: Putnam's Sons, 1971), p. 86.
9. Bruce Williams, "The Lost Pharaohs of Nubia" *Nile Valley Civilizations,* ed., Ivan Van Sertima (New Brunswick: Journal of African Civilizations, 1985), pp. 29–46.
10. T. G. H. James, *Archaeology of Ancient Egypt* (New York: Walck, 1972), p. 24.
11. Elizabeth Payne, *Pharaohs of Ancient Egypt* (New York: Random House, 1964), p. 44.
12. Arensa Sondergaard, *My First Geography of the Suez Canal,* (Boston: Little Brown, 1960), pp. 29–30.
13. Harris, *Gods and Pharaohs from Egyptian Mythology,* pp. 16–17.
14. Robert Silverberg, *Before the Sphinx* (New York: Thomas Nelson, 1971), p. 67.
15. Payne, *Pharaohs of Ancient Egypt,* p. 25.

16. Ruth Warren, *The Nile* (New York: McGraw Hill, 1968), p. 21.
17. Carl Boyer, *A History of Mathematics* (New York: Wiley, 1968), p. 23.
18. Robert Silverberg, *Before the Sphinx — Early Egypt,* p. 20.
19. Charles A. Robinson, *Ancient Egypt, a First Book,* revised by Lorna Greenberg (New York: Franklin Watts, 1984), pp. 18, 21.
20. Ruth F. Jones, *Boy of the Pyramids* (New York: Random House, 1950); Enid L. Meadowcroft, *Scarab for Luck* (New York: Crowell, 1964).
21. Robert E. Alter, *Treasure of Tenakertom* (New York: Putnam, 1964); Erick Berry, *Honey of the Nile* (New York: Oxford, 1938).
22. Rosemary Harris, *Bright and Morning Star* (New York: Macmillan, 1972).
23. Alice W. Howard, *The Princess Runs Away* (New York: Macmillan, 1934).
24. Zilpha K. Snyder, *The Egypt Game* (New York: Atheneum, 1965).
25. Beatrice Lumpkin, *Young Genius in Old Egypt* (Chicago: DuSable, 1979); *Senefer and Hatshepsut* (Chicago: DuSable, 1983).

BOOKS SURVEYED BUT NOT CITED IN NOTES ABOVE

Nonfiction

Cottrell, Leonard. *The Secrets of Tutankhamen's Tomb* (Greenwich, Conn.: New York Graphic Society, 1964).
Fenton, H. Sophia. *Ancient Egypt — Book to Begin On* (New York: Holt, Rinehart and Winston, 1971).
Haag, Michael van. *Egypt, the Land and the People* (London: Silver Burdett, 1975–77).
Halliburton, Richard. *Second Book of Marvels — the Orient* (New York, Bobbs Merrill, 1938).
Hawkes, Jacquetta. *Pharaohs of Egypt* (New York: Harper & Row, 1965).
Henderson, Larry. *Egypt and the Sudan* (New York: Thomas Nelson, 1971).

Macauley, David. *Pyramid* (Boston: Houghton Mifflin, 1975).

Stuart, Dorothy M. *The Boy Through the Ages* (Edinburgh: Doran, 1927), pp. 31–53.

Swinburne, Irene and Laurence Swinburne. *Behind the Sealed Door* (New York: Sniffen Court, 1977).

Taylor, Alice. *Egypt* (New York: Holiday House, 1953).

Wallace, John A. *Getting to Know Egypt* (New York: Coward McCann, 1961).

White, Anne T. *Lost Worlds* (New York: Random House, 1941), pp. 93–165.

Fiction

McGraw, Eloise J. *Mara, Daughter of the Nile* (New York: Coward McCann, 1953).

Militarism in Juvenile Fiction

Donnarae MacCann

Among its many uses, children's literature provides a road map for cultural historians—a means of measuring society's basic assumptions. Prevailing ideas tend to be mirrored in children's books, and the books then reinforce the ideas.

One way to see how this phenomenon operates is to consider children's fiction about war. It was not until the 1950s that the simplistic patriotism that appeared in early works was somewhat rectified, although many books still contain a nostalgic dimension which obscures the real horrors of war. Some aspects of this cultural history have been more thoroughly examined than others, but the record so far shows the persistence of militaristic codes, untempered nationalism and nostalgic visions of suffering and triumph.

In "The Dark Mirror: War Ethos in Juvenile Fiction, 1865–1919," Peter A. Soderbergh shows that reconciliation characterized post–Civil War novels, and books tended to stress the rightness and reasonableness of both contenders in that war. After 1898, however, Theodore Roosevelt's notion that war was a "great adventure" predominated. "It is no exaggeration," writes Professor Soderbergh, "to say that, by 1918, the cheery adolescent of 1895 had been transformed by the writers into a war-crazed instrument of national policy."[1] He pinpoints a growing militarism and notes the influence of imperialistic novels by British journalist George Henty, who aimed to cover in juvenile fiction "all the wars, great and little" since 1688. Widely available in the U.S., his seventy-odd titles included *With Clive in India* and *With Lee in Virginia.*

Reprinted from *Interracial Books for Children Bulletin*, 13, nos. 6/7 (1982), 18–20 by permission of the publisher.

Donnarae MacCann, a member of the *Interracial Books for Children Bulletin* advisory board and a contributor to *The Arbuthnot Anthology of Children's Literature*, is a columnist for *Wilson Library Bulletin*.

Edward Stratemeyer modeled his Spanish-American War stories (*Under Dewey in Manila, Fighting in Cuban Waters,* etc.) after Henty's works, and ended his career in 1930 with more than seven hundred titles, a stable of writers and some sixty pseudonyms. By the end of World War I, Stratemeyer protagonists had become wholesale slaughterers; they did not hesitate, for example, to glee-fully let floundering German soldiers sink with their ships. ("What a relief," notes one character, "that more of the loathsome beasts have been removed from a decent world.")[2]

Similar themes appeared in series books by Percy Keese Fitzhugh, inventor of the noble slum kid, Tom Slade. Tom is given up for lost in flaming planes and troop ships; he is in and out of prison camps; he revives his collapsing French sweetheart by describing the hardiness of U.S. Camp Fire Girls:

> ". . . they don't scream when they get into a boat, and they ain't afraid of the woods, and they don't care if it rains, and they ain't a-scared of noises and all like that. You got to be one of them tonight. . . ."
> "No more am I afraid. I will be zis fiery camp girl—So!"[3]

Since Fitzhugh was endorsed by the Boy Scouts of America, it is not surprising that Tom continuously demonstrates the beauty of Boy Scout training: he can break barbed wire by coating it with sal ammoniac, locate enemy cannon by finding a splinter of bark on a dud shell and identifying the type of tree, and calculate his position by the timbre of a locomotive whistle.[4] Nonetheless, as in the Stratemeyer works, the Hun's "brutality," "loathsomeness," "murderous disposition" and propensity for bombing hospitals are vividly portrayed.

Heroes from earlier pulp novels were recruited in the literary World War I war effort. For instance, in *Tarzan the Untamed,* Tarzan puts his pet lion on a starvation diet and then feeds it German captives for dinner.[5] In the more genteel publications for children, characterization and setting are more naturalistic, but plots are just as propagandistic. In one *St. Nicholas Magazine* story, the crew of an armored tank named Little Cutey go into "the scrap" with "grins wrapped round their faces," hailing "with delight" the approaching battle. The Yanks get captured in this "scrap" (a euphemism for grim trench warfare), but no matter: "All the lost ground was recovered, and most of the prisoners the Germans had made were rescued" the next day.[6]

The publishers of these early works were quite clear about their motives. As one advertisement read: "There is no better way to instill patriotism in the coming generation than by placing in the hands of juvenile readers books in which a romantic atmosphere is thrown around the boys in the army. . . ."[7]

Similar works appeared in Britain as children's literature supported "national interests." In the decade prior to World War I, Germany was singled out as the enemy in much popular English fiction, and in fact William Le Queux, author of *Invasion of 1910,* collaborated with a British Field Marshall in working out details of an imagined German invasion. In order to increase readership and profits, Lord Northcliffe, who serialized the story in the *Daily Mail,* changed the tale's military strategy so the German troops march through all the English towns! Similar "invasion stories" were printed in *Boys' Friend, Boys' Herald, Magnet* and in Northcliffe's popular boys' papers, *Gem* and *Marvel.* According to Cadogan and Craig, "If by 1914, the boys of Britain and the empire were not raring to go and have a crack at the Kaiser it was certainly not the fault of Lord Northcliffe or his authors."[8]

The myth of white superiority has been an element in children's fiction throughout U.S. history. Novels about war often reinforce this theme; in the earlier works in particular, a character's appearance is usually enough to induce quick sympathy or repulsion (assuming of course that the reader was a proper, white, Anglo-Saxon child).

A black skin inevitably signaled a villain. In *The Battleship Boys' First Step Upward* (1911) two Hawaiian crewmen who desert ship are referred to as "niggers," as "those black-faced fellows from the other side of the world," whose "black goes all the way through; I'll bet they're black clear to the bone."[9] (It is interesting to note that the U.S. "annexed" Hawaii in 1898).

Countries dominated by the U.S. after its war with Spain were often treated paternalistically in fiction—the indigenous population portrayed as childlike and needing a Great Protector. For instance, a Mexican is described as a "stupid-looking, undersized man, evidently of the peon class" (*The Boy Scouts of the Air in the Lone Star Patrol,* 1914).[10]

The early novels also reflected the ideology of this country's "manifest destiny" on this continent, glorifying the U.S. cavalry's role in the conquest of Indian lands. U.S. policies toward the indigenous population were justified by depicting Native Americans in inhuman terms.

The Chinese were consistently stereotyped as ominous opium peddlers and as coolies "just like horses; it's hard to realize that they are really human beings."[11] Until World War II, the Japanese generally fared better—they were sometimes even considered the "Yanks of the East."

"Half-breeds" and white people who fraternize with people of color were also often singled out for special condemnation. White men in a Philippine bar have "sunk so low they are no longer any part of a white man," and the hero's underworld contact is a hideous creature with "all the bloods of the Far East in his veins" (*Dave Dawson in Singapore,* 1942).[12]

In general, the images of girls and women in these early works reflect the sexism of the times. Typically the protagonists wring their hands and cry, "Oh, if I could just put on a uniform, and take up a gun and—and—go after those awful Huns!"[13] There are, however, some exceptions to the "passive female." For example, girls are allowed to outwit spies and even land in France in *Red Cross Girls.*

In the U.S., as in other countries, there has been a tendency for novels—and other media—to reinforce the movement of women into public spheres during wartimes and a counter-campaign "to bring them home" when the wars ended. (See, for example, the Cadogan and Craig study of British novels and Betty Friedan's *The Feminine Mystique.*)

Following World War I, jingoistic novels continued to circulate through mass market channels, but serious, unmelodramatic children's novels about World War I were not numerous. People were beginning to share Ernest Hemingway's perspective: " . . . there is nothing sweet nor fitting in your dying [for your country]. You will die like a dog for no good reason."[14]

As the U.S. became involved in World War II, portrayals of Germans shifted slightly in pulp fiction. In his study, " 'The Foreigner' in Juvenile Series Fiction," J. Frederick MacDonald notes that whereas Germans had been brutally inhuman in World War I novels, they became "cunningly inhuman" in World War II. Brutality was shifted to "those dirty brown devils," those "throat-slitting sons of Nippon" (*Dave Dawson with the Pacific Fleet,* 1942).[15]

Snow Treasure by Marie McSwigan (Dutton 1942) and *Twenty and Ten* by Claire Huchet Bishop (Viking 1952) were among the few serious examples of U.S. war fiction during the 1940s and early 1950s. They were both based on factual events, the first describing how gold was smuggled from Norway, and the second giving an account of how ten Jewish children were rescued. By the late 1950s books of European origin began to appear in U.S. editions, and the traditional war ethos began to change slightly.

Before considering some typical books of this period, it is worth noting an outstanding antiwar allegory published in 1958: *Tistou of the Green Thumbs* by Maurice Druon (Scribner 1958).[16] Tistou can instantly produce flowers with his magical thumbs and manages to halt an impending war: "What could be done with rifles that flowered, with bayonets that you couldn't poke . . . ?" His clear-headed logic annoys his elders when he comments on the war:

> If I've understood properly, the Go-its and the Get-outs are going to fight a war for oil because oil is an essential material for fighting wars. . . . Well, it's stupid. . . .

Among the many novels in a realistic style for children is Ian Serraillier's *The Silver Sword* (Criterion 1959, reissued as *Escape from Warsaw*, School Book Service 1972), which depicts refugees struggling to reach Switzerland. It breaks with conventional war narratives by including a sympathetic portrait of a German family whose son is in the army and it shows how children had to fight starvation (a theme treated in even starker terms in Erik Haugaard's *The Little Fishes*, Houghton Mifflin 1969). Female protagonists have relatively strong roles in *The Silver Sword* and in another novel based on fact, *Ceremony of Innocence* by James Forman (Hawthorne 1970), which chronicles Sophie and Hans Scholl's martyrdom after they become anti–Nazi pamphleteers at their German university.

Friedrich by Hans Peter Richter appeared in German in 1961; it was published in this country in 1970 (Holt, Rinehart & Winston) and won the American Library Association's Mildred Batchelder Award. A detailed treatment of the Nazi harassment of German Jews, *Friedrich* is written with exceptional skill.

Summer of My German Soldier by Bette Green (Dial 1973) also departs from the conventional works by presenting a sympathetic portrayal of an "enemy soldier," but the book is marred by racism. The fat Black "mammy" who works for the protagonist's family is a singing, Scripture-quoting caricature with a minstrel dialect ("I ain't nevah 'fore cast me no 'spersions on the other folks' folks").

Rifles for Watie by Harold Keith (Crowell 1957), which won the Newbery Prize, is similarly bigoted, and it should be noted that the racist images are presented as author perceptions, not character perceptions (a very crucial distinction):

> A Negro woman, huge and billowy, her shining, blue-black hair bound in a red handkerchief, waddled into the room,

wheezing heavily at every step. . . .
Rolling her eyes in fear, she wrapped her heavy black arms nervously in her blue apron. . . .

Cross-Fire by Gail B. Graham (Pantheon 1972) is one of the few children's books about the Vietnam War. It is a biased story of a U.S. soldier who encounters four Vietnamese children outside their bombed-out village. Some degree of trust develops between the soldier and a thirteen-year-old girl, but eventually the baby dies, the soldier dies trying to protect another child and the rest of the family is shot by U.S. troops mistaking them for the enemy. The author makes it clear that everything could have turned out differently if all the men of the village had not gone off to Saigon to enrich themselves with U.S. dollars, and if the remaining elderly man—a Communist—had not brainwashed the children.

My Brother Sam Is Dead (Four Winds Press 1974), an ALA Newbery honor book, appears to have been inspired by the antiwar movement of the 70s, although the book is about the American Revolution. Young Timothy cannot decide whether to be a "Patriot" like his beloved brother or a Tory like his beloved father. In the climactic incident, Timothy's brother, Sam, a dedicated member of the Continental army, is suddenly executed by his own commanding general because of an alleged theft. Authors Christopher and James Lincoln Collier seem to be trying to stun the reader with a triple-layered irony: Sam's arrest for a crime he didn't commit, his indictment for literally stealing from himself and his death at the hands of his compatriots. The unrealistic plot complications reduce credibility, and the book comes close to what Albert Guérard has defined as propaganda: A book that "tries to snatch an intellectual decision by means of a sentimental appeal."[17]

In children's books death typically occurs "off stage" or happens only to minor characters. Because children tend to think of life as part of a conscious benevolent design—a scheme that means punishment for villains and rewards for the righteous—authors usually keep tragedy at a distance. They indicate that war leads to psychological adjustment in a protagonist or a new level of maturity. Unfortunately, this can give war a certain glamor. When young protagonists are depicted as growing up overnight and shouldering responsibilities far beyond their usual capacity, children find the whole idea appealing. They would like to be the fifteen-year-old shepherd who rescues twenty kidnapped children from an Albanian camp and brings them back to Greece despite the incredible hardships and Greek Communist guerrillas (the book's predictable villains), as occurs in *Ring the Judas Bell* by James Forman (Farrar 1965).

In Margaret J. Anderson's *Searching for Shona* (Knopf 1978) two girls trade identification tags during World War II. This enables one girl to escape to Canada, where she becomes thoroughly unscrupulous. The girl who suffers the experiences of war becomes an exemplary person. Wartime stress—like poverty—is often presented as a character-builder, thus glossing over the realities of war.

It should be noted that almost all children's books about World War II published in the U.S. are misleading for another reason. Because most of these books focus on European experiences, they deal with a war free of nuclear attacks. Thus they are concerned with a war that fits neatly into a novelistic framework—a war with a beginning, middle, and end. In Japan, on the other hand, the effects of the nuclear bombing of Hiroshima and Nagasaki are without end. Children need to learn about this dimension of nuclear war.

Novelists are still, according to Cadogan and Craig, attracted to "an extraordinary amalgam of insecurity and exhilaration" about the war years, and critics seem to be trapped in the same nostalgia. In *The Tragic Mode in Children's Literature,* Carolyn T. Kingston maintains that children's war novels have a cathartic effect. She becomes positively rapturous, stating that war within a narrative welds "generally disassociated groups into a marvelous unity, a state of mind prolific of acts of self-sacrifice for the common cause. Emotional pitches of mystical ecstasy are reached." Kingston adds that when books give insights into this "ecstasy," "the results are worth climbing bomb-devastated ruins."[18] Ruth Kearney Carlson praises the "heroic image" a book can give to childhood, and cites "deeds of prowess" in medieval legends as a way to stimulate it.[19]

A better critical approach would be a program of research that focuses on links between cultural history and children's books. As for example: George Orwell's discoveries about a 1910 worldview in boys' magazines of 1939,[20] Nicholas Johnson's study of war comics,[21] a study of George Henty's imperialistic novels by G. D. Killan,[22] and a study of English novels, comics, and newspapers by Ann Dummett.[23]

A sensitivity to what is historically authentic is at the same time a sensitivity to the art of the novel. The good writer sustains the links between real human experience and the invention of fiction. Irish novelist Elizabeth Bowen writes: "The novel lies in saying that something happened that did not. It must, therefore, contain uncontradictable truth, to warrant the original lie"—the original lie being the fabricated characters' situations and locales. Finding an "uncontradictable truth" presupposes a concern with many aspects of the human scene. In war fiction it presupposes a quest for the knowledge that will disarm bigotry, militaristic biases and nostalgic delusions.

NOTES

1. Peter A. Soderbergh, "The Dark Mirror: War Ethos in Juvenile Fiction, 1865–1919," *University of Dayton Review* 10, no. 1 (Summer 1973), 14.
2. Ibid., p. 20.
3. Arthur Prager, *Rascals at Large, or, The Clue in the Old Nostalgia* (Doubleday, 1971), 178.
4. Ibid., pp. 173, 175.
5. Ibid., p. 184.
6. C. H. Claudy, "A Match for His Captors," in *The Second Nicholas Anthology,* edited by Henry Steele Commanger (Random, 1950), 405, 411.
7. Soderbergh, p. 17.
8. Mary Cadogan and Patricia Craig, *Women and Children First: The Fiction of Two World Wars* (London: Victor Gollancz Ltd., 1978), 27–31.
9. J. Frederick MacDonald, " 'The Foreigner' in Juvenile Series Fiction, 1900–1945," *Journal of Popular Culture* 8, no. 3 (Winter 1974), 535.
10. Ibid., pp. 535, 537.
11. Ibid., p. 543.
12. Ibid.
13. Soderbergh, p. 18.
14. Ernest Hemingway, quoted in *Esquire* (September, 1935).
15. MacDonald, p. 539.
16. This book is a modern French classic, available in four editions in France, but now out of print in English.
17. Albert Guérard, *Art for Art's Sake* (Lothrop, 1936).
18. Carolyn T. Kingston, *The Tragic Mode in Children's Literature* (Teachers College Press, Columbia Univ., 1974), 94, 98.

19. Ruth Kearney Carlson, "Ten Values of Children's Literature," in *Children and Literature*, edited by Jane H. Catterson (International Reading Association, 1970), 33.

20. George Orwell, "Boys' Weeklies," in *The Collected Essays, Journalism and Letters of George Orwell: An Age like This, 1920–1940* (Harcourt, 1968).

21. Nicholas Johnson, "What Do Children Learn from War Comics?" in *Suitable for Children? Controversies in Children's Literature*, edited and introduced by Nicholas Tucker (Univ. of California Press, 1976).

22. G. D. Killan, *Africa in English Fiction, 1874–1939* (Ibadan Univ. Press, 1968).

23. Ann Dummett, *A Portrait of English Racism* (Penguin, 1973).

Part 6. Lives of Great Men
— and Women — All Remind Us . . .

What's Left Out of Biography for Children

Marilyn Jurich

Biography is hard to write. Resurrection may be more difficult than creation. The biographer "assays the role of a God, for in his hands the dead can be brought to life and granted a measure of immortality."[1] Not only must he revive persons — and particularly one person — but he must breathe back past times — not so much a panorama of ceremonies and battles, but the trivia that are significant to most people.

Biography for children is especially difficult to write because it is supposed to recreate and at the same time provide a guide to success, to encourage the child "to make something of himself" by giving him a believable model who "made it."[2] Thus, the biographer is supposed to be a psychologist or a moralist or both. At the same time, he is dealing with a necessarily imperfect subject about whom the young reader wants to know as much as possible. As Richard Ellmann writes, "More than anything else we want in modern biography to see the character forming, its peculiarities taking shape. . . ."[3]

In the preface to *Literary Biography,* Leon Edel cites that difficulty besetting all biographers: keeping a perspective somewhere between sterile objectivity and shrieking subjectivity. If one interprets the facts, may not he be inventing new facts? In straining to be truthful, there is always the danger of inventing the facts beforehand out of one's own prejudices. De Voto, in 1933, attacked

From *Children's Literature,* 2 (1973), 143–51. Reprinted by permission of the publisher. This paper was originally presented at the Seminar on Children's Literature of the Modern Language Association, Chicago, Illinois, December 27, 1971 and is an excerpt from a larger study by its author.

Marilyn Jurich is assistant professor of English at Suffolk University, Boston.

this "intuitive" form of biography: "Biography," he wrote, "is different from imaginative literature in that readers come to it primarily in search of information."[4]

Yet that very information, André Maurois believes, should in modern biography contain a moral lesson, if only to prove something about life, its difficulty, its frustrations, its end result of becoming what we did not choose. He feels that a special lesson is contained in exceptional lives. "Great lives show that, in spite of all, it is possible for a man to act with dignity and to achieve internal peace."[5]

Many of these exceptional lives, particularly as they are presented to the child, are made into heroes whom the child cannot only admire but extravagantly worship. For children, biographies are often like those for adults in Victorian times, when Carlyle pronounced that "it was in great men's actions, fully as much as in their pronouncements, that lessons of great wisdom could be read."[6] Indeed, psychologists or child experts frequently tell us children must have ideal beings after whom to pattern their behavior.

It seems to me, however, that there is need today for more biographies of ordinary people—not the Victorian type of biography which was written to affirm middle-class values, but biographies enabling a child to identify with the figure in the biography and so endure—something of the kind of thing one finds in drama in Brecht's *Mother Courage*. Thus, I do not altogether agree with Harold Nicolson, who believes that "the life of a nonentity or mediocrity, however skillfully contrived, conflicts with primary biographical principles."[7] We are no longer a complacent Victorian audience. We find it more difficult, perhaps, to define "nonentity" or "mediocrity." Further, since ideals as absolutes can never exist, in past or present, one might suggest that hero making is ethically wrong simply as a falsehood. The effects of hero worship might also be questioned. What happens when the child finds he cannot become even close to the ideal? Does he destroy himself or the society that seemingly prevented the attainment of this end? What happens when the hero is discovered to be an ordinary man or even a fraud? Does the child become so disillusioned that he gives up the possibility of positive change, or does he decide that, after all, the dishonest way "to the top" still gets you there—or gets you there more easily? I believe that the antihero is a legitimate subject of the biographer who works for children, that passivity or even outright failure can be interesting, imaginative, and even inspiring.

According to children's writer, Jean Karl, one of the attributes that makes a children's book distinct is "outlook." She finds that "A children's book looks at life with hope, even when it is painting the most disastrous of circumstances. . . . It does not believe that everything is always fine. But it is willing to hope that something can be done, that life can be better."[8] Such an outlook means not only that certain subjects would necessarily be considered improper, but certain portions of the lives of eminent people might be excluded. If the subject's weaknesses or failings were included, the reader might question whether the contribution was, in fact, worth it. Other lives might be censored, not because their examination leads to existential despair, but because their "sexual irregularities" might inspire to youthful orgy. According to Lillian Hollowell, the editor of a well-known anthology of children's literature, the complete lives of a Brahms or a Shelley "do not bear close inspection."[9] She is eager to maintain, however, that "A good biographer neither distorts nor suppresses; he may give a partial life, but he portrays his subject truthfully, noting both virtues and shortcomings."[10] One may ponder on whether exclusion is not a delicate form of suppression.

May Hill Arbuthnot, probably the most widely known writer on the subject of children's literature, also sanctioned "limited biographies," for, paradoxically, giving a more accurate view of the whole man.[11] "Adult peccadilloes," she maintained, will distort the essential character. One instance she cited was of "one of our historical heroes" who—as other frontiersmen—took an Indian wife and then deserted her. One might well ask whether a typical practice can be ignored (or even justified) merely for its "normality"; whether on the contrary, if the incident were included in the book, the child might gain better understanding of the plight of the American Indian. If the "hero" were, except for this part of his life, a decent sort, the child might still feel him worthy of reading about. My own feeling is that such heroes *need* humbling. Elsewhere, May Arbuthnot agreed that while a biography was, by her definition, a story of a hero, that hero should be presented with weaknesses and obstacles. Such a presentation, she felt, would give young people "courage to surmount personal or social difficulties."[12] She did not mention what these weaknesses were.

Some persons are never mentioned, are never subjects, for children's biographies. Those people whose sex lives were "irregular" are not considered appropriate: George Sand, Oscar Wilde, Lillie Langtry, or Casanova. Nor are "love-linked" people given twin billing: Nicholas and Alexandra, the Duke and Duchess of Windsor, Scott and Zelda Fitzgerald. Those who have led violent lives outside the "establishment" are also disqualified— Dillinger, for instance. Most show people who are "entertainers" rather than "legitimate" actors are considered too "trivial" to be models for children. Often their psychological background is considered disturbing: Marilyn Monroe, Lana Turner, Tiny Tim. Prominent political figures are excluded on the grounds that they are uninteresting: Governor Rockefeller. Other people whose lives may be worthy and inspiring are excluded or not examined because their contributions are considered too difficult for young people to grasp: Thorndike, the psychologist; Simon Weil, mystical philosopher; Horace Walpole, writer and art collector; and James Joyce. Among these left-out subjects for children, there seem to be no lives of cooks or critics, farmers or pharmacists, mothers or merchandisers.[13]

Biographers for children not only differ in what material is selected or in what person is regarded as an appropriate subject but in how the chosen material is structurally included. If a work is categorized as biography rather than biographical fiction, it follows a plot closely parallel to the life, usually chronological, of the characters and incorporates valid situations and behavior which can be documented or deduced from sources. (Rarely, however, are these sources listed in biographies for children.) What is distinct in a biography for children is the extensive use of dramatic devices rather than narrative or expository ones—imaginary conversation to convey essentially accurate facts, behavior, or actions. Information or description is also frequently injected to supply a clearer or more vivid account of the people or times. In a life of Pocahontas, the author pauses to describe how herbs are used to make healing drinks and ointments, and to describe how the young "squaws" look when they perform a dance for Captain John Smith.

A comparison of the way a life is told for an adult and for a child is interestingly clarified in "News Notes from the Feminist Press." Reah Heyn, the writer of *Challenge to Become a Doctor: The Story of Elizabeth Blackwell,* discovered how she needed to revise her book to appeal to children:[14]

> BEFORE: Best of all, Elizabeth now had a partner. Her name was Marie Zakrewska, called by everyone Dr. Zak. Marie had been chief-midwife and professor at a hospital in Germany, but lost her job due to the jealous anger of the men doctors. Dr. Zak than travelled to America, hoping to find more opportunity, but her friends kept telling her to be satisfied with a nursing career.

AFTER: On the morning of May 15, 1954, a young Polish woman walked into the dispensary. She could hardly speak English, but Elizabeth knew enough German to understand her.

"My name Marie Zakrewska," the woman said. "I came to America . . . continue medical work . . . from German."

Elizabeth was astonished. "Tell me your background."

Groping for the correct words in English, Marie described her past. "Age 23, I was chief midwife . . . professor at hospital Berlin. Students devoted . . . but much jealousy among doctors . . . they say I should be nurse. Support myself for year by sewing. Someone told me your name . . . I come for guidance."

Elizabeth took a deep interest in this determined woman. "First, I shall give you English lessons, and then you must go to college and get your medical degree. Meanwhile, would you like to assist in the dispensary?"

Obviously overjoyed, Marie replied, "Oh yes, Dr. Blackwell. Been very depressed . . . I date my new life in America from this visit."

Such biographies, though not necessarily less scholarly in research, are necessarily less complex in detail and less comprehensive in coverage. Writing in *Commonweal,* Elizabeth Minot Graves comments that these very limitations often require more writing skill than biographies for adults, since the writers must write clearly, and with pace, must make the individuals come to life. The biographer must write this way consistently, or he will lose his young readers.

Arnold Adoff's book on *Malcolm X* (New York, 1970) is essentially a picture book which glosses over the early life of Malcolm and barely suggests his real impact as a Muslim and as the leader of the Organization of Afro-American Unity. The book for adults — *The Autobiography of Malcolm X* — is so far superior in what it includes that it would seem advisable for the child to wait until he can read this account. A book on Martin Luther King by Margaret Boone-Jones (Chicago, 1968) is also too vague in conveying either the vitality of the individual or the nature and extent of his political and spiritual influence. King simply works, for example, "to have bad laws changed for better ones."

Though Langston Hughes experienced poverty and suffered the usual indignities inflicted on his race, Charlemae Rollins in *Black Troubadour* (Skokie, Illinois, 1970) sees the poet as having a rather favorable environment. While some facts are included to indicate economic hardship, the suffering is made conducive to artistic success. The idea is that if you work hard, regardless of background, you will succeed. Milton Meltzer's *Langston Hughes, A Biography,* also written for teenagers, does not gloss over the poet's difficulties, nor does it see the American way of life with such blurry optimism. The physical and psychological brutality suffered by Hughes as a child is gone into, as are the conditions of the Black ghetto in Cleveland during the earlier part of this century. Later, as Meltzer indicates, during the era of McCarthyism, Hughes was cited as a communist (a charge never proved) for his "radical books." As a result of his having appeared before the "Un-American" Committee, he lost lecturing jobs. Not for epitomizing the American Dream is Hughes acclaimed in Meltzer's book, but rather for giving voice to social injustice, to the importance of the Black "soul," to the causes of the migrant workers and other deprived groups.[15]

For older children and adolescents, surely figures of economic or political importance are capable of being humanized, but they tend to disappear as people in the panorama of chronology, genealogy, contemporary personalities, politics, and statistics. We are often only faintly aware of the physical person, his environment, his family relationships. The aim of the biographer is to present palatable history, but usually the effect is to present an enigmatic figure moving through a muddled sequence of events. *Zapata* by Ronald Syme (New York, 1971) is certainly both an oversimplification of character and a mystification of Mexican history. *Leader at Large: The Long and Fighting Life of Norman Thomas* by Charles Gorham (New York, 1970) is more satisfactory as history as well as in humanization, but the author often loses Thomas to circumstances and political experiences. When Thomas does reappear, the author views him less as a man than as a movement to be pondered on and praised. Harry Fleishman's book, *Norman Thomas* (New York, 1970), an "adult" source to which Gorham admits some indebtedness, is also enthusiastic in its endorsement of Thomas the man and of the socialism Thomas advocated. But the book is more acceptable as a biography because it provides a fuller perspective of the subject—the child, student, husband, and social reformer.

As an "establishment" figure, Andrew Carnegie provides a startling contrast to Thomas in his complete acceptance of a social code through which he eventually finds personal satisfaction and vast public success. In *Andrew Carnegie* (New York, 1964), Clara Ingram Judson reveals the reasons for Carnegie's achievement, but also promotes the work ethic. Carnegie may have lived by the Calvinist doctrine, and the writer here makes him into the allegorical American figure of "the go-getter." The repeated implication to the child is, "If you work hard, have strength and resolution, show initiative, are proud of what you are doing, are persistent in your effort, uncomplaining in your unremitting diligence, never refuse the opportunity to better yourself, show honesty and thrift, undertake responsibility, show, above all, ambition to better yourself—you, too, will make your million." Carnegie may have been devoted to such principles, but it is questionable as to whether his devotion was this fanatic. However Carnegie felt, the obvious didacticism here makes the character unbelievable.

Written by Clara Judson's daughters, the foreword to this book explains their mother's aim in writing her numerous biographies—to reveal how these "leaders," "threads in the tapestry of America," helped realize the beliefs that Americans hold: faith in government by the people; devotion to freedom; belief in education; and the conviction that each individual is important. Andrew Carnegie, then, is one of the threads in that glorious American flag, an embodiment of nationalistic goals.

Carnegie's treatment of labor is never critically or fairly examined. However amiably Carnegie exercises a tyranny over his workers, he is still a tyrant. In accepting the idea of a union in writing, yet advising that all mills be nonunion to prevent disputes over wages, he reveals some duplicity; and his so-called "interest and concern for workers" (p. 124) is never convincingly demonstrated. The so-called champion of workingmen actually denied the Homestead workers a national union, and gave all workers an inadequate wage, determined by "a sliding scale." In 1892, after the Homestead strike, the leaders lost everything, and rates for the workingmen were cut even further. Workers labored seven days a week on a twelve-hour shift. As a biographer for adults points out, "And Carnegie went on giving libraries and wondering why so few adults made use of his magnificent gifts."[16]

Clara Judson refers to *The Gospel of Wealth* as a truth. This work affirms Carnegie's notion that wealth in the hands of a few can elevate the race much more effectively than wealth distributed more equitably. Mrs. Judson seems, then, to confirm this notion that the "man of wealth" is "a trustee in the community" and deserves to be since he is obviously much superior to "his poorer brethren." This was a concept particularly common among Calvinists of the period, and one still held by many people, but not all, and it can only be maintained in Carnegie's biography by allowing for certain omissions from the whole story, as I have cited above.

If Carnegie is the American hero, the self-made man and the fulfillment of the American dream, then Karl Marx is the arch-villain, the Satan who throws down all who would ascend the ladder to the golden heaven, where the God of the Dollar reigns supreme. Written for adolescents, *Karl Marx, The Father of Modern Socialism* by Albert Alexander, is not really a biography but a diatribe against the economic philosophy Marx espoused and a defense of the American system. It is a "loaded" book. Marx is hateful because he represents a hated doctrine. As a child, he was totally unlikable; as a college student, he was totally ir-responsible; as an adult, he is best characterized as an atheist who, unable to bear most people and incapable of understanding life in general, escapes from living through philosophical abstraction.

The author implies that the ten-point program in *The Communist Manifesto* is somehow invalid because many of the goals in that program have since been accepted. Marx's thinking is criticized as being confined to the era in which he lived, derived from Marx's observance of hopeless conditions of that day—not in any sense a far-reaching explanation which can have relevant application. *Das Kapital* is disapproved of for revealing how wealth can come to be concentrated in a few hands. Income and inheritance taxes are viewed by the author as effective means of preventing such ac-cumulations. Thus Marx, as a philosopher, is pictured by Alexander as a self-deluded, selfish individual who simply plays games with abstractions in order to avoid honest work.

Generally, if one is to be an honest-to-goodness hero—either in this country or elsewhere—he must have known some kind of eco-nomic deprivation. Riches are not justified if the rags have not been flaunted beforehand. In biographies of Andrew Carnegie for children, written either by Katherine Shippen (New York, 1958) or by Clara Judson (discussed previously), the hero's early life is marked by poverty. Poor from what perspective, one might well ask. How *comparatively* poor as immigrants in the mid-nineteenth century? And is one really poor with relatives and friends in Pittsburgh, close by, who can lend money, give jobs, provide contacts?

Financial difficulty is also a means to strength of mind and inspiration to effort in *Explorer of the Unconscious: Sigmund Freud* by Adrien Stoutenburg and Laura Nelson Baker (New York, 1965). The assumption seems to be that a lack of funds necessarily means poverty. Actually when Freud had "no money available" and was "worried about debts," he was, at the same time, collecting primitive sculpture, taking long summer vacations, and sporting stylish clothes. His contribution to psychology did not depend on either his id, ego, or superego having known "real" want.

Even the poverty of George Washington is stressed. Elsie Ball in *George Washington, First President* (New York, 1954) sees poor George at eleven inheriting only "a large tract of land which was not very fertile" (p. 14) and Ferry Farm—not really his, but to be used as a family homestead. George, then, has "to make his own way in the world."

This misleading notion that fame and fortune come to those who work hard and long and that, conversely, those that have fame and fortune always deserve it, can well arouse psychological and even physical violence, once the realistic situation is confronted by the child and he recognizes how he has been biographically brainwashed.

Presenting a cultural and chronological perspective can diminish the possibility of distortion. In other words, if the person *is* poor, why poor, how poor, and, perhaps, how comparatively poor *today?* Why brave, how brave, and to whom? How brave *today?*

Sitting Bull by La Vere Anderson (Champaign, Illinois, 1970), for the eight to eleven age group, is a clear and lively book, sympathetic to an understanding of the values of Sioux life. In the Sioux battle with the Crows, "Slow" (the hero's original name) is regarded as *brave* after he is the first to strike a Crow Indian from his horse. Killing, in this case, is regarded as respectable, even deserving of reverence, as it probably always has been so long as the death comes to an *enemy.* To his own people, though, Sitting Bull is always gentle and compassionate. He abolishes slavery in his band. He tells stories, creates pictures, composes songs. He is wise. How comes such a man—or any man—to kill?

Perhaps the biographer needs to regard violence and its particular value to this Indian tribe; perhaps he should suggest how certain types of destruction are worshipped today. Peace-abiding citizens and "family men" may also destroy and yet be acclaimed heroes.

One would need a team of researchers working for some years to cover every facet of the treatment of biography for children. More research needs to be done on how a "life" is viewed for the young as compared with how the same life is viewed for the adult. More studies need to be made of the treatment of evil in children's books. Also, an investigation is desperately needed of the hiatus in the treatment of sex in all children's books, including biographies. The supposedly "brave" children's biographies of the pioneer in birth control, Margaret Sanger, have a curious habit of omitting her rich love life, including her marriages. Certainly these had some bearing on her crusade.

All in all, I see two major needs. The first is to encourage the writing of biographies of great human beings who are not famous, and who may be greater for this very reason, that they did not seek or obtain renown. We all have known such people and could wish for nothing more for our children than that they be like these quiet great ones. The second need is to give the subjects of biographies for children a fuller treatment—not to talk down to the child. The danger in the half truths of so many current biographies for children is that when that child reads the total account of the life in an "adult" book, he is understandably likely to distrust all adult information and instruction, and throw the good out along with the bad.

NOTES

1. John A. Garraty, *The Nature of Biography* (New York: 1957), 28.
2. Learned Bulman, "Biographies for Teen-Agers," in *Readings About Children's Literature,* edited by Evelyn R. Robinson (New York: 1966), 412; reprinted from *English Journal* 47 (Nov. 1958), 487-94.
3. Richard Ellmann, "That's Life," *New York Review of Books,* 17 (June 1971), 3.
4. Garraty, p. 140.
5. André Maurois, "The Ethics of Biography," in *Biography and Truth,* edited by Stanley Weintraub (New York: 1967), 50.
6. Richard D. Altick, *Lives and Letters: A History of Literary Biography in England and America* (New York: 1965), 85.
7. Harold Nicolson, *The Development of English Biography* (London: 1928), 146.
8. Jean Karl, *From Childhood to Childhood: Children's Books and Their Creators* (New York: 1970), 7.
9. Lillian Hollowell, ed., *A Book of Children's Literature* (New York: 1966), 241.
10. Ibid., p. 242.
11. May Hill Arbuthnot, *Children's Reading in the Home* (Glenview, Ill.: 1968), 261.

12. Ibid., p. 259.
13. See for instance, Doris Solomon, compiler, *Best Books for Children* (New York: 1970).
14. As discussed in "News Notes," *Feminist Press* (Baltimore) (Spring 1971), 7.
15. Milton Meltzer, *Langston Hughes, A Biography* (New York: 1968).
16. Joseph Frazier Wall, *Andrew Carnegie* (London: 1970), 579.

Living Proof: Children's Biographies of Marie Curie

Wendy Saul

The meritocratic paradigm virtually dominates the lives of educators. Educational institutions continue to be billed as the key to adult success. Children are told that if they are talented and work hard in school, recognition and profit will follow. How-to books for parents and teachers describe the importance of dealing consistently and fairly so that youngsters understand how specific actions lead to deserved punishments and rewards. Behaviorism, the philosophical model of our era, is premised and builds on this notion of "just deserts."

Research by Jencks, Coleman, Bowles and Gintis, Bond, and others, however, powerfully demonstrates that family income and affiliation are better predictors of vocational and academic success than either native ability or effort. And the findings of these scholars are not alien to what most of us have learned through experience. The implication here is unsettling — without major changes in our economic and political system, there is little hope for improving the lot of the poor, ethnic minorities, or women.

For scholars and practitioners who are guided by critical theory, neo-Marxist traditions and phenomenology, a serious question arises about what to tell children regarding their pasts and futures. Should curricula focus on the grim and hardly palatable fruits of inequality, or should attempts be made to instill hope in children through historical and biographical accounts of people, like themselves, who have been successful?

A slightly different version of this essay was published in *School Library Journal* 33 (Oct. 1986), 103–8 with whose permission and that of the author, Wendy Saul, the present version is printed here.

Wendy Saul is the author of *Butcher, Baker, Cabinetmaker, Photographs of Women at Work*, associate editor *The New Advocate*, and assistant professor at the University of Maryland-Baltimore County.

Because pessimism seems antithetical to our notions of both childhood and education, there is a general and often unspoken agreement among educators to celebrate success. The argument appears to be based on some variation of the self-fulfilling prophecy; if those statistically less likely to succeed see that others of their kind have been successful, they are more likely to pursue productive goals. To this end, Black History Month has been officially added to the school calendar, Martin Luther King's birthday is designated a holiday, and children's books about the achievements of minority heroes and heroines are available from every major publisher. Similarly, organizations such as "Women in Science" visit schools to offer advice and encouragement to female students. This thrust is reinforced by juvenile nonfiction titles such as *What Can She Be?, Saturday's Child,* and my own *Butcher, Baker, Cabinetmaker: Photographs of Women at Work.*[1]

Thus, critics of the status quo can delight in the increase of juvenile biographies about women and minority group members. It would seem that the past is finally being retrieved and made available to children. This paper, however, is designed as a cautionary footnote to that movement. In this preliminary study of biographies of Marie Curie it appears that biography is being used as "living proof" that the system can and does work for us all. As the formula for recognition—talent plus effort equals achievement—is repeated again and again, the reader is invited to see his or her family's lack of success as a personal problem. Furthermore, specific incidents which threaten an optimistic, bourgeois interpretation of current values are either downplayed or omitted entirely.

Moreover, biographies, by their very nature, are a selected retelling and interpretation of events, and children's biographers in particular have great latitude in choosing which events they portray as typical and important. And finally, because publishers and reviewers are usually not field experts, but instead are trained to consider how the child will feel after reading a particular work, historical accuracy is rarely called into question.

To evaluate a biography, one need have more than a passing familiarity with the person and the discipline being described. For this reason, I have chosen to focus on biographies of Madame Marie Curie, the most lionized scientist on the shelves of the public or school library. Robert Reid's adult biography, which has received critical acclaim from scientists and historians alike, Eve Curie's adoring and important portrait of her mother, and numerous collective biographies which include segments on the Curies were all readily available. Furthermore, personal access to

University-affiliated chemists familiar with the syntheses and theory used by the Curies, as well as my interest in Curie as a woman, made her an appealing character for this study.

The sample of juvenile biographies of Marie Curie includes the five titles listed in the 1985–1986 *Subject Guide to Children's Books in Print*,[2] as well as seven others catalogued in the children's room of an independent, suburban library in an upper-middle class mid-western community.

Marie Curie is, in many ways, an excellent choice for Americans anxious to prove that the diligence and talent of women are justly rewarded. Unlike the almost forgotten Rosalind Franklin, whose work was probably as important as that of Watson and Crick in analyzing the structure of D.N.A., or Barbara McClintock, whose theories on plant genetics were scorned in the best journals until she recently won the Nobel Prize at an advanced age, Marie Curie won her first Nobel award for a discovery she made while pursuing her dissertation research, and a second Nobel prize for her dogged pursuit of an aligned problem. Moreover, Curie came from a relatively poor family in an oppressed country, and died a world-famous scientist and heroine of her adopted, free country, France.

The theoretical basis for this approach is best explained and exemplified by Raymond Williams, neo-Marxist literary critic and sociologist who describes how cultures legitimate and give preeminence to certain traditions, values, and interpretations:

> From a whole possible area of past and present, in a particular culture, certain meanings and practices are selected for emphasis and other meanings and practices are neglected or excluded. Yet, within a particular hegemony, and as one of its decisive processes, this selection is presented and usually successfully passed off as 'the tradition,' 'the significant past.' What has then to be said about any tradition is that it is in this sense an aspect of *contemporary* social and cultural organization, in the interest of the dominance of a specific class. It is a version of the past which is intended to connect and ratify the present. What it offers in practice is a sense of *predisposed continuity.*[3]

Williams' comments guide the critic to look for emphases and omissions. Surprisingly, however, that kind of subtlety found little place in many of the accounts considered here. Curie biographers were either so ill-informed or intent on promoting a particular vision of success and appropriate behavior, that they felt remarkably free to stray, to turn their backs on historical fact. In short, although the Curie biographies dramatically instance Williams' claim that a version of the past predisposes readers to a particular view of the present, it should be noted that scholars with a completely different literary and social orientation might also balk at the factual distortions evidenced in these texts. For example, all of the juvenile biographies provide vivid accounts of how the late nineteenth century attempt to Russianize Poland personally effected the Sklodowski family (Marie Curie was born Manya Sklodowska). Eleven out of thirteen describe a specific incident in which Manya, always an excellent student, was called upon to recite before a Russian school inspector. Manya performed beautifully, the inspector left satisfied, and the patriotic Polish teacher was relieved. At this point the young Curie, in an atypical show of emotion, publicly wept for her country and herself.

Although this incident clearly typifies Marie Curie's long-standing and deep pro-Polish sentiments and loyalties, it may also be included because it is one of the few recorded instances in which the future scientist shows any "feminine" form of emotion. If this story of oppression were being told about a male child, for instance, there is some question about whether the crying would be emphasized.

An even more blatant example of historical distortion is found in *The Value of Learning: The Story of Marie Curie,* which portrays the czarist inspector with a hammer and sickle on his hat!

In still other instances, Williams' claim is clearly evidenced. Every account includes mention of the death of Manya's eldest sister and her mother; both deaths occurred within six months during the year the girl turned nine. These deaths were important in shaping Curie's character and values, and should undoubtedly be mentioned in any adequate description of her early life. While virtually every biography mentions how difficult it was to grow up with a consumptive mother who avoided kissing her children for fear of contagion, only one of the accounts, Mollie Keller's 1982 version intended for children in grades seven and up, mentions that it was after these two deaths, at a very young age, that Marie Curie gave up religion for good. Curie's antireligious sentiments are important in understanding her attitude toward science and her abiding attraction to positivism. A loss of religious faith is also something young children could understand and relate to (better perhaps than they can understand and relate to the purification and measurement of radioactive isotopes), and yet this fact is simply omitted.

Although there are many other incidents which are naively or purposefully distorted in Curie biographies designed for children, the remainder of this paper will explore only two others in detail — the Marie/Pierre romance, and the scientific honors bestowed upon Madame. For the record, however, I cite the following omissions and observations that support a meritocratic version of experience.

1. Little mention of the nervous breakdown Curie experienced after graduating top in her gymnasium class at age sixteen.

2. Radium sickness is mentioned only casually and never connected to the radiation sicknesses with which most children are familiar, such as the effects of the bomb.

3. Marie Curie was the mother of two children, neither of whom saw her as much as the average suburban child sees his or her nonworking mother.

4. An attempt is made to show Marie Curie's interest in the regalia of femininity, although, in fact, Curie never owned more than two dresses at a time, and was never concerned with domestic responsibilities.

5. It was expensive for Marie Curie to work. A questioning child might ask why a famous scientist was offered public charity after her husband's death. Marie Curie received few of the rewards most American children, who dream of fame, imagine.

But given the American dream, romance is surely one of the rewards which should come to a hard-working and brilliant woman; fittingly, biographers have portrayed the relationship of Pierre and Marie in terms that perfectly reinforce that romantic ideal. Robin McKown, author of two of the Curie biographies, puts it this way: "It was as if they (Marie and Pierre) were two parts of a chemical compound, meant to be united. Their thoughts, their dreams, their ambitions seemed to flow from a single source. They were supremely happy."[4] Mollie Keller, author of the least romanticized of the biographies describes the marriage of the Curies by adding that "Pierre and Marie were bound by more than temperament, ideals, and interests. They were also bound by love."[5]

Although it seems clear that Pierre and Marie Curie had a very good marriage, their relationship was in most respects atypical of the classic romance. First, Pierre and Marie were, before all else, scientists. At the time they met, both were engaged in studies so consuming and intense that marriage, even dating, seemed a horrible waste of time. Although most of the children's biographies describe the Curies' courtship as contributing to, rather than taking away from, their scientific studies, there is a definite implication that for every deserving human being, there is a perfect complementary partner of the opposite sex waiting somewhere.

Second, we are implicitly told that because Marie and Pierre were willing to wait, diligently pursuing their studies, until they found the perfect mate, they were graciously rewarded with romantic love, which is seen as distinct from shared temperament, ideals, habits, and interests. Both Marie and Pierre had had earlier relationships which never came to fruition; in Marie's case the son of her former employer in Poland was kept from marrying her because she was not of his class. If we entertain the possibility that Manya and Casimir had married, the female member of the team would never have achieved international recognition — women were simply not allowed to pursue their studies in Poland. And even if Manya had gone abroad to study as a married woman, the laboratory space and French associations provided by Pierre would not have been available to her.

Marie's relationship with Pierre then was productive partially because, by the time they met, both had developed a lifestyle and intellectual commitments the other understood and respected. Within their relationship, there was never a question of Marie's career being secondary to Pierre's. On the contrary, when it was Marie's good fortune to stumble onto and then vigorously pursue the unusually intense radioactive emissions from pitchblende, Pierre realized that her work was potentially more important than his own, and he dropped his crystallographic studies to collaborate with her. In each publication, and there were many, both authors were absolutely explicit in citing which aspects of the work each had been responsible for. The Curies never saw themselves as one scientist with one mind.

When Pierre was accidentally killed as he walked in front of a horse-drawn vehicle one rainy afternoon, people expected that Marie's science would change. When, in fact, it did not, they saw her continuing efforts as a fitting tribute to Pierre's memory. Neither in newspaper accounts of the day, nor in children's biographies over the past twenty years, is Marie Curie described as a scientist whose work was as important to her as any human relationship. If Marie had been the one killed, there is serious doubt whether Pierre's continuing work would have been described as a tribute to his wife.

Curie's early brilliance and the intellectual propensities of her family are attributes that all the biographers choose to include. These facts, plus Curie's diligence, are generally portrayed as equations in a formula that lead to the only possible solution — scientific fame and recognition. The book jacket description of Lorraine Henriod's Curie biography for beginning readers is typical: "In school, Marie Curie always answered correctly. When she grew up she became a scientist. Then she knew the right answers, too—to questions no one had ever asked before." These biographies make it appear inevitable that anyone who can read at the age of four, and whose intellectual gifts are nurtured, will someday become great. Conversely, they suggest that questioning and disobedience are anathema to science.

The Curie descriptions uniformly point to the fact that wealth has no place in this formula. Keith Brandt's *Marie Curie: Brave Scientist,* a 1983 publication, begins, "The Sklodowski family did not have much money. They were not famous or very important. But these things did not matter to them. To the Sklodowski family of Warsaw, Poland, what *did* matter was education." Several other retellings suggest that the Sklodowskis' economic problems were in fact a boon to the aspiring scholar—for instance, her abilities to concentrate developed as she lived in small quarters with her large, intellectual family.

This insistence that Marie Curie's poverty provided the perfect soil in which her genius could grow is reinforced later in each of the biographies. All of the tales give great weight to the impoverished conditions in which Mademoiselle Sklodowska lived as a student—she had to lug her own coal from the basement, her garret was often so cold that ice formed in her wash basin, she ate little and had few furnishings—but as Robert Reid points out in his account of Curie's life, these were the conditions in which many scholars at the Sorbonne lived. The interesting fact, and again Mollie Keller is the only one to point this out, is that if Curie had wanted to share a room with other students, her costs would have been considerably reduced, and her living conditions greatly improved. Here we see yet another instance in which Curie's antisocial character is denied, and her poverty is romantically emphasized.

Science, even for a woman as talented and disciplined as Marie Curie, cannot be divorced from social circumstance as it is in virtually every biography for children. Marie Curie's first Nobel Prize was awarded jointly to Henri Becquerel, Pierre and Marie Curie. About half of the children's biographies do not even indicate this fact. Moreover, the Curies were too physically sick from their work to attend the ceremony, although in Henriod's account for young children illustrator Fermin depicts Madame Curie accepting the coveted prize. Other biographies simply omit information about the actual presentation of the award.

Furthermore, both Curies were humiliated by the scientific establishment of France. Pierre, whose education was somewhat nontraditional (he worked with private tutors instead of going to the "right" schools), had been proposed for membership in the Académie des Sciences. Because he believed that election would help the standing of his work, he agreed to make the social calls necessary to enlist the support of members. This kind of activity was painful to Pierre; the fact that his candidacy failed by a vote of twenty to thirty-two surely did not help his science. After winning the Nobel award, Pierre again let his name be entered into candidacy; this time, after the mandatory social calls, he was admitted by a small margin.

To members of the Académie, Marie was not even a viable candidate at this time. Six years after Pierre's death, the Nobel laureate submitted her name for candidacy to the Académie. She was the first woman ever considered for membership, and the male establishment came out in angry force against her. She was attacked as a woman, a foreigner, a Catholic, and a Jew, and was finally denied membership by a slim margin. It was at this point that Marie Curie was awarded her second Nobel Prize. This award has to be seen as a political statement—the work for which Marie was given the prize, the purification of radium, though difficult, was not considered either as original or as extraordinary as other scientific achievements of the day. In short, no biographies for children even address the social and political character of scientific accolades.

Children's biographies also make little attempt to connect the kind of science Marie undertook to the extant social and political climate. Although there are many comments about Madame Curie's preoccupation with thoroughness, and some discussion of Pierre's inventive and imaginative mind, none of the presentations sees these circumstances as due to anything but temperament. Logic suggests, however, that given the fact that Marie Curie was being attacked on virtually every scientific front, the kind of science she would undertake would be both careful and methodical so that no one could question its correctness. For Marie Curie to engage in speculation or untested leaps, would be to invite disregard.

Finally, few of the biographies attend to the economic circumstances that make scientific research possible. This issue was important to Madame Curie; during her own working life, science changed from an enterprise in which individuals could be successful, to one in which expensive equipment and materials made institutional affiliation a necessity. By the time the radium institute was established, Curie had modified her views on the role of the scientist. To raise money for her research, she uncomfortably paraded across America, and fought unflinchingly to make sure that she, rather than the University, had complete control over the precious material.

Although every biography, even those written for very young children, stresses that the Curies never became wealthy through their scientific research, and that both Marie and Pierre were able to make gigantic scientific leaps with virtually no funds, working under the worst conditions, Marie's last attempts to insure the continuation of her personal scientific goals are given almost no attention. Even when her trip to the States is mentioned, it is as if Marie were simply accepting another honor, like the Nobel Prize, but in this instance the award was a gram of radium. In fact, the money to buy the radium was raised largely through the efforts of a journalist, Marie (Missy) Meloney, who was distressed by the constraints under which the famous scientist worked.

Upon her death, Madame Curie willed the radium that remained to her daughter and colleague, Irene Joliot-Curie, rather than to the University. In doing so she told the world that she still trusted individuals rather than an institution to continue her work. This fact is never mentioned in the biographies for children, and given little attention in the biographies for young adults. On the contrary, in the Mollie Keller's *Marie Curie,* generally a reliable source, there is a gross misrepresentation in this particular matter. Keller tells readers that: "The gift (Marie) had travelled so far to get came on May 20, 1921. The night before, Meloney ran through the ceremony and showed Marie the deed of gift. Marie's eyes were not too tired to notice that the deed gave the radium to her personally, and not to the Institute. She was horrified. She had never and would never own any radium. In the middle of the night she sent Meloney to find a lawyer and a notary to change the deed so that radium could be 'consecrated for all time to the use of science'."

This interpretation and these quotes are hearsay, apparently taken from Eve Curie's emotional biography of her mother.

The story, according to the more scholarly Reid, goes like this: Before embarking for America, Curie sent Meloney a letter asking that the recipient of the gift of radium be specified. Missy (Meloney), cognizant of the scientist's concern that the material would be given to the University of Paris instead of to Marie, replied in writing: "The gram of radium is for you, *for your own personal use* [italics used in the original communication] and to be disposed of by you for use after your death. I shall be glad to be of use to the University of Paris if it needs assistance, but for the present my time and energies are concerned only with your personal interests."

Let me be clear: in these misinterpretations and misrepresentations I do not charge malice. My guess is that in an attempt to reify Curie and the brand of selfless science these authors wish her to represent, they could not themselves believe that there was a real need for Marie to protect her work and her assets. In a just system, in a meritocratic system where excellence is valued, such protections would simply be unwarranted. But Marie Curie knew that she did not live in such a world. Throughout her career she had been impeccably clear in delineating just what was hers, and what was to be attributed to others. Her radium, the possession which concretely represented and allowed for her science, was not to be trusted to the socially and politically affected University.

The point here is not that Marie Curie was selfish and self-seeking. To the contrary, she scrupulously maintained her positivist ideals and her feeling that scientists should not become involved in politics. She knew, however, that other scientists did not share her views, and saw her personal ownership of the radium as a way of insuring the kind of disinterested science in which she so fervently believed. But the children's biographies of Curie do not even entertain the possibility that scientists may view their work differently, or that the world might have changed so dramatically from the time of Curie's death to the present that her apolitical stance might reasonably have changed. This could be done, for instance, by noting that Irene Joliot-Curie, came to see the inappropriateness of the "disinterested science" model as she witnessed Hitler's rise to power.

Science is also presented in children's biographies of Curie as a specialty for the brilliant. To do well in science, these books imply, one must also be utterly disciplined, ready to lead a life of sacrifice, and willing to die early of terrible diseases. Although this description of the scientist applies well to Madame Curie, the authors make no attempt to compare Marie's efforts, style, and successes to those of other well-known figures. (Rutherford, Einstein, and Becquerel, for instance, achieved recognition in markedly different ways.) Through such a comparison readers would be invited to speculate on why Marie Curie became the kind of scientist she did. The answer, I contend, has to do with the fact that Curie was a woman working in a totally male-dominated world. None of the biographies even suggests this explanation as a possibility.

A librarian informant tells me that nine-and-ten-year-old girls regularly come to her asking if there are any biographies of Helen Keller, Marie Curie, or Marilyn Monroe. At first this lumping together of three such disparate figures seemed both funny and bizarre. But on further reflection, I see questions embedded in the queries of these children which authors of biographies need to address . . . How do women become famous? Did these famous figures somehow enjoy the suffering they endured? How did they brace themselves against an unsympathetic or hostile world? Was it worth it?

Library literature suggests that children go to life stories for inspiration. This common-sense notion dominates the field of biography; biographical accounts are designed and intended to leave readers with lumps in their throats. Reviewers, too, tend to focus on how successful a given text is in uplifting the reader. In an effort to give Black, Native American, Hispanic, and female children hope for the future, authors, publishers, and those who dispense children's texts tell readers that if they try hard, if they are truly deserving, they will be rewarded. Children come to books for living proof that sustained effort is rewarded, and we provide them, again and again, with the "facts" they "need."

But there are alternatives to this vision. What if, for instance, we assumed that the purpose of biography was to answer questions such as the ones posed earlier: How *did* famous women, Blacks, Hispanics, or Native Americans brace themselves against an unsympathetic and hostile world? In this case, the implied reader would have radically changed his or her stance, and authors, publishers, and reviewers might respond in kind. What if, instead of steering away from a volatile issue such as Marie Curie's antireligious sentiments, an author worked to find those moments when the biographical subject said no to the norms and values she saw as unrewarding, and antithetical to her goals and ideals? In writing and publishing a biography of this sort, children's literature professionals would, I contend, be attending more fully to the psychological and historical reality of the subject, *and* the interests of the reader. From a critical perspective, an adequate biography of minority or female success would have to attend specifically to strategies used by the hero or heroine to combat prejudice, and to the points in the maze, those fissures, where a clever and determined and very lucky person was allowed to slip through.

NOTES

1. Gloria Goldenreich, *What Can She Be?* series, illus. (Lothrop, 1972–1979); Suzanne Seed, *Saturday's Child,* illus. (O'Hara,

1973); Wendy Saul, *Butcher, Baker, Cabinet Maker,* photographs of women at work by Abigail Heyman (Crowell, 1978).
2. *Subject Guide to Children's Books in Print 1985–1986,* (Bowker, 1985).
3. Raymond Williams, *Marxism and Literature,* (Oxford Univ. Press, 1977), 115–16.
4. McKown, 1971, p. 46.
5. Keller, p. 30.

WORKS CITED

Brandt, Keith. *Marie Curie: Brave Scientist.* Troll Associates, 1983.
– – –. *Marie Curie, Woman of Genius.* Illustrated by Cary. Garrard, 1970.
Eberle, Irmengarde. *Radium Treasure and the Curies.* Illustrated by William Sharp. Crowell, 1942.
Farr, Naumerle. *Marie Curie – Albert Einstein.* Pendulum, 1983.
Greene, Carol. *Marie Curie, Pioneer Physicist.* Children's Press, 1984.
Grey, Vivian. *Secret of the Mysterious Rays.* World, 1977.
Henriod, Lorraine. *Marie Curie.* Illustrated by Fermin Rocker. Putnam, 1970.
Henry, Joanne L. *Marie Curie, Discoverer of Radium.* Macmillan, 1968.
Johnson, Ann D. *The Value of Learning: The Story of Marie Curie.* Illustrated by Stephen Pileggi. Value Communications, 1983.
Keller, Mollie. *Marie Curie.* Watts, 1982.
McKown, Robin. *Marie Curie.* Illustrated by Karl W. Swanson. Putnam, 1971.
– – –. *Marie Curie.* Illustrated by Lili Rethi. Putnam, 1959.
Sabin, Louis. *Marie Curie.* Troll Associates, 1985.
Veglahn, Nancy. *The Mysterious Rays: Marie Curie's World.* Illustrated by Victor Juhasz. Coward, McCann & Geoghan, 1977.

Part 7. Children and Language

"I Play It Cool and Dig All Jive"* Languages in Children's Books

Betty Bacon

I received private lessons from Miss Ryan in a narrow hall off the classroom. . . . She read to me about sheep in the meadow and a frightened chicken going to see the king, coaching me out of my phonetic ruts in words like *pasture, bow-wow-wow, hay,* and *pretty,* which to my Mexican ear and eye had so many unnecessary sounds and letters. . . . When we came to know each other better, I tried interrupting to tell Miss Ryan how we said it in Spanish. It didn't work. She just said "oh" and went on with *pasture, bow-wow-wow,* and *pretty.*

— Ernesto Galarza describes the first grade at Lincoln School, Sacramento, California, in 1916, in his autobiography, *Barrio Boy.*

There is a potent magic in language. In other societies, I might keep my real name a secret because, if you know it, you have the power to do me intolerable harm simply by uttering it in the wrong tone of voice. In modern society, my pronunciation and grammar tell you who I am, where I come from, and how you need to see yourself in relation to me. The emotion that this calls forth in both of us determines our initial (and perhaps subsequent) reaction to each other. And much, if not all, of this reaction we learn as children, absorbing it along with milk and soft drinks, vitamins and Twinkies, from our families, friends, teachers, television, and books.

Parents, teachers, librarians, and the general public debate fiercely about what kinds of language should and should not be learned—

*The title is taken from Langston Hughes' poem, "Motto."

and by whom. In a conversation with me an eminent scholar once extolled standard English as the only adequate medium for culture, ideas, science, and technology. She felt Black children should be forced to study and speak only standard English.

Such reverence for the standard English, as written, if not always spoken, by the white U.S. middle class today, ignores a thousand-year process of drastic and continual change. It's a long way from "Sumer is icumen in, / Lhude sing cuccu!"[1] in the thirteenth century to Langston Hughes in the twentieth century affirming, "For I'se still goin', honey, / I'se still climbin', / And life for me ain't been no crystal stair."[2] And in between, the language of Chaucer evolved to Shakespeare to Pope to Walt Whitman to James Joyce. And picked up words like *xylophone* from the Greek, *crag* from the Welsh, *rug* from the Norwegian, *beef* from the French, *alkali* from the Arabic, *bungalow* from the Hindustani, *yam* from the West African,[3] and so on and on. English is spoken with a wide variety of pronunciation, vocabulary, and grammar from the Australian "jumbuck in the tuckerbag" to the young cockney whose courteous street directions in Southeast London I could not understand at all to the back-country Appalachian "step-husband" to California's popular "flautas" and "burritos" — not to mention the by-now world-wide term, "Reaganism." Under the circumstances, to confine children and their books to standard English would be a far more limiting form of censorship than banning all mention of sex.

Indeed, verbal variety and sexual frankness are not necessarily unrelated. An instructive example is a Victorian monstrosity, *Buttercup's Visit to Little Stay-at-Home,* produced in 1881 by one L. Clarkson. With appropriate drawings of plump, pink, well-draped infants, Clarkson writes:[4]

> What's 'at — Did I tum in,
>   Jes' now, wif' ze Tide?
> Dess I don't know very
>   Much 'bout at ride?
> Mus' been as'eep when
>   I sailed from ze sky;
> When I woke up, I was
>   High and dry.

Ah, the darling little ones with their adorable baby-talk! If only we could teach them all to be just like that!

Compare this with *My Special Best Words* by John Steptoe, a creative and fearless young Black artist and writer. Steptoe's little boy and girl are certainly *not* like that. They are nothing if not *real,* and their language has all the candor of live, twentieth-century children—loud, warm, affectionate, vulgar. They talk about food and fathers—and especially about every fluid from every bodily opening. Three-year-old Bweela, pictured with a big toothy laugh, says:[5]

> My best words is WHATSHAPPENINMAN and IWANT-SOMEWATERDAD and IDONTWANTTOTAKEANAP and my special best word for Javaka [her one-year-old brother] is YOUADUMMY! Javaka's best words is TAKEABREAK and SPAGHETTIOS and PICKMEUPDADDY.

Steptoe is obviously depicting his own children. He has a sensitive ear, and he is not afraid to write things down (nor to draw them) as they really are—from the car to the dining room to the bathroom. Adults are startled, often shocked, but this is real child language. The book also has the rhythms of Black English.

And Black English is where society's emotional responses get more and more shrill. It originated in the language of slavery and, hence, the rural South. It is now spoken by many Blacks throughout the country and is generally recognized as a native tongue. It is sometimes characterized as a dialect, a variant, but also as a special language.

The main differences between Black English and standard English are three:[6]

1. *Word choice.* Examples: *nitty-gritty* and *jazz,* which have passed into the vocabulary of standard-English speakers; *man* as a form of address as in Steptoe's book quoted above.

2. *Pronunciation.* Examples: *ant* (ahnt) the British pronunciation for *aunt,* instead of the American *ănt;* dropping the final *t* from words like *rest* and *soft* and the final *g* from words ending in *ing.*

3. *Grammar.* Examples: no inflectional *s* ending for plural nouns; use of the nominative pronoun for the possessive (e.g. *he foot*); manner of expressing time and duration without tense inflection (as in *They mine* for short-term duration, meaning either *They were mine* or *They are mine* depending on context; also *They be mine* to express habitual or long-time duration). (Similar constructions are found in other languages, e.g., Russian.)

Though Black English is distinctive, it can also serve as a medium of communication with speakers of other kinds of English. As poet June Jordan wrote:[7]

> I am talking about a language that will tell you simply "They Mine." (And incidentally, if I tell you, "they mine," you don't have no kind of trouble understanding exactly what I mean, do you?)

These words come from an article, *Black English, the Politics of Translation,* and politics is the root of the matter. Politically, the downgrading of Black English as an inferior distortion of "real" English is an instrument in the economic and social discrimination and racism inflicted on American Blacks. The Black defense of linguistic legitimacy is an expression of the political and economic struggle against racism.

Somewhat parallel is the stubborn and spirited vindication of Scottish English as a defense of political independence and resistance to economic exploitation. It was sparked in particular by Robert Burns in the eighteenth century after Scotland finally succumbed officially to British governance. And American children can belt out Burns's "Auld Lang Syne" on appropriate occasions without finding his Scottish language an undue hindrance.

Drawing into themselves a patronizing attitude with the air they breathe, standard-English speakers react with indignation to the fact that Black English is *different.* The linguistic authority, Dwight Bolinger, puts it this way:[8]

> The standard, naturally, is the way we ourselves talk. . . . Our primitive social desire for uniformity continuously asserts itself. The pressure to abolish differences in behavior—above all in linguistic behavior—is unrelenting.

The American tradition of the melting pot gave a veneer of social benevolence to this linguistic pressure. It was not only necessary for the new immigrant to learn a useful means of communication with earlier immigrants, he or she also had to become like them in every other way. Under these conditions, a language that came out of a number of African languages, filtered through the common experience of slavery, was not likely to win recognition from the rest of the population. But the vigor of this language could not be totally contained, and *jive* talk, for instance, has made its way into general usage.

The patronizing attitude toward Black English was passed down to children through succeeding generations. In the classroom and in the library, they learned about Longfellow and Tennyson, but a cloud of silence surrounded Paul Laurence Dunbar for many years after his death in 1906. Yet he was one of the great pioneers in using Black English for a serious literary purpose. Some of his poems were collected in a volume for children, including "When Malindy Sings," which aims a sarcastic barb at the white mistress:[9]

G'way an' quit dat noise, Miss Lucy—
Put dat music book away;
What's de use to keep on tryin'?
Ef you practice twell you're gray,
You cain't sta't no notes a-flyin'
Lak de ones dat rants and rings
F'm de kitchen to do big woods
When Malindy sings.

For a century, children throughout the country encountered Black folk tales and Black language through the "Uncle Remus" stories set down by white newspaperman Joel Chandler Harris. Although the tales were indeed there, they were presented in the context of the white child listening to the Black slave. Moreover, Chandler's effort to reproduce the sound and rhythm of Black language through a system of spelling as elaborate as Dunbar's made his texts very hard to read.

The work of Black anthropologist and folklorist Zora Neale Hurston was unknown to most adults—much less to children—until Julius Lester and other contemporary writers made use of her research. This began the process of restoring her to her rightful place in the development of American literature.

Up until the 1960s, a few Black writers did turn their talents to writing for children as well as adults—notably Langston Hughes, Gwendolyn Brooks, and Arna Bontemps. They could pass back and forth with practiced ease between Black and standard English, thus enriching the linguistic experience of their young readers. Then the civil rights movement opened the door for a whole new Black literature for youngsters (a development in which the Council on Interracial Books for Children, founded shortly after World War II, played a significant part). At last, Black writers could use Black English with a chance of reaching their audience.

In prose fiction, some writers put conversation in Black English, while narrative and descriptive passages are in standard English. Brenda Wilkinson uses this combination of language in *Ludell.*[10]

> Mama . . . changed linen on both beds, then came and stood between the kitchen and the front room, looking around while sweat poured from her brow.
> "Mama, you never gon sit down?" Ludell asked.
> "Yeah, I reckon I oughta," she said. "Even a mule do that."

Lucille Clifton employs the same technique in her picture book for young children, *Amfika,* when she writes:[11]

"He waking up now." Mama's voice sounded all happy and dancing. Amfika opened his eyes wide.

The full richness of Black English as a literary expression is especially evident in those books which are written entirely in Black language. Alice Childress was a playwright and a newspaper columnist before she wrote her first book for young teen-agers. *A Hero Ain't Nothin' but a Sandwich* is a highly complex novel about a boy in Harlem—his family, his school, his friend, his dreams and struggles, and his drug addiction. The reader sees Benjie, the hero, in a series of dramatic scenes, each told in the voice of one of the characters. Here is Benjie himself, remembering the moment of terror when he was about to throw himself off the roof of his house:[12]

> Hangin by one hand from a roof edge ain't no joke. Lookin down six, seven stories over a concrete backyard will blow your mind if your brain ain't in strong condition. My grandmother ast me what I was thinkin while hangin like that. No way for me to say cause I can't clear remember any one thought comin behind another, thassa fact. Day by day I'm losin some more of what little I did remember. Night by night I be dreamin it over again. One night I dream Butler drop me and I was fallin straight down to get smattered on concrete. I woke up just in time, with such a jump till I fell outa bed.

The language changes as we enter the thoughts of Benjie's stepfather, his teacher, his ambitious friend, his troubled mother, his old grandmother. Each has a distinctive accent that serves as an essential ingredient of character delineation—much as Alice Walker uses nuances of language to mark the progress of *The Color Purple*.

A totally different mood is created by Julius Lester in his retelling of the tale of "High John the Conqueror" in his *Black Folktales:*[13]

> Way back during slavery time was a man named John. High John the Conqueror they called him. And he was what you call a *man*. Now some folks say he was a big man, but the way I heard it, he wasn't no bigger than average and didn't look no different than the average man. Didn't make any difference, though. He was what you call a *be* man—be here when the hard times come, and be here when the hard times are gone.

Here the language is used to project strength—down to earth, irre-pressible.

June Jordan begins her story of two teen-age lovers, *His Own Where,* with an outpouring of feeling in the form of a prose poem:[14]

> You be different from the dead. All them tombstones tearing up the ground, look like a little city, like a small Manhattan, not exactly. Here is not the same.

> Here, you be bigger than the buildings, bigger than the little city. You be really different from the rest, the resting other ones.

> Moved in his arms, she make him feel like smiling. Him, his head an Afro-bush spread free beside the stones, headstones thinning in the heavy air. Him, a ready father, public lover, privately at last alone with her, with Angela, a half an hour walk from the hallway where they start out to hold themselves together in the noisy darkness, kissing, kissed him, kissed her, kissing.

Rich and passionate, the language draws the reader at once into the story by its creation of mood, person, and place. Jordan uses the grammar to create a singing cadence, and the cadence pulls the reader along with its special musical quality. It is untranslatable.

For all their differences, the three quoted passages have one thing in common: They make use of standard English spelling. No Uncle-Remus-type barriers are put in the way. Pronunciation is left to the reader. The sound of the language arises from rhythm and grammar and the reader's voice. Obviously, these writers, too, can move back and forth between Black and standard English. Their particular method of suggesting the sound of Black language makes it possible for standard English speaker—whether child or adult—to experience its rhythmic quality and even to read it aloud.

But what of the children who will read these books? First of all, let us in no way underestimate the importance for children to find their own native way of speaking put down in a book. This has much to do with learning to read, it has much to do with self-respect. Your own language, your own usage, in your own book has a great influence in how you feel about books in general. Are they something of yours, or are they alien?

It is a ruling class myth that working class kids are nonverbal, and that they have great trouble learning to read because they are unaccustomed to using words. Nothing could be further from the truth. The English folklorists, Iona and Peter Opie, asked two fourteen-year-olds in the north of England for the names they called their classmates. The youngsters came up with a list of thirty-one, ranging from "phumph," "squarehead," and "chubby cheaks," to "gilly," "Bullet Head," and "cominist."[15] Street talk is just that—talk; and it uses words. In fact, it uses them in all kinds of unusual and ingenious ways. Black teen-agers in the city learn to "play the dozens," a complex word game of mutual insult in rhyme. The playground poetry of Black youngsters in Houston, Texas, fills an entire book:[16]

> Eat a piece of candy
> Greedy greedy
> Jump out the window
> Crazy crazy
> Don't wash the dishes
> Lazy lazy
>
> Vaccination
> Education
> Does it hurt
> Or does it sting
> It don't hurt or anything

Obviously the assumption that Black children and working class children are nonverbal is erroneous. It gives rise to a further assumption that working class youngsters are incapable of understanding and using a wide variety of words. Anything unusual will confuse them—or so a school librarian evidently thought, when she refused to buy the very funny British stories about Paddington the bear[17] because they contain such exotic words as *lorry* for *truck*, *shillings* for *quarters*, and *underground* for *subway* (to name only a few horrible examples).

It gives rise to the teacher who will not read *The Tale of Peter Rabbit* to her Black kindergarteners because they will not understand the literary English of the text that includes such statements as "some friendly sparrows . . . implored him to exert himself."[18] As if the children could not guess from the illustration or as if she could not enrich their language by explaining to them!

The same kind of disdain was demonstrated by the kindly nursery school teacher who wanted to translate *Peter Rabbit* into Black English. Her good intentions ignored the fact that no language is richer in rabbit stories than Black English, so there was no pressing need for another one, and the parallel fact that a minimum of explanation would make Beatrix Potter's masterpiece entirely comprehensible since it is a simple, direct narrative illustrated in detail.

Her assumption is that Black kids should get books *only* in Black language. The reverse of this is the librarian in a white middle-class suburb who refused to buy books in Black language, or even with Black subjects, "because we have no Black patrons, so the children won't be interested." (Similarly, following their own prejudices, adults are comfortable giving children collections of Chinese folk tales about China halfway around the world, but *Pie-Biter*,[19] a folk tale about the Chinese in California in the 1850s, is rejected because "only Chinese-American children would read it.")

Carrying the limitation of language to the extreme is the controversy over bilingual education, especially in areas with substantial Hispanic populations. Ignoring the fact that Spanish was the language of large sections of the United States long before English, the education of children in both languages is condemned on the excuse that this would be "cutting them off from the mainstream."

The provincialism of the monolingual approach was pointed up by the Mexican-American historian and educator, Julian Nava, when he told a group of California children's librarians, "Only in the United States is a bilingual child considered culturally deprived." (This is not entirely accurate as the same attitude prevails in other countries where the language of the working class differs from that of the ruling class—for example, South Africa.) Education in more than one language is considered routine in many countries less geographically and linguistically isolated than the United States. In Surinam, South America, it is normal to be fluent in half a dozen languages—in fact, necessary for the conduct of the daily routine by everyone from businessmen to longshoremen. Bilingual education has been the rule among national minorities in the Soviet Union since the 1920s, and children's books are sometimes published in as many as seventy languages.

Ideally, all children deserve education in many varieties of language—their own and other people's. The rich culture of the world should be theirs, and they should have the tools to deal with it—including pride in their own language and pleasure in crossing its boundaries. As Margaret Schlauch says: "The best heritage of poetry belongs, like the best of all the arts, to all the people who enjoy it. Under more favorable circumstances, I am convinced that this would include vast numbers who never hear about their heritage today."[20] Elsewhere she quotes grammarian Charles Fries who advocates an education that provides "a language experience that is directed toward acquaintance with and practice in the rich and varied resources of the language."[21]

Professor Kenneth Goodman wrote in 1972:[22]

> Authors and editors of children's books can base language decisions on a single pervasive principle: it must be real language as people really use it. It has taken . . . more than a decade to realize that if Black is beautiful, so is the way Black people talk. . . . It is not just the Black child or the Chicano child or the Appalachian child who needs books portraying real people telling it like they do. All children need to encounter the richness in language, culture, and experience that is America.

The late Soviet poet, Kornei Chukovsky, was a minute observer of children's use of language and their responses to its peculiarities. He wrote:[23]

> We must not forget also that part of our task in helping the child acquire knowledge of his spoken language is the constant enrichment of his speech with more and more new words. Since a child's mental growth is closely connected with the growth of his vocabulary, it is easy to see how important this task is. In this sense, to teach a child to speak well means also to teach him to think well. One is inseparable from the other.

It would be a poor civilization indeed in which we gave *A Hero Ain't Nothin' but a Sandwich* with its subtle permutations of Black English only to Black children or *The Hobbit* with its literary English-English only to the families of professors at Oxford or Harvard. Children have a right to the *whole* world. They have a right to see their own lives — including their language — reflected in their books, but they also have a right to go beyond that to other people, other times, other places, and other languages. "His own where," "lorries," "tuckerbags," and "implored him to exert himself" are not insuperable obstacles but guideposts to the rich life of our planet.

With grateful acknowledgment for help, criticism, advice, and especially thinking, to Dr. Julian Boyd, Professor of Linguistics, English Department, University of California, Berkeley.

NOTES

1. *Oxford Book of English Verse,* p. 1.
2. Hughes, p. 73.
3. Pyles and Algeo, pp. 297 ff. passim.
4. Clarkson, p. 6.
5. Steptoe, p. 12.
6. Pyles and Algeo, pp. 234–35; Schlauch, *The English Language,* pp. 198–99; Dillard, pp. 51–52.
7. Jordan, *Library Journal,* 15 May 1973, 1632.
8. Bolinger, p. 276.
9. Dunbar, p. 7.
10. Wilkinson, p. 53.
11. Clifton, p. 24.
12. Childress, p. 111.
13. Lester, pp. 93–94.
14. Jordan, *His Own Where,* p. 1.
15. Opie, p. 154.
16. *Apple on a Stick,* pp. 23, 19.
17. Bond, *A Bear Called Paddington.*
18. Potter, p. 33.
19. McCunn, *Pie-Biter.*
20. Schlauch, *The Gift of Tongues,* p. 257.
21. Schlauch, *The English Language,* p. 199.
22. Goodman, *Library Journal,* p. 3425.
23. Chukovsky, p.17.

BIBLIOGRAPHY

Apples on a Stick: The Folklore of Black Children. Collected and edited by Barbara Michels and Bettye White. Illus. by Jerry Pinkney. Coward-McCann, 1983.

Bolinger, Dwight. *Aspects of Language.* Harcourt Brace Jovanovich, 1968.

Bond, Michael. *A Bear Called Paddington.* Illus. by Peggy Fortnum. Houghton Mifflin, 1958, 1960.

Childress, Alice. *A Hero Ain't Nothin' But a Sandwich.* Coward, McCann & Geogham, 1973.

Chukovsky, Kornei. *From Two to Five.* Translated by Miriam
    Morton. Rev. ed. Univ. of California Press, 1968.
Clarkson, L. *Buttercup's Visit to Little Stay-at-Home.* New ed. rev.
    and enl. Illus. by the author. E. P. Dutton & Co., 1881.
Clifton, Lucille. *Amifika.* Illus. by Thomas Di Grazia. E. P. Dut-
    ton, 1977.
Dillard, J. L. *Black English: Its History and Use in the United
    States.* Random House, 1972.
Dunbar, Paul Laurence. *Little Brown Baby: Poems for Young
    People.* Selections, with biographical sketch, by Bertha
    Rogers. Illus. by Erick Berry. Dodd, Mead, & Co., 1895,
    1940.
Galarza, Ernesto. *Barrio Boy.* Univ. of Notre Dame Press, 1971.
Goodman, Kenneth. "Uptight Ain't Right." In *Library Journal* 97
    (15 Oct. 1972): 3424–26.
Hughes, Langston. *The Dream Keeper and Other Poems.* Illus. by
    Helen Sewell. Alfred A. Knopf, 1932, 1963.
Jordan, June. "Black English, the Politics of Translation." In
    Library Journal (15 May 1973): 1631–34.
– – –. *His Own Where.* Thomas Y. Crowell Co., 1971.
Lester, Julius. *Black Folktales.* Illus. by Tom Feelings. Grove
    Press, 1970.
McCunn, Ruthanne Lum. *Pie-Biter.* Illus. by You-shan Tang.
    Design Enterprises of San Francisco, 1983.
Opie, Iona and Peter. *The Lore and Language of School Children.*
    Oxford Univ. Press, 1959.
The Oxford Book of English Verse, 1250–1918. Chosen and edited
    by Sir Arthur Quiller-Couch. New ed. Oxford Univ. Press,
    1940.
Piaget, Jean. *The Language and Thought of the Child.* World Pub-
    lishing Co., 1955.
Potter, Beatrix. *The Tale of Peter Rabbit.* Illus. by the author.
    Frederick Warne & Co., n.d. [1906].
Pyles, Thomas, and John Algeo. *The Origins and Development of
    the English Language.* 3rd ed. Harcourt Brace Jovanovich,
    1964, 1971, 1982.
Schlauch, Margaret. *The English Language in Modern Times (since
    1400).* Warsaw: PWN-Polish Scientific Publishers; London: Oxford
    Univ. Press, 1959, 1967.
– – –. *The Gift of Tongues.* Modern Age Books, 1942.
Steptoe, John. *My Special Best Words.* Illus. by the author. The
    Viking Press, 1974.
Wilkinson, Brenda. *Ludell.* Harper & Row, 1975.

Part 8. Writers Speak for Themselves

Creating In and For a Pluralistic Society

Mildred Walter

Pluralism emphasizes equality of organizations formed out of citizens' needs and interests. Lack of equality of organizations in this country has led to charges that the system in the United States is not pluralistic. Customs, beliefs, and traditions in this country confirm those charges.

In spite of the wide variety of peoples in the United States, traditions, beliefs, and customs are grounded in western ideology. Individualism is the ultimate. Free enterprise and competition are esteemed. The English language in a "correct" form is deemed the best for conveying images and recording experiences. Values set by the "majority" are perpetuated, and the institutions, both public and private, enforce those values by consensus and/or control.

Now, how do these values and ideology affect me, a woman, a Black, and a product of the rural South? How do I create in this diverse, complex society where competition, free enterprise, and individualism are supreme, where conflict activism is contained or controlled by consensus? I belong to a racial, sociopolitical group whose members' needs and interests vary widely. However, because of the overriding concerns with racism and a continual struggle for social equality, participation in this group is often necessary.

Some Blacks find their interests and needs met better outside the

Excerpt from a paper delivered at the Every Child Conference in New York City in 1985. By permission of the author.

Mildred Walter is the author of seven books for boys and girls, ranging from retellings of African folk tales to junior novels about contemporary young Black people in the United States. She is the recipient of the 1987 Coretta Scott King Award.

group. Others may choose to identify with the group, finding their interests and needs satisfied. My experience in the group has caused me to conclude that pluralism in this society is an illusion. And my experiences as a Black have led me to develop beliefs and customs that are alien in a society that glorifies individualism, competition, and free enterprise.

I was born in a small Louisiana town where my relationship with the ruling majority was a "them and us," or a master-servant one. My family, my school, my church, my community, my friends, and my direct adversaries were all Black. I don't remember ever not knowing that where the paved streets began was the white quarters. Unless you worked in that area, or had official reasons for being there, you didn't go.

In Louisiana, with an admixture of French, Indian, Black, and Caucasian, there was a wide range of "colors" among Blacks. I don't remember ever not knowing that the closer one came to looking white the more beautiful one was considered. The standard of beauty was white skin, thin lips, patrician nose, thin bodies, and reserved manners.

I played with and loved white dolls, and there was a time when I denied myself the pleasure of walking and running freely in the rain because water did "terrible" things to pressed hair. And I remember the time when I wished to look like a girl admired for her long curly hair and olive tinged skin. My mother, apparently annoyed because of that wish, responded, "You're prettier than she will ever be."

I didn't believe her, but a seed had been planted. There were sprouts of confidence, of self-awareness, and a feeling of worth. The sprouts took roots and grew into an acceptance of myself which was the beginning of acceptance of others.

T. S. Eliot said, "A novelist need not necessarily understand people better than most of us, but he must be exceptionally aware of them." These words can easily apply to being Black in this system. For survival I had to develop skills that gave me the ability to interpret what I see, hear, and feel in a way that what I reveal outwardly is not detrimental to me or my group.

I learned that competition breeds distrust; cooperation creates confidence and friendship. Cooperation with, not conquering, nature increases bounty, enhances beauty. We are one with the universe— one with all things dead, living, and to be born. The elderly are esteemed for they are the link between that which is and that which has been.

I learned that sharing cements harmony with nature. As nature gives the elements of earth, air, water, and fire without condition, so must we give of our talents and goods.

You are probably anxious for me to get on with how I create in this society. I must say it is not easy. Those of you who work with words are probably muttering, "So what's new? It's not easy for any of us."

My proposition is that creating in this society is more difficult for me because I am Black. I write books for all children about people and places I know best. When I create I seek my material in a collective consciousness that is at variance with western ideology. My characters speak to me the way southern Black folks say things. Then I must translate.

When I create, my characters insist on exclaiming, "I am not free unto myself. I am part of a whole, interdependent, seeking an identity with my group knowing that because we are, I am. If I break away without approval, I am lost."

Further, when I create, I am reluctant for I know that my creation is likely to be delivered by hands that know little about me, my beliefs and customs. The very life of my creation might depend upon one who feels that the way Black folks say things is jarring. To quote Zora Neal Hurston, "It is ridiculous to decorate a decoration." It is unpolished to repeat words rhythmically as jazz musicians repeat a note to emphasize a simple refrain. To write a story simply with no hidden meanings, no symbols to be unearthed may be deemed of little literary value. These are the fears that are always in the back of my mind when I create.

"Why do you fear?" you may ask. "Your work is published, your work is read, and often well received."

It is not for me, or my work alone that I fear, but for my group. In the year 2000, it is projected that almost a third of the U.S. population will be peoples of color. Blacks will comprise the largest percentage of that group. Further, in the year 2025, thirty-five percent of the total population will be peoples of color. With a third of the total population sixty-five years or older at that time, the market for children's books will have changed drastically. For all practical purposes, one half of the children's book market will be directly affected by peoples of color.

That fact has serious implications when, today, less than two percent of published writers are people of color and when there are even less that number as editors, marketing specialists, and executives making decisions.

In the publishing business, as in all businesses, the bottom line is, "Is it salable?" If that future market is going to be cornered, steps must be taken now; otherwise, the influence of the publishing industry will be greatly reduced.

To create a profitable reading clientele among peoples of color, I submit to publishers that a commitment to the creation of positive images of us must be made now. That commitment will manifest itself in the use of our talents, now; in the appreciation of our styles, now; and in the investment of time and resources right now to persuade peoples of color to consider your products.

When these efforts are joined the inevitable need for editors, managers, market specialists, and yes, decision-makers from our groups will be met. In the process of securing future changing markets, a wider base for a pluralistic society to become a reality also will be in the making. A pluralistic society, like a good book, is a challenge to create. It is a goal to pursue. And, like a good book, it is never finished, but still we find pleasure in striving to attain a perfect ending.

Those who work with words, whether by creating or marketing, have great influence over those who wield power in this society. We are the ones, for better or worse, who form and shape opinions. The task is to make this society a truly pluralistic one in which organizations formed out of needs and interests are balanced. And one in which individuals, within those organizations, are able to create and to act with courage knowing that they can make a difference.

Children's Responses to Illustrations of Poetry

Agnia Barto

Drawing and verse. Artist and poet. Two different people, two different creative personalities, pooling efforts to produce a book for the child reader. Though I cannot say I have ever studied children's responses to the illustrations in my own books, I have had occasion to discuss things with numerous illustrators and have often had the opportunity to watch children responding to books. Generally speaking, I attach great importance to what the child reader thinks, and often child audiences are the first to hear me recite new poems. As soon as they start fidgeting, I realize that I must ruthlessly delete even lines which I might think well-written to maintain the suspense and brevity, and not let attention flag.

The way children—especially small children—express themselves is through smiles, laughter, happy cries, remarks, or bored eyes. Sometimes their remarks are most valuable. One day a certain writer was asked to read a new story to a kindergarten audience. Response was sluggish. One little boy said, "I've read that before!" "But it hasn't been published yet!" the writer objected. "I know I've read it!" the little boy insisted. How straightforward, yet how killing, an assessment of a stereotyped story!

For the child reader to take to a book, it is essential, as I see it, for poet and artist to share a common feeling of what I would call the childlike. It is also very important that the two grasp one another's creative intent. Wherever you have this inner unity, the resulting book is sure to offer the child much; it will teach him to think, to see, and to feel. On the other hand, I do not think it at

Reprinted from *Children's Literature in Education* 32 (Spring 1979), 11–17, by permission of the publisher, Agathon Press.

Winner of the Lenin Prize for Literature, the late Agnia Barto was a distinguished Russian poet especially active in promoting international cultural exchange.

all essential for every event I describe in a poem of mine to be necessarily faithfully illustrated. It is for the artist to select at his own discretion what he thinks would make an interesting picture. The important thing here is how well he is able to grasp the substance and single out the main points.

I shall always feel grateful to one tiny reader of mine who, it should be said, still did not know his letters. This was a long time ago. I was informed by the editors at the Children's Literature Publishing House that a fine artist, Konashevich, would himself illustrate my poem for small children, "The Toys." He showed me his drawings, and I took a great fancy to them though there seemed to me to be something missing in the excellently executed drawings that would be most appealing to children. The poem was (in rough translation):

> Teddy was dropped on the floor.
> Teddy lost his paw.
> But I won't desert him,
> Because he's such a good fellow.

In the accompanying drawing, the teddy bear was depicted squatting on a pink quilt. Its paw was bandaged, and on a little table put together of toy blocks was a toy vase with flowers in it and a toy cup.

"Perhaps you could draw the teddy bear without its paw?" I inquired of the artist. He replied that that would be too naturalistic. Now, as I was afraid of that and also felt humbled in the presence of such a famous artist, I agreed. What is more, I could not find any arguments to show that I was right. At a kindergarten later on, I read from this book while the children turned over the pages with the pictures on them. One little boy said, "The teddy bear's paw doesn't hurt, it's been pasted on and bandaged, and the teddy bear's now going to have a cup of tea." He indifferently turned over the page. It struck me that my concept differed from that of the artist. The artist had not wanted to upset the child, intimating that now nothing hurt the teddy bear, and all the unpleasant things were gone. I, on the other hand, had desired to evoke empathy and compassion, as I had thought to convey the idea of devotion. Nor was there any organic bond between drawing and verse. Happening to mention this to Konashevich several years later, he said, as if amazed, "Yes, evidently I deprived the child of the possibility to act." Only later did I come to realize what he meant by this very apt remark.

"The Toys" came out in more editions with illustrations by

different artists. Here is a rough transcript of children's responses
to the pictures provided by the artist N. Kuznetsov:

"The torn off paw can be fixed back on again!"
"We must ask the doctor to help."
"It's all bandaged up, but it must hurt awfully!"
"My little Bunny has no hair on its head, just like my Grandpa,
but I'll never leave him."
"Give me a pencil and I'll make the teddy bear whole."

When children take to a drawing, they will stick up for it.

"The cornflower is really blue, but here in the drawing it's almost
white." The kindergarten teacher shook her head. "It faded in
the sun," tiny Lena returned on the spur of the moment.

Not infrequently the children's responses reveal each child's personality. A leading Soviet cartoonist, Kanevsky, once showed me
the transcript of a discussion of his drawings by eight-year-olds.
The conversation was about a volume of my poetry and, more specifically, the drawings illustrating the poem, "Lyoshinka,
Lyoshinka." (Lyoshinka is the Russian endearing diminutive for
the name Alexis).

First, some extracts from the poem:

"Lyoshinka, Lyoshinka,
Please show you're able
To learn, my Lyoshinka,
The multiplication table!
Sonny boy, my darling,"
Mother begged her son.
Dogging little Lyoshinka
Is the entire Young Pioneer group.
The Counselor gasped,
"A poor mark in his progress report!
Which means we've not been paying
Enough notice to the little boy.
Lyoshinka, Lyoshinka,
Would you please be able
To learn, our little Lyoshinka,
At least the first inflection?"
Little Lyoshinka replied,
"Beg me all the harder!
A boy without a conscience, me,
A boy who always lags behind!"
Lyoshinka, Lyoshinka . . .

Kolya: "She certainly looks like a real mother, with hand on her heart."

Galya: "How on earth do you know? Are you also a little Lyoshinka?" (*Laughter*)

Kolya: "No, it isn't me. This isn't a drawing of me." (*Laughter*)

Tanya: "I'd punish him for being so naughty. I wouldn't let him watch the TV."

Vera: "Look at the Counselor in despair!"

Nikita: (*Letting his imagination run riot*) "Our soldiers also have a boy like this, so they got him a specially trained dog which leads him to school on a leash." (*Laughter*)

The transcript further demonstrates that the children began to imagine all sorts of things and to think up funny stories. Kanevsky took such a liking to one of these child fancies that he felt he must turn it into a picture. And here you have a very curious thing—the drawing acts on the child's imagination, and this in turn evokes a creative response from the artist. Here you have a kind of feedback.

I think it is a good thing when children look at pictures without any adults around. The mental imagery they may create may be purely arbitrary at times, but it isn't suggested or imposed by the excessively rational thinking of an adult. A nice little boy came to see me recently, quite precocious for his age of four-and-a-half. There was one thing that surprised me: he had a rational way of thinking which is not very characteristic of small children. In my study he spotted the figure of "The Jolly Pencil," which, made of variously colored cardboard, had been presented to me by the editors of a Soviet magazine for children. The figure is dressed in an orange blouse and has bright orange hair and a colored pencil for a nose. The little boy touched him, and in a most businesslike way, asked me, "Can he write?" "No," I said. The little boy chuckled and shrugged his shoulders and said, "Why have him around, then?" Perplexity was dissipated when the boy's mother, a young lady with a Master of Science degree in mathematics, picked up a new book of mine illustrated by the lyrical drawings of that fine artist, Miturich, and began to show the boy the pictures inside. Now, these were poems for schoolchildren, which were naturally too advanced for the boy. The young mother showed the boy a picture of a virtually full-page Santa Claus and two boys, with a glimpse through the window of a crescent moon against a background of sky.

"That's Santa Claus!" the little boy said happily. But his

mother was not interested in that. "Tell me," she said, "what would that crescent moon look like tomorrow?" "A bit fuller," the little boy confidently replied. In another picture, the little boy's mother wanted him to say what season of the year it was, and in still another, to indicate the species of the birds depicted.

"Why, do you think I'm showing him the pictures wrongly?" she inquired of me, evidently sensing my disappointment. I did not bother to disillusion my visitor, but as we said goodbye I advised her to read more fairy tales and lyrical poetry to the little boy. I greatly regretted that I didn't have at home at the time a new book which Miturich had illustrated. It had some poetry which the little boy would have been able to understand, and it would have been interesting for me to watch the boy's response to the artist's lyrical drawings. I must say that Miturich seems to be a born illustrator of poetry, as he capably grasps its substance, intonation, beat, and mood.

Let me give you now an excerpt from the poem, "The Sorrowing Swan":

> In a bleak, cold park
> Amidst the ice
> Winters a swan,
> All alone.
> Did it hurt its wing?
> Did it break it, perhaps?
> Poor, unlucky chap,
> Unable to fly.

and, further,

> I keep thinking about him,
> Race off to see him on the pond,
> I made up my mind to pretend
> I'm also a swan.
> I'm also white,
> All in snow.
> I stretch my neck
> As far as I can,
> Snow sweeps
> Across the pond.
> I cry, "Listen!
> We'll swim together,
> Only I on the ground . . ."

The boy realizes that all his pretenses are futile, and that the swan is lonely and sorrowful. Here, now, are the responses "The Sorrowing Swan" evoked from five-to-seven-year-olds:

> "What a pretty picture!"
> "It's pretty for you, but the swan's all by itself. Only sky, water, and the swan."
> "I can stretch my neck still further than that boy!"
> "Couldn't I think that this would be a half-swan, half-boy?"
> "Why didn't any of the other swans wait for him? And why did none of them come back to him!"
> "Daddy left us for good, but then came back again."

What deep insight on the part of the artist! The children realized that the drawing was not only beautiful but dramatic, and saw the boy almost as a fairy tale "half-swan, half-boy" personage. But the chief thing here is that Miturich's presentation of the swan's loneliness is so impressive that the child senses the bird's sorrow as his own, comparing it to his own feelings, noting, however, that whereas his Daddy came back, the swan is still all alone.

Research into children's responses to illustrations and pictures represents a concern of paramount importance, and I think that the time is ripe to study most attentively the impact on children's minds of the immoral content of the plethora of comics. After all, in general, the comic is a sort of picture book. There is no denying that there are some attractive and quite innocent samples in this genre, although one cannot call them Artistic Literature. But I refer to the gangster stories propagating violence, cruelty—the variants of the notorious Superman themes. "The impression one gains," one artist once remarked, "is that all this was drawn by a robot, not by a human being!" Cheap, but pernicious, immoral, and inartistic, this trash is read also by little children and the captions are presented in mediocre versification. Could we possibly research and clarify children's responses and pool information as to the impact of this poisonous junk on young readers in different countries? I think this would be of value for many parents who are too careless or, by contrast, too preoccupied with everyday cares to really understand what their children read.

Not wishing to end on such a sad note, allow me now to share with you a few excerpts from letters which children have sent to writers and artists and to the Children's Book House.

> "My dream is to have peace on earth and for myself to become a librarian in order to hand out books to read. That's also very

important, but the first thing is more important. Is my dream the right sort of dream to have?" (from a twelve-year-old schoolgirl)

"Here is my drawing for your poem. I know it's not very good, but my imagination might end. Mummy says that it begins to end from the age of six, and it'll soon be my eighth birthday." (from a seven-year-old boy)

"I want to have two Winnie-the-Poohs that would be the same. I want to have two books. Because something might suddenly happen to one of them, but I want Winnie-the-Pooh to always be with me." (from a seven-year-old girl)

From a letter to me:

"My five-year-old daughter would like to know this, as she said, 'Are you an Auntie or a book?' "

And, finally, from a letter to a favorite poet:

"I love you and wrap you in paper, and when you tore, I pasted you together."

Part 9. Inspiring Creativity

First and Foremost Books

Vassily Sukhomlinsky

One of the essential principles in my teacher's creed is boundless faith in the educative power of books. Education involves above all words, books, and meaningful human relationships. . . . Books are powerful tools without which I should be dumb or tongue-tied, for I should be unable to tell a child a hundredth part of what he needs to be told and what I actually do say. An intelligent inspired book can often be decisive in relation to a man's future.

Reading is a window through which children see and come to understand the world and themselves. It is opened to a child only when, apart from actual reading, and even before he is first shown books, painstaking work on words is carried out, work which should embrace all spheres of children's activity and emotional life — work, play, communication with Nature, music, creativity. Without creative work that gives rise to beauty, without fairy-tales and fantasy, play and music, it is impossible to imagine reading as one of the spheres of a child's intellectual life. . . . A child will remain blind to the beauty of the world around him if he has not been made aware of the beauty of words read from books. The path to a child's heart and mind can take two forms, which at first glance might appear to contradict each other: it can lead from books, from reading to oral speech, or from living words, that have become part of a child's intellectual life, to books, to reading, and to writing.

From Vassily Sukhomlinsky, *On Education,* translated by Katharine Judelson (Moscow: Progress Publishers, 1977), 248–58. Reprinted by permission of the publisher.

A school principal in the Ukraine, Vassily Sukhomlinsky wrote extensively on education. His best known work is the prize-winning *To the Children I Give My Heart.*

Life in the world of books is quite different from the ordered diligent performance of homework. It is possible for a child to leave school with flying colors in his exams and yet with no inkling of what intellectual life involves, and without having experienced that profound human joy to be derived from reading and thinking. Life in the world of books introduces us to the world of beautiful ideas, enabling us to delight in the riches of our cultural heritage and to ennoble our character.

Do not be afraid of devoting whole hours of classwork to books. Do not be afraid of devoting a whole day to a journey round the "ocean of books." Let books thrill young hearts and capture young imaginations!

One of the causes of spiritual poverty is a lack of real reading which enthralls a man's mind and heart and stimulates thinking in relation to the world outside, in relation to man's inner world. . . . How should an intelligent and beautiful book be made a means of self-education? What should we do to insure that young people are held captive not only by tape-recorders and radio programs, dance halls, and cinemas but also by intelligent and beautiful books?

Let the most joyous of a school's celebrations be its Book Festival. On that day our local collective farm makes presents of books to the pupils. . . . Encourage children not only to want to read but to read and reread their favorite books. Let the rereading of good books become an intellectual need of older pupils just like repeated listening to favorite pieces of music.

Yet how should we set about this? Vital in this connection, of course, is good literature teaching.

It is impossible to assess pupils' views and convictions from the answers they give to their teachers' questions. (If it were possible to mold a child's outlook by having him learn wise maxims by heart, education would be a very easy undertaking.) Still less can we draw conclusions relating to children's interpretation of the world from the answers they proffer during literature lessons. I was always afraid of forgetting even for a minute the important principle that literature is studied not so that a few years after leaving school a young man or woman is still able to repeat what he was made to learn by rote at school. Life confronts the individual with "exams" at every step, and it is through his behavior and activity that he is able to show he is equal to the test. The ultimate goal for the study of literature is the molding of man's inner world — his morals and his cultural and esthetic sensitivity. When I observed how pupils in their early teens could be thrilled and almost overwhelmed by literary characters, and how after listening to works of literature they would start pondering on their own lives, this was infinitely more important than the precision of their answers on the text in hand. Perhaps that is to a certain extent an exaggeration, but for the last thirty years now I have been constantly aware of the fact that putting questions to pupils after they have read a work of literature is sometimes just as ill-advised as asking them after they have been listening to music to reproduce in words what they have just heard.

Without reading there can be no true and worthwhile communication between teacher and pupil. . . . When I was making a close study of what and how pupils in their early and late teens read, I was horrified to see that they had no idea that real reading involved thoughtful penetration of a book's meaning and mental exertion. They were only used to one kind of reading — reading textbooks. . . .

I have realized that adolescents need to be taught how to read. In our school we set aside a special "Thinking Room." Here we brought together over three hundred of the "cleverest books" we could find. In practice it meant we had a small reading room.

The room's very name aroused interest among the pupils for whom it was designed. When we first opened that room I told the pupils about an interesting book which dealt with the life of Lomonosov. I also showed the pupils the list of books I had read which I had been keeping for over twenty years. I depicted the supreme happiness for the educated man and woman — happiness of communion with books.

Reading in the "Thinking Room" was always a quiet occupation, for no one was allowed to disturb the peace; speaking was forbidden and, furthermore, the room was specially set up in a quiet corner of the school garden.

Some of our reading time was specially set aside for poetry. I used to recite from some of the finest poetic works that have become part of the world's cultural heritage: verses by Pushkin, Lermontov, Zhukovsky, Nekrasov, Fet, Shevchenko, Lesya Ukrainka, Schiller, Mickiewicz, Heine, Béranger, and various other poets. The children were soon eager to learn by heart a poem that had particularly appealed to their imagination. In the course of four years' poetry sessions, the pupils learned a good number of poems. Yet they never started memorizing them before they had come to appreciate their breath-taking beauty. . . .

The children were particularly fond of having long works read to them in installments. *The Adventures of Tom Sawyer* was spread over several weeks. The setting in which the children listened to the book enhanced their enjoyment. Other books which I read in installments included Maxim Gorky's *Childhood,* Valentin Kateyev's

A White Sail Gleams in the Distance. . . (referred to on p. 6 of this volume as *The Lonely White Sail—Ed.*) and P. Bazhov's *Malachite Casket.*

A library was provided even for the pupils in the primary grades. It consisted of four sections. The first contained stories that were, in my opinion, particularly valuable for the children's moral, intellectual, and esthetic education. (We used to buy enough copies of each book to be used at lesson-time.) In the stories which were selected there was a profoundly humane message easily accessible to the child and conveyed through vivid artistic images. . . .

The second section of that class library was made up of stories by modern Russian and Ukrainian authors: about our daily life, the work of Soviet men and women, the peace movement, the exploits of heroes during the Great Patriotic War (1941–45), and about child heroes. My pupils showed particular interest in the verses of Sergei Mikhalkov and Samuil Marshak and the stories of Gaidar, Kassil, Nosov, Prilezhayeva, Trublaini, Yanovsky, Zbanatsky, Linkov, Ivanenko, Voronkova, Zhitkov, and Alexandrova.

The third section was reserved for fairy-tales, poems, and fables. . . .

The fourth section of the library contained Greek myths. Here after a lengthy search we had assembled books containing the myths of Ancient Greece presented in a form accessible to children. Ancient mythology has an important part to play in children's intellectual and esthetic education. Not only does it unfold before children a fascinating page from the history of man's culture, but it stimulates the imagination, stretches the mind, and encourages interest in the distant past.

Youth is an age of poetry in the broad sense of that word. . . . Boys and girls in their late teens sense the poetic element not only in lyric verse but also in prose. True poetry unfolds before them in works that reflect not only real life, with all its joys and sorrows, but also in works permeated with the conviction that life's truth will triumph. A work can depict profound grief experienced by its heroes, a plot may have a tragic ending, but even death is interpreted by pupils in the senior classes as the supreme act to affirm life, if the hero dies in the name of those who shall live after him. By the time boys and girls have reached their late teens they have already formed mature views on this subject. They scornfully dismiss works which tend to present everything through rose-colored spectacles, and round off the plot with a happy ending. "Such things don't happen in real life," they say after reading works of this kind.

There is a noticeable tendency for each new generation on approaching adulthood to adopt an increasingly uncompromising stand on the purity of intimate emotions. Boys and girls in their late teens hope to find in poetic works portrayals of love that is loyal and ennobling and strong enough to overcome all tribulation.

A fast-moving plot in a work of fiction does not satisfy readers of this age group if it is not accompanied with profound ideas; ideas which throw light upon the philosophical aspect of social relations, or men's emotional and intellectual lives, are not only read and reread time and time again, but excerpts from books containing them are recorded for future reference and the ideas are analyzed and interpreted. Pupils often look for opportunities for engaging in polemics with authors. . . .

As they approach adulthood, boys and girls not only feel a greater need for esthetic experience, but also for esthetic activity. . . . Many try their hand at poetry. The boys' verses are usually concerned above all with intellectual and philosophical assessment of phenomena from the world around them. They contain no expression of their feelings as yet, no descriptions of Nature. Verses by girls from twelve upwards are distinguished by more subtle, emotionally intense expression of feelings, particularly expression of love for Nature.

Unfortunately, there are still large numbers of literature teachers whose pupils are unable to write compositions. In their efforts *to force* pupils to write compositions, these teachers swing from one extreme to the other: either they present their pupils with ready-made models borrowed from teaching manuals, or on the contrary, they demand that what a child writes be produced "absolutely independently." The upshot of all this is that nothing is achieved for the simple reason that the teacher himself cannot write compositions and that his pupils have never heard from him a single vivid word that is *all his own.*

It would be naive to expect a child to be so spurred on by the beauty of his environment that he will sit down and write a composition straight off. Creative activity is not something that children engage in intuitively or instinctively: it has to be taught. A child will only put together an essay after he has heard a teacher describe a natural scene, for instance. The first composition which I read to my pupils was composed on a quiet evening as we sat at the edge of a pond. I aimed to help the children understand and sense how a visual image could be conveyed in words. At first the children merely reproduced my own compositions, but gradually they progressed to independent descriptions of scenes from Nature which had impressed them: individual creativity was emerging. In this process it is very important that children should be made aware of the emotional and esthetic nuances of words. A child will learn to write a composition only when each word before him is like a little brick which has a previously appointed place. Children will then select the only brick that is suitable in a given context. They will never be able to pick the first words which happen to come into their heads: Their emotional and esthetic sensitivity will prevent them from doing so.

During childhood each boy or girl is a poet. . . . I am not one of those who go into raptures over children's natural talent, and am far from the belief that every child is a poet by nature. Man's awareness of the beautiful brings out the poet in his soul. If this awareness is not nurtured a pupil remains indifferent to the beauty of Nature and the beauty of words, a creature for whom there is no difference between the acts of throwing a stone into a pond and the singing of a nightingale. Introducing a child to the joy of poetic inspiration and awakening in his heart the living seeds of creativity is just as important as teaching a child reading and arithmetic. In some children the source of creativity is richer and in others poorer. I have observed how in some cases children's poetic inspiration is not a short-lived soaring heavenwards, not an explosion, but a constant inner need.

Once more I must stress that children's poetic creativity should not be regarded as a sign of talent. It is just as common and natural a phenomenon as the ability to draw: it is something all children work at, it is something every child experiences. Yet poetic creativity becomes a commonplace phenomenon in a child's life only when a teacher opens up to his pupils the beauty of the world around them and the beauty of language. Just as love of music cannot be fostered without music, so love for poetic creativity cannot be fostered without creative activity.

A man who loves the works of Pushkin, Heine, Shevchenko, Lesya Ukrainka, who seeks *to express beautifully his impressions of the beauty* which surrounds him, whose search for the right word has become for him as essential a need as his need to contemplate the beautiful, for whom the concept of the beauty of man finds expression above all in respect of human dignity, in the affirmation of the most just—communist—relations between men, can never become coarse or cynical.